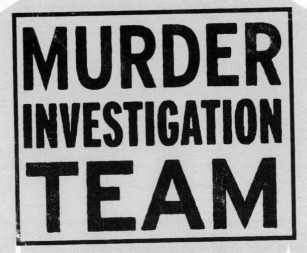

MURDER INVESTIGATION TEAM

HOW KILLERS ARE REALLY CAUGHT . . .

FORMER SCOTLAND YARD DETECTIVE INSPECTOR
STEVEN KEOGH

JB

First published in the UK by John Blake Publishing
an imprint of Bonnier Books UK
4th Floor, Victoria House
Bloomsbury Square
London WC1B 4DA
England

Owned by Bonnier Books
Sveavägen 56, Stockholm, Sweden

www.facebook.com/johnblakebooks
twitter.com/jblakebooks

First published in paperback in 2022

Paperback ISBN: 978-1-78946-642-3
Ebook ISBN: 978-1-78946-643-0

British Library Cataloguing-in-Publication Data:

A CIP catalogue record for this book is available from the British Library.

Design by www.envydesign.co.uk

Printed and bound in Great Britain by Clays Ltd, Elcograf S.p.A

1 3 5 7 9 10 8 6 4 2

Text copyright © Steven Keogh 2022

John Blake Publishing is an imprint of Bonnier Books UK
www.bonnierbooks.co.uk

I dedicate this book to all those on MIT, who give everything in the pursuit of justice for those taken from this world.
And to the loved ones left behind. Your courage is truly humbling.

All information is correct at time of publication

CONTENTS

PREFACE

If you're reading this, I'm guessing that you have an interest in all things murder. You may even describe it as a fascination. Well, you're not alone. That's something we both have in common.

People's interest in murder is not a new phenomenon, and it's certainly not niche. Edgar Allan Poe published the first detective short story in *Graham's Magazine* in 1841, 'The Murders in the Rue Morgue'. Since then, the subject has spawned thousands of films, TV shows, books, board games, video games and podcasts. *Serial*, one of the very first true crime podcasts, set a record-breaking 340 million downloads for its first two seasons.[i] It's a subject that truly captures people's imaginations.

Some of these are very good at demonstrating how a murder case unfolds, be that the intricacies of an investigation, the experiences of those left behind or even a closer look at the killers themselves and their motivations. The problem is that most are produced by people who have never been part of a murder investigation themselves. They haven't lived and breathed a case from beginning to end, witnessing first-hand the trauma that murders cause. Only those at the coalface can appreciate how difficult it is to solve a case, and how much harder it is to achieve a conviction at court. In fact, for a topic so prevalent in popular culture, it is surprising how little is actually known about the true inner workings of a murder investigation team.

In this book, I want to put that right. Here, I will give you a unique insight into how modern-day Scotland Yard investigates murders. I will take you on a journey from crime scene to trial; through all the steps needed to take a case from the initial investigation to a conviction at court. We will delve into a level of detail that doesn't exist elsewhere; a glimpse behind the curtain into the hidden world of a real-life detective. But this isn't just a manual on how to investigate murder. I will guide you through more than twenty murder cases that I was involved with, demonstrating how that theory is put into practice. I will also dispel some of the myths that are associated with murders, putting straight some of the glaring inaccuracies perpetuated by TV, films and books.

I served for thirty years as an officer with the Metropolitan Police. More than half of that time was spent as a Scotland Yard detective, investigating both murder and terrorism. I was part of more than a hundred murder investigations, during which I built up a huge well of knowledge of how these cases are solved.

An important point to make is that every case you will read about has been to court, so I am not breaching any confidentialities. As a former officer who signed the Official Secrets Act, I wouldn't be able to publish a book that divulged any confidential information. More importantly, I wouldn't want to break the confidence of those bereaved families whom we helped in the most desperate of times. It is because of this that I won't use the names of victims in this book. Through the descriptions I use, it may be possible to identify cases. It would be very difficult to write about an investigation without giving away some clues as to who the victim was. But, for me, it is important that those family members don't see their lost loved one's name in print.

Other than that, I will be honest with you about the highs and lows of a murder investigation. Scotland Yard has a fantastic record for solving murder cases, with around nine in ten ending with someone being caught for the killing. But things aren't always easy, and we didn't always get things right.

By the end of this book, you will have a true understanding of what real murder investigations involve. When you see a news report on TV about a killing, you will know what the detectives beginning that investigation will be thinking. When you see footage of a crime scene with people walking around in paper suits, you will know who those people are and what they are up to. When you hear about a murder trial, you'll understand what's at stake and how fragile the situation is for both police, prosecution and the family.

But murder investigation is a huge topic, one that could fill many, many books. So, while I want to give you everything there is to know here, that just isn't possible. If, after reading this book, there is more you wish to learn, please head to https://murderacademy.com, where you can delve even deeper into one of the most fascinating subjects in the world.

Steven Keogh

CHAPTER 1

INTRODUCTION

A JOURNEY INTO THE UNKNOWN

Nothing ever happens on a Monday, especially in the morning. Or so we thought. We were crewing a homicide assessment team, better known by its acronym, HAT. There are several specialist police vehicles like this dotted around London, ready to take on-call detectives to the scene of a murder or a suspicious death as quickly as possible. London is covered twenty-four hours a day and 365 days a year by four of Scotland Yard's murder investigation teams (MITs), each ready to respond at a moment's notice. In reality, though, most days you won't be called upon, which can lead to a false sense of security. That's how I was feeling that morning. Each team spends seven days as a HAT, and this was our last. Generally, if you get through the weekend without a murder, you are OK.

In situations like this, when you think you've got away without picking up a new enquiry, there is one word you don't mention. It is known as the *Q word*. You just don't say it. *Why would you? Who would tempt the gods of fate?* But, that morning, somebody did: 'I can't believe how quiet the weekend was.' In response, cries went up around the office, but half-hearted ones. It was a Monday morning, after all.

Then the phone rang. That's what it was known as: *the phone*. The only people who would call us on *the phone* were the police control room. *Surely, it's just a call for advice?* But as soon as my colleague starting speaking, I knew it was much more than that. I knew that look; that tone of voice. Another murder on the streets of London. We waited for the call to finish to be told more. It was a stabbing. A woman had been killed in a shopping area in South London. *On a Monday morning?* That made no sense. My immediate thoughts were of an argument in a shopping queue or a domestic incident. At that stage, we had no idea it was something far more unusual and extremely tragic.

We gathered what we would need and headed to our car. We had to get to murder scenes quickly, otherwise important evidence could be lost. We drove using blue lights and sirens. It's difficult to talk in a car with that much noise around you so there wasn't much conversation. We were all deep in thought. I couldn't say what my colleagues were thinking, but I always used these journeys to focus my mind on what was to come. I've been to dozens of crime scenes, but I still now experience the same buzz that I did the very first time. I always knew that, if the feeling went, it was time to move units.

There are steps that all murder investigators go through at scenes, and I was rehearsing those in my head. As the senior officer, most decisions would fall to me. I learned the hard way that those decisions would be pored over by lawyers. Lawyers who would have months to second-guess the decisions I had to make on the spot. Some of the most uncomfortable moments in my career were standing in the witness box at the Old Bailey, having my decisions scrutinised. That's why I needed that buzz. The moment I started to relax and take the job for granted was the moment mistakes would start to creep in.

Each crime scene was different from the last. Sometimes we would walk into scenes of absolute chaos, at other times complete calm. That feeling of going into the unknown created adrenaline.

As we pulled up to the crime scene, we were met by a familiar sight. Blue lights, uniformed officers, crime scene tape. This was an area I knew well, and at this time on a Monday morning it would usually be a hive of activity. Not this morning. Other than a few officers, the streets were eerily quiet. No cars, no people.

We sought out the officer best placed to tell us what happened, which would either be one of those first on scene or the person in charge. In this instance, it was a uniformed inspector who had arrived soon after the first officers. This was important as, to make the best decisions, you needed the best information.

He pointed across the road to where I could see a body. There was also blood, lots of blood. He told us the lady had been killed by someone using a large knife. He then pointed to the other side of the road, where I could see a woman in handcuffs standing with uniformed officers. We were told she was the one who attacked the lady in what appeared to be a totally random murder. She seemed to be in her late twenties and had long, dark hair. I had to look again just to be sure of what I was seeing. What jumped out at me was how calm she looked, with a half-smile on her face. *Had she really just killed someone?* She looked more like someone waiting their turn at the cashpoint.

In any murder detective's career, there will be cases that stay with them. For me, this was one of those. But that was nothing compared to the impact this incident was going to have on so many other people.

We quickly became aware of who the victim was and where she lived. I sent two of my officers to her home and to where her poor husband was about to have his world torn apart. This was the wife he had just said goodbye to, taken from him in the most callous of acts imaginable.

And so we set about our work. Work that would ensure that lady's family could one day get the justice they deserved.

BEFORE WE START OUR VOYAGE THROUGH MURDER

The call to that murder was one of many in my career, but it meant a lot to me for various reasons. We will revisit that case later in the book.

Those calls were always the start of a much longer journey: one for justice. I will show you what that journey looks like. To do that, I have separated the book into three sections: The Crime Scene, The Investigation and The Trial.

But, before we begin, there are a few matters we need to make sure you are aware of.

The first is a look at what murder actually means. It is a

central theme of the book, so we all need to understand how it is defined. I will then explain what MIT is aiming to achieve. This may seem obvious, but there is more to our mission than is commonly appreciated. I'll then outline the different categories of murder investigation and, finally, I will introduce you to some of those who make up the investigation team.

Did You Know? *The rate of homicide per 100,000 population in the UK is 1.2. In the United States the rate is 5.3. In Canada it's 1.8 and in Australia it's 0.8. In New Zealand it's only 0.7. In Brazil, unbelievably, the rate is 30.8.*[ii]

WHAT IS MURDER?

As I said earlier, I'm guessing you already have a keen interest in the subject of murder. You've probably watched many TV shows that deal with the subject, and perhaps you've read some books. You'll almost certainly have followed cases on the news as they garner so much media attention. But how many of us actually know what murder is? During my research for this book, I asked a cross-section of people about their understanding of the offences of murder and manslaughter. Almost all said they felt murder was an *intention to kill* someone, while manslaughter was killing someone *unintentionally*. There are elements of truth to both statements, but, as with most things in law, both offences are a bit more complicated.

Throughout this book, we will be talking about murder and, to a lesser extent, manslaughter. So a look at those offences, as they are legally defined, is a good place for us to start.

This isn't a law journal, so it won't be a long and in-depth dive into all of the nuances of both offences. I'd like to impart just enough so that it's clear what each offence involves and the defences that might be put forward at court.

Defining Murder

The law in England and Wales has a definition as to what constitutes murder. It's rather old and, as you're about to see, it isn't written in the most user-friendly language. Murder is committed:

Where a person of sound mind and discretion unlawfully kills any reasonable creature in being under the Queen's peace, with malice aforethought.

Hmmm. So, *what does that mean?* Well, let's look at each element in turn.

'Of sound mind and discretion'

This means the person was sane or, in other words, not suffering from insanity. I will explain the meaning of insanity shortly in the section on Defences to Murder below.

'Unlawfully kills'

In simple terms, this is causing someone's death without justification in law or having a reasonable excuse. This can be broken into two parts:

1. 'Unlawfully'

There may be some instances where taking a person's life would be lawful, so the killer would not be guilty of murder. Some examples of this are:

- If someone kills a person out of self-defence.

- If a police officer killed someone while acting in line with their duties, as long as they didn't go beyond those duties or use excessive force. For instance, if an officer was to shoot and kill an armed bank robber who pointed a gun at them, that would be *justification* in law.

But, if I were to kill my neighbour because I was angry that he was playing music loudly, there would be no justification in law, no matter how annoying he was being. It wouldn't be a reasonable excuse, so this would constitute an unlawful killing.

2. 'Kills'

This may include either an *act* or *omission* that led to a person's death.

An *act* would usually be an assault, such as a stabbing, shooting or beating, etc.

An *omission* would be someone not carrying out a duty of care. For instance, this might be a doctor who deliberately held back treatment that would have saved a person's life.

In order to prove murder, there has to be a direct link between the act or omission and the death of the victim. Although the act or omission doesn't need to be the sole cause of death, it must be shown to be a major contributing factor. It's useful to think of it in this way: *If that act or omission hadn't happened, would the person have died?* If the answer is *no, they would still be alive*, then it is likely to be murder.

As an example, consider someone receiving a serious head injury in an assault which resulted in them having a fatal seizure. If the assault can be shown as causing the seizure, this is likely to constitute murder.

'Any reasonable creature'

Put simply, this is a *human being*.

'In being'

This defines the victim as a person who is born alive and who has taken a breath from their lungs. So, the killing of an unborn foetus would not constitute murder.

'Queen's peace'

This means that the killing was not carried out during a war, i.e. a soldier killing the enemy in battle.

'Malice aforethought'

This concerns what was in the mind of the killer, or *mens rea*. For them to be guilty of murder, their intent must have been to *kill* or *cause grievous bodily harm* (otherwise known as GBH). For the purposes of this book, I will refer to that element as *really serious harm* as they have the same meaning. This second element of murder is something most people are unaware of. It means a person can be guilty of murder even if they had no intention to kill. Intending *really serious harm* is enough.

So, that's the definition of murder broken down into its key elements. But, going forward in this book, I will concentrate on only two aspects of the definition.

'*Of sound mind and discretion*' will not be relevant as all defendants are presumed sane unless evidence is presented otherwise. We can discount '*Queen's peace*' as nothing we will talk about is from a war zone. We can ignore '*reasonable creature*' as every case will involve a human being, and we can also leave out '*in being*' as all cases involve a person who has been born and taken a breath from their lungs.

When we look at what constitutes murder, I will concentrate on two simple elements that drive our investigations and eventual arrest of suspects.

For a person to be guilty of murder, they would need to both:

- unlawfully kill a person; and
- intend to *kill* **or** *cause really serious harm*.

This is a much simpler way to look at the offence, rather than getting bogged down in complicated legal terms.

Did You Know? *You may be wondering what the difference is between 'homicide' and 'murder'. In simple terms, murder relates to one specific offence, as we discussed in the last section, whereas homicide is a term that covers all unlawful killings, such as murder, manslaughter and corporate manslaughter.*

Defences to Murder

In the law of England and Wales, when it comes to murder, a number of statutory defences exist. These include full defences of insanity and self-defence, and partial defences of diminished responsibility, loss of control and suicide pact. I will explain the meaning of each of those in this section.

Insanity

As we saw from the definition above, for a person to be guilty of murder they need to be *of sound mind and discretion*. So, if a person is deemed to be insane at the time of a killing, then they are not guilty of murder by reason of insanity, making this a complete defence.

A complete defence means the defendant will be found not guilty of any offence in relation to the killing. This is different to partial defences, where the defendant will be found guilty of a lesser charge of manslaughter.

But what would constitute insanity?

For insanity to be accepted, they would need to be suffering a *defect of reason*, from a *disease of the mind*, so as to be unable to understand what they were doing or unable to understand what they were doing was wrong.

What that means, simply, is that the killer either had no idea that they were killing somebody or, if they did, they didn't know it was wrong. An example would be if a person was suffering from hallucinations and believed they were killing a monster, when in fact it was a person. Or, perhaps they killed a person while they were having an epileptic episode, with no idea what they were doing.

In reality, this does not happen very often. The majority of cases that come to court where mental illness has played a part would not fall under this defence. In reality, people rarely kill without knowing what they are doing or that it is wrong.

A finding of insanity has to be decided by a court. In cases of murder, that would be by a jury in a Crown Court.

Self-Defence

We know that if a person kills someone and they're deemed to be acting in self-defence, they wouldn't be acting unlawfully, so they wouldn't be guilty of murder. But *what constitutes self-defence?*

If a person finds themselves in a violent situation, they may defend themselves using force that is *reasonable* in the circumstances.

What is reasonable? There are two tests and both must be passed:

- Firstly, does the person using the force honestly believe it was reasonable and necessary? *This is a subjective test, as it is based on what was in the person's mind at the time.*

- Secondly, does the jury consider that a reasonable person would regard that force as reasonable and necessary, given the facts the defendant believed to be true? *This is an objective test, as it is based on what the jury decide a reasonable person would believe.*

Let's consider an example. A defendant says he saw the victim holding a knife and he honestly believed he was going to get stabbed, so he stabbed him first. That satisfies the first test. If the jury decide that a reasonable person, in that same situation that the defendant believed himself to be in, would also stab the victim, that satisfies the second test.

In that example, the defendant would not be guilty of murder.

Partial Defences to Murder: Defining Voluntary Manslaughter

There are other defences to murder where, if accepted, the defendant would be guilty of *voluntary manslaughter* rather than murder. These are known in law as *partial defences* because, unlike *self-defence* and *insanity*, a person would still be convicted of a crime, albeit a lesser one. In these cases, they will still have committed all the elements needed to prove murder.

Diminished Responsibility

The first partial defence is *diminished responsibility*. This is the defence most used in cases where a defendant for murder was suffering from mental illness.

This defence hinges on the defendant's state of mind at the time of the killing. To have this defence available to them, they would need to show they were suffering from an *abnormality of the mind* at the time of the murder which *substantially* impaired their ability to understand the nature of what they were doing, form rational judgement or exercise self-control.

An example of this would be a person suffering from psychosis who believed the person they killed was involved in some sort of conspiracy against them. That reaction was completely uncalled for and unlawful, but the psychosis substantially affected their rational judgement in that situation. So, even though the act would satisfy all the elements to prove murder, this defence, if accepted, would lower the conviction to one of manslaughter.

You may ask, '*what is the difference between insanity and diminished responsibility?*' In simple terms, the bar for insanity is much higher. A person who is not sane at the time really doesn't understand that they are killing a person or doesn't know it's wrong. With diminished responsibility, this isn't the case, but their state of mind brings them to the point of killing.

Loss of Control

Another partial defence is *loss of control*. This is where a person is in fear of serious violence, or where they feel seriously wronged and go on to act in a way that another person in a similar situation would consider reasonable. For example, in one case a man who had raped a woman was taunting that woman's boyfriend about how she had wanted to have sex. He reacted angrily, stabbing the rapist. He was acquitted of murder but found guilty of manslaughter.

Suicide Pact

There is a third partial defence, known as a *suicide pact*. This is a rarely used defence, however, and self-explanatory, so we won't look at this in any detail.

All three of these defences lead to a finding of guilt for *voluntary manslaughter*.

Defining Involuntary Manslaughter

The main difference between this offence and murder is the intention to *kill* or *cause really serious harm*. If someone is killed unlawfully, but without either of those intents, this is known as *involuntary manslaughter*.

There are two types of involuntary manslaughter:

1. By an unlawful and dangerous act (known as
    constructive manslaughter)

2. By gross negligence

A classic example of an *unlawful and dangerous act* is when the victim is punched once, falling to the floor and banging their head, with the bang to the head causing their death. As there was no intent to kill or cause really serious harm, they would be guilty of *constructive manslaughter*.

Gross negligence is often used in work environments. As an example, consider a gas engineer fitting a boiler that is far below acceptable standards, leading to someone dying from carbon monoxide poisoning.

I hope that's clear and not too confusing. I will only touch on the law when necessary, but I feel it's important to understand what the murder investigation teams (MITs) set out to prove in each case they deal with.

Did You Know? *The homicide rate is higher in London than in any other part of England and Wales. The following figures are per million of population: London 16.5; East of England 15.4; West Midlands 13.0; Wales 12.4; North West 12.3; East Midlands 10.5; North East 10.5; Yorkshire and The Humber 9.4; South East 8.3; South West 6.0; England and Wales (average)11.7.*[iii]

WHAT IS THE AIM OF THE INVESTIGATION?

All teams, no matter what industry they're in, need an objective that everyone is working towards. For MITs, that is no different. Within the team, each member will have individual targets, all contributing to that overall aim.

I call this approach: *big goal, little goals*.

In murder investigations, the *big goal* is a fairly obvious one, but with a slight proviso attached: *Secure a safe and proper conviction at court.*

Why do I say safe and proper? Well, that goal can't come at any cost. It must be the right conviction, secured ethically. I'm not suggesting the MIT would try and secure a conviction in any other way, but that message still needs reinforcing. There is usually a *quick way* to success and the *right way* to success. All teams should take the *right way*. That is the same in any industry, profession or sport.

Each murder investigation is unique, with different characteristics, methods and challenges. But that *big goal* will always be the same.

WHAT TYPES OF MURDER INVESTIGATION ARE THERE?

What is a typical murder investigation? The answer to that is there isn't one. No two murders are the same. There are, however, general types of investigation that most enquiries would come under:

- Domestic homicides: by partners or from within the family
- Mental health
- Gang related
- Criminal activity: robbery, burglary, drug dealing, sex attacks

- Confrontation: pub fights and disrespectful looks

There are other, less common types too, such as serial killers, terrorism and mass homicide.

Each MIT will take on between six and ten murders a year.

WHO MAKES UP A MURDER INVESTIGATION TEAM?

Myth Buster: *In popular fiction, it's usually a detective chief inspector (DCI) or a detective inspector (DI) who cracks the case. They are often shown running around in the field, fighting with the murderer and putting their life at risk. They solve the case through their outstanding bravery and detective ability. As dramatically satisfying as this is, it's completely and utterly inaccurate. Being a DCI or DI is actually about formulating strategies, making high-level decisions and doing what you can to help those on your team achieve their goals. As a DI, the biggest risk to my life was getting an infected paper cut.*

In the Metropolitan Police, murder investigation teams (MITs) became permanent in the early 2000s. Until then, teams were formed from a pool of detectives taken from various departments as and when they were needed. There are now twenty permanent MITs based in different locations across London.

You will often hear the term *Scotland Yard detectives*. In reality, murder detectives are no longer based at the headquarters in New Scotland Yard. It is now the domain of senior officers. However, that name is still used to describe detectives from the Metropolitan Police, so I will use it in this book.

Each team consists of around thirty people, including a DCI, two DIs, four detective sergeants (DSs) and 18 detective constables (DCs). In addition, there are four or five non-police officers (known as police staff) whose roles relate to a computer system known as HOLMES (Home Office Large Major Enquiry System). We will look at that in further detail in Chapter 3.

All officers must apply to join the MIT. They will go through a selection process that involves a written application and interview.

During an investigation, each officer will have individual roles and responsibilities. Below is a selection of those roles, some of which we will look at in more detail later:

Senior investigating officer (SIO): This is usually the DCI, although it may be the DI. They will have overall responsibility for the investigation from a strategic point of view, and they are the name that will be associated with a case for media purposes (the face of the case). At the start of an enquiry, they will make the majority of high-level decisions, but as the case progresses, they usually delegate this responsibility to the investigating officer (see below). They will undertake training to qualify as a nationally-recognised SIO for the purposes of investigating serious crime. That is a four-week course that requires proof they performed certain tasks before it can be awarded.

Investigating officer (IO): One of the DIs would perform this role, working closely with the SIO in setting investigative strategies and decision-making. Think of them as the deputy SIO. As the case progresses, they will usually be the one making the high-level decisions on the enquiry. With the high number of investigations each team takes, it would be difficult for one person to perform the lead role in every case, so the responsibilities are shared. A Scotland Yard IO will usually also be a nationally-qualified SIO, able to fulfil both roles.

Case officer: This role would be carried out by one of the detective sergeants (DSs). Their job is to ensure all officers are working towards the investigative strategies. They are usually the ones who prepare reports for the Crown Prosecution Service (CPS) and will be the point of contact between them and the murder investigation team (MIT). When it comes to trial, it is the case officer who represents the team at court.

Family liaison officer (FLO): Murders have a huge impact on bereaved families. The loss of a loved one at *any* time is hard, but to lose someone through an act of violence is even more difficult. Specially trained officers carry out this role, acting as the point of contact between family and investigation team.

Exhibits officer: During the investigation a large amount of evidence will be collected, known as *exhibits*. It is this officer who has responsibility for managing these. They receive advanced training and are present at crime scenes and post-mortems.

CCTV officer: Closed-circuit television (CCTV) is all around us. Virtually every commercial premises will have a CCTV system, as do many homes. Cameras are on many streets, and buses and trains have their own systems. As a result, this form of evidence has become an essential tool in murder investigations. This officer will ensure footage is obtained, viewed and presented as evidence at court.

Intelligence officer: Intelligence can be vital in solving murders and comes from many sources. These can include police databases, criminal records and registered informants. This officer will be responsible for pulling the intelligence together, maintaining records and presenting their findings to the SIO. They will also be the link between the MIT and partner agencies who may hold intelligence. In cases that are more difficult to solve, this role can be vital in guiding the team in the right direction.

One of the most important tasks when gathering intelligence relates to the victim. A picture will need to be established of their life, including relationships, friends, interests, places frequented, jobs, phones used, vehicles, any criminal activity, etc. This is commonly known as *victimology*. As a majority of murders have a link between victim and suspect(s), this work can be vital in solving a case. The officer will be aided in this task by a *researcher* and an *analyst*, members of police staff trained in the gathering of intelligence. They are not formally attached to the MIT.

Disclosure officer: The police have a duty to retain all material generated during investigations. This officer is charged with reviewing this material. They will also make decisions around what should be provided to the Crown Prosecution Service (CPS) for disclosure to the defence.

Communications officer: Modern communications have become a central element in murder investigations. Everyone has a mobile phone, and the information they provide can be vital. The communications officer will be responsible for pulling together all of the phone evidence, including making the necessary applications to obtain call data from the phone companies. At trial, they will usually present this evidence to the court.

Interviewing officer: The interviewing of suspects in police custody plays an important part in all criminal investigations. Every officer is given training in how to interview, but some go on to learn more advanced techniques. We will explore this subject in detail later, in Chapter 3.

If you were to ask me what my favourite role was, it would have to be case officer. I've performed most roles, including SIO and IO. But for me, case officer is the most rewarding. You are the person who knows the case inside and out, you are there from start to finish and you are able to represent the MIT at trial. You live and breathe the investigation more than any other detective on the team. When I took promotion to DI, knowing I would never perform that role again took some getting used to.

Myth Buster: *The rank structure in MITs is far less formal than portrayed on TV. The DCI/DI may be referred to as sir/boss/guv/ma'am, although more often than not, people will just use their first name. A DS will also be referred to by their first name, as opposed to sarge or skipper. Non-detectives, i.e. the officers you see in uniform, tend to be more likely to use those more formal terms.*

Did You Know? *The first detectives (and, indeed, police force) in England were known as the Bow Street Runners, who were formed in London in 1749 by a magistrate called Henry Fielding. They were established to help tackle highway robbery and, at its foundation, consisted of just six men. The Metropolitan Police was formed in*

1829. However, the Bow Street Runners remained in existence until 1839, when the two organisations merged. The Metropolitan Police didn't introduce a detective branch until three years after that, in 1842.

CONCLUSION

In this chapter, we have laid the foundations for what is to come. Having looked at the law around murder, we can now define it and how it's distinguished from manslaughter. We've discovered the many roles within a murder investigation team and what our overarching aims are. We will now take a closer look at where that investigation begins: the crime scene.

CHAPTER 2

THE CRIME SCENE

INTRODUCTION

In most walks of life, how you begin something has a serious impact on how successful you are likely to be. If you don't lay proper foundations when building a house, it's likely to fall down. If a marathon runner doesn't eat and sleep properly before a race, they're unlikely to finish. It is exactly the same for a murder investigation: everything starts with the crime scene. If investigators get that part wrong, the chances of gaining a conviction are likely to be seriously impacted. For that reason, it is where the majority of training is focused. It is where strict structure has developed. In this chapter, I'll take you through those processes, showing you how they are implemented to give us the best chance of conviction. We will look at what evidence is being sought and how it is secured.

WHAT IS THE INITIAL RESPONSE
TO A CRIME SCENE?

Whenever we attended a murder, there was usually a scene of chaos. Our job was to bring order and make sure all potential evidence was secured. This is known as the *initial response*.

So, *how does the murder investigation team (MIT) do that*? As I said, these incidents can be messy, confusing and stressful. Important decisions will be made, and if you get them wrong, the consequences can be huge. The way you get through that is by using two tools available to you: your *experience* and a *structure* to follow.

Experience: Nobody joins a MIT without having dealt with other serious crime. At local police stations, often referred to as the Criminal Investigation Department or CID, detectives learn their trade by dealing with serious assaults and sexual offences. In these investigations, they are responsible for crime scenes and are tasked with managing the investigations all the way through to court. So, by the time they're dealing with murders, they have a large bank of knowledge to fall back on.

Structure: MIT officers follow a series of steps that have been developed to allow a systematic approach to the initial investigation. All murders are different, but this process can be followed at every scene. It is called the *five building blocks*. These steps are:

- Preservation of life
- Preservation of scene
- Securing of evidence
- Identifying the victim
- Identifying and arresting suspects

Let's go through each in turn and explore both what they mean in practice and why they are so important.

Preservation of Life

In any situation, preservation of life is the priority for police. When officers first arrive at a scene, the victim may still be alive. If so, they will most likely be taken to a hospital. Sometimes, emergency treatment is given at the scene. The helicopter air ambulance, which often attends, will have a doctor perform procedures such as thoracotomies. This is where they open the chest to gain access to internal organs, usually the heart, in order to stabilise the victim. It's very much a last resort operation and has a low survival rate.

If a victim is pronounced dead at the scene, their body will remain until it can be removed without the loss of forensic evidence. That may take hours, which can be extremely upsetting for families. Nobody would want a loved one remaining in that position for any length of time, but it is necessary.

If family members attend the scene, it can be a difficult situation. There were times we had to physically restrain relatives from getting to the victim. You understand why they want to. They need to hold their child one last time or know for sure it was them. But you also know you can't let them as it could compromise evidence. It was always a heartbreaking experience, one of the hardest things I had to do as a detective.

Case File: A teenager had been accosted by a group while playing basketball and was stabbed to death. Somehow, word got back to his mother and she had run to the scene, just a few blocks away from her house. She was hysterical, understandably, demanding to be let past the police cordon, which is a line of tape, set up to prevent people entering and interfering with the scene. She wanted to see her 'baby' as she cried out his name. Initially she tried to reason with us, and when that didn't work, she tried to slip past the cordon to see him for herself. We had to remain firm, stay in control and explain how important it was to preserve the scene. Communication is the most important skill that a detective can possess, and there is no bigger test than a situation like this. Stopping a parent from holding their child one last time made me feel like the worst person in the world. As a parent myself, it would be all I would want.

Preservation of Scene

Crime scenes are where the most important evidence is obtained, so properly securing them is crucial. The period of time straight after a murder is known among detectives as the *golden hour*. It is when evidence will be most abundantly available. If certain opportunities aren't capitalised on now, or evidence secured, it is likely they never will be.

What is a crime scene? That may seem obvious, but it's not as simple as you think. When murder investigators refer to crime scenes, there are various types:

- **The location of the murder**: Probably the most important crime scene as it is where most evidence is likely to be recovered.

- **Where the victim is found**: This may not necessarily be where the attack occurred. A victim can walk or run some distance before collapsing. Sometimes a murderer may move a body to another location, in which case that place is referred to as a *deposition site*.

- **The victim**: It may seem odd referring to a murder victim as a *scene*, but that is what they are. They are a potential source of evidence, which is likely to be lost if they are not properly secured.

- **The suspects**: For the same reason, they will be treated as scenes. They may have forensic evidence on them, which can link them to the murder.

- **Vehicles**: Any cars or other vehicles used by the suspects or victim may have important evidence in, on or around them. That can include forensics, weapons and phones.

- **Where the weapon is found**: Suspects are likely to discard weapons used in a murder. They may have some awkward questions to answer if caught with them. The location they are found in is treated as a separate crime scene. This is called a *weapon deposition site*.

As you can see, the list of potential crime scenes is endless. The best way to think of them is that if there is a place, person or vehicle with the potential for providing evidence, it will be treated as a crime scene.

Did You Know? *In the year ending 31 March 2020, the places in which murders in England and Wales occurred included the following: In and around a dwelling, 46 per cent; in the street, 31 per cent; open outdoor area (park/car park) 8 per cent; other public places (shops/schools/hospitals, etc.), 4 per cent; licensed premises (pubs/clubs/restaurants), 4 per cent; residential homes 3 per cent.*[iv]

How are Crime Scenes Preserved?

That depends on the type of crime scene. If it's inside premises, it is quite straightforward. The building can be locked down until all necessary work is carried out. If it is outside, police cordon tape is used to close off the area. Tents will often be used to protect the body from weather and bystanders wanting to see what is happening. If the scene is a live person, then they will have their clothing seized and swabs taken from areas where DNA evidence may be recovered. Swabs are like giant ear buds, wiped over an area to pick up traces of DNA. Vehicles are lifted onto a truck and taken to a secure warehouse for a full examination.

Securing of Evidence

When the murder investigation team (MIT) arrive at the scene, they will be looking to secure evidence. If they don't, there is a danger it can be lost forever. The main types are:

- **Witnesses**: They need to be spoken to as soon as possible, while events are still fresh in their minds. The longer this takes, the more likely they are to forget details.

- **Closed-circuit television (CCTV)**: By viewing CCTV early, it may be possible to identify footage of suspects, the victim or, if you're really lucky, the murder itself.

- **Weapons**: Quite often, weapons are discarded, although they are not normally easy to find. Police dogs can be used to carry out an initial search of the area. They are trained to pick up human scent, which can lead them to discarded objects.

The way I approached the search for evidence was to stand close to where the attack happened, then look around. That may seem obvious, but I've seen many detectives who do not do this properly. I would look at buildings, cars, street lights, poles, pavements, gutters and bins. You would be amazed by what you spot when you take the time to properly absorb your surroundings. CCTV cameras might be there, cars that look out of place, corners where weapons could be discarded, potential witnesses, escape routes, blood spots, ballistic damage or passing buses. There are so many opportunities to gather evidence that could be lost if you're not observant. The same goes for identifying the routes in and out of a crime scene and, thus, where a suspect may have come from or where they may have escaped to.

Another trick is to revisit the scene at the same time but on a different day. By the time we arrive, after a murder takes place, the police have already been there for some time with cordons in place. The circus around a crime scene gives a false idea of what the area is really like and can be distracting. If you return later, however, when it has returned to normal, you may get a feel for what a location is really like. People will be out and about, and you can stop and chat to them. It is amazing what you find out when you take the time to talk to locals. For whatever reason, they may not have been spoken to before, but they could reveal all sorts of relevant information.

Case File: We were called to a housing estate in Woolwich, South East London. A man had been stabbed next to a block of flats. Witnesses saw the suspect running away but couldn't give a detailed description. I walked the area with our CCTV officer. We looked at every building and every route in and out. We talked to people as we went, asking them if they'd seen anything. Within a short space of time, from these conversations with locals, we had identified where the suspect had come from and where he had fled. We also saw various opportunities for CCTV coverage that we made sure was viewed straight away. From this, not only did we obtain footage of the suspect, but we also caught the murder itself on camera. The video showed the suspect robbing the victim at knifepoint, then a fight between the pair a short distance away. Armed with a good image of the killer, we were quickly able to identify him. He was arrested shortly after, allowing us to obtain evidence that would otherwise have been lost, which included blood from the victim at the suspect's home and the clothing he was wearing at the time. The footage we obtained left very little doubt as to what happened and, indeed, this evidence led to the suspect being convicted of murder.

Identifying the Victim

Sometimes the victim's identity is known straight away but if it isn't, *how can that be established?* Here are some of the ways that can be achieved:

- Identification documents may be on the victim, such as a driving licence.

- The victim's mobile phone may be at the scene, providing personal information.

- Witnesses to the murder may know the victim and can be interviewed.

- The victim's fingerprints can be checked. Mobile devices are available that can search the criminal records database, although this only works if they have been arrested in the past.

- Missing person reports can be reviewed for a match. Any scars or tattoos they have would be important for this.

Once the victim is identified, the investigation team can:

- **Obtain phone billing information**: With this, they can see who the victim has been in contact with.

- **Check police intelligence**: There may be reports of previous incidents involving the victim or ongoing tensions indicating the motive for the killing.

- **Speak with family and friends**: They may hold key information.

Once the identity of a victim is established, the family can be contacted and informed of the death. Telling relatives their loved ones have been murdered is hard. You know the next words that come out of your mouth will change their lives forever, and they are unlikely to ever forget what you say. That makes choosing the right words so important. There is no easy way and no right way, but there can be a wrong way. For me, it was always a balance. A balance between leaving them in no doubt and being as sympathetic as possible. If you're too matter-of-fact, you come across as harsh and cold but if you try too hard to minimise the impact of your words, you run the risk of them not grasping what you're saying. In terms of how they react, I feel like I saw every response possible. You may have heard of the five stages of grief: denial, anger, bargaining, depression and acceptance (the Kübler-Ross Grief Cycle). To me, that is so true, and I have seen them all. Denial – '*no, there is no way that is my boy*'; anger – even to the point where I had to restrain a dad who came at me in a violent way; bargaining – '*this is my fault, I knew I should have taken him away*'; depression – one victim's mother had an instant breakdown and it took days before we could speak to her; and, finally, acceptance, which is the one that often threw me and happened more than you'd expect. I say that with no judgement as, until you are in that situation, you have no idea how you yourself would react.

Identifying and Arresting Suspects

Arresting suspects is a priority. Everything the MIT does is to *secure a safe and proper conviction at court*. The sooner an arrest happens, the more likely that is.

Imagine the potential evidence from a suspect arrested a few minutes after a murder. They could have the victim's DNA on them. They may be wearing the same clothing as they did during the murder or have a mobile phone that can put them at the scene. If a weapon was used, they may still have that on them. If robbery was a motive, they may still possess the stolen property.

What If the Arrest Was Made Days or Weeks Later?

All that valuable evidence is likely to be gone. If hands are washed, DNA will be lost. The same goes for clothing. In the majority of murders, suspects dispose of their phones. They may even change their appearance, such as hairstyles and facial hair. They will have time to ask others to provide alibis for them.

This is why early arrests are so important to investigators.

EXAMINING THE CRIME SCENE

Watch any murder story on the news and you're bound to see footage of the crime scene, usually with people wandering around in paper suits and carrying bags of evidence. Have you ever wondered, *Who are those people and what are they doing?*

Who Is in Those Paper Suits?

This is a question I get asked a lot. First off, it isn't just paper suits. They also wear masks, gloves and overshoes. This outfit is referred to as *full-barrier clothing*, and it protects the crime scene from contamination.

News reporters usually describe these as *forensic officers*. But *what does that mean*? Well, which experts enter a crime scene depends on the circumstances of the murder. The list you're about to read covers most experts who *could* be called to a scene. The first four will attend every murder:

Crime scene manager (CSM): Those who examine crime scenes used to be the unsung heroes of murder investigations, with detectives taking all the limelight as the stars of crime dramas. That was until recently, however, when forensic examiners became famous in their own right, being front and centre on TV shows like *CSI: Crime Scene Investigation*. Within Scotland Yard murder enquiries, the lead crime scene investigator is known as the crime scene manager (CSM). Their job is to assess the scene and ensure the relevant experts are used. They work as the link between the investigation team and the supporting forensic services. When it comes to crime scenes, they are the experts, and, as investigators, we would look to them for specialist advice. A CSM is not a police officer but a member of police staff.

Exhibits officer: This would be a detective constable (DC) from the MIT. They are specially trained in the handling of evidential exhibits. The exhibits will be packaged at the scene, in sealed bags. Each is given a unique reference, made up of the officer's initials. If the exhibits officer's name was John Alan Smith, for example, he would use his initials with consecutive numbers. So, JAS/1 for the first exhibit and JAS/2 for the second, etc. They will log all exhibits taken from a scene in a specially designed book. This book records the movement of exhibits – for instance, if they are sent to a laboratory for examination. Known as *continuity of evidence*, this is extremely important when the case comes to court.

Photographer: Photography is essential for several reasons. Few people will be allowed into the scene, but it will be important for others to know exactly what the scene looked like. This would include where the victim was found, the layout of the location, any disturbance, where weapons were found and bloodstains, etc. This is for the benefit of investigators as well as those at trial, including witnesses, jury, barristers and judge. The first task is to record the scene in the state it was found, including the body. Next is exhibit locations. You will have seen those yellow markers with letters on them used to record locations of relevant finds. They say a picture paints a thousand words, and that is never truer than at a crime scene.

Crime scene examiner: These people go by various titles. I always knew them as scenes of crime officers (SOCO). They work under the direction of the crime scene manager (CSM) and are responsible for recovering forensic evidence, including fingermarks and DNA. In today's world of budget cuts, they also carry out photography. They are also police staff rather than officers.

So, these four roles are ever-present. But who else might you see there? The following experts attend *some* crime scenes but only when their specialist knowledge is required:

Forensic scientist: The majority of the work a forensic scientist carries out will be in a laboratory. There may be instances where they will be required to attend a crime scene.

This is usually to do with the finding, recovery and inter-pretation of blood. Blood pattern analysis is possible from photographs, but that work would ideally be carried out at the scene.

Forensic pathologist: Most deaths result in a post-mortem unless somebody dies shortly after an illness. If a person dies in suspicious circumstances, a special post-mortem (SPM) will be carried out. More thorough than regular post-mortems, they're conducted by Home Office-approved forensic pathologists. These experts provide evidence to courts as to how the death occurred. Although they conduct most of their work at a mortuary, they can attend crime scenes, if necessary, where they will examine the body *in situ*.

Forensic entomologist: Entomology is the study of insects. This can be used to determine when a person may have died and if the body has been moved from one place to another. When a person dies, it doesn't take long for flies to land, laying eggs in body orifices and wounds. These eggs will go through various cycles before they become fully-grown flies. Examining insects and interpreting their life cycles makes it possible to give estimations on timelines of death. If these insects are not natural to the surroundings, it may also indicate the body has been moved.

Forensic anthropologist: Anthropology is the study of the human skeleton. By looking at bones, it is possible to establish certain facts including age, gender and race. They may also be able to establish a timeline of death from decomposition. If there are injuries to the skeleton, they may also assist in providing a cause of death.

Forensic odontologist: I'm sure you have heard of victims being identified via dental records. If that form of identification is used, it would be carried out by a forensic odontologist. For this method to work, you need an idea of who the victim is, as their dental records are required for the purposes of verification. They can also be used where a victim has bite marks on their body, comparing these to dental impressions of any suspect.

Forensic palynologist: Forensic palynology involves the study of pollen and spores from plants. If, for example, a body is found in woods, plant grains can help establish if it has been moved. A suspect may also be linked to a particular location if spores are found on them or possibly their vehicle. Cases have been proved by material found in car tyres.

Specialist search officers: Thorough searching of scenes is needed to recover all potential evidence. These search officers are highly trained and use specialist equipment. They are known as POLSA, which stands for police search advisor. If you ever see footage of police officers crawling along on their hands and knees, this is them.

Case File: A man, suffering from mental health issues, had been released by the hospital. His family were trying to get him readmitted as they were concerned for his welfare (an all too familiar story). He had a young child with a woman and their relationship was somewhat volatile. A few days after being discharged, the pair met at his flat. They were drinking and taking drugs. He suffered from paranoia, which he seemed

to direct at his child's mother. This resulted in him
violently attacking her, apparently grabbing the nearest
weapon he could find: a breeze block. He used this
to continually pound this poor woman's face. Police
were called some hours later, after concerns were raised
by the woman's family. They forced entry to his flat
and found him sitting on a sofa, feet from where the
woman's dead body lay. Her injuries were so severe
that it would have been impossible for her family to
identify her. She had no police record, so fingerprints
could not be used. Although we were confident it was
her, a high level of proof is required by the coroner.
Because an inquest would be necessary to investigate
the cause of death and support the prosecution of her
murder, her identity could not be in doubt. To reach
this standard, we obtained her dental records. A forensic
odontologist attended the mortuary and compared the
teeth of the dead woman with the dental records to
provide conclusive evidence. Without this, we would
have sought DNA from her home, possibly from a
toothbrush, and a DNA profile could have been created
for comparison. That is a long process. Odontology
allowed us to make a formal identification much more
quickly. This was important for her family as well as
the coroner. As long as any doubt remained, they could
have held false hope that their daughter was still alive.

What Are They Doing?

In essence, the job of these professionals is to *interpret* the scene.
To tell the story of what is likely to have happened.

Why do they need to do that?

In most murders, the suspect doesn't give an account of what happened. Even when they do, you can't trust what they are telling you because they will most likely have an agenda. It is unusual to get an account from the victim (although not unheard of, as you'll see below). There may be no witnesses to what happened, and even when there are, you can't rely on them not to get things wrong. Occasionally, the murder may be caught on CCTV but not often.

So, forensic examination of a crime scene is crucial to the investigation. Let's consider some of the key facts they are looking to establish:

- The identity of the victim
- The sequence of events
- The cause of death
- The identity of the suspects and how they can be linked to the scene

Case File: I said it isn't unheard of to obtain an account from a victim and we had one such case. A mother and son were living together. He was suffering from poor mental health and she was trying desperately to get him the help he needed (as I said in the previous case file, a far too common scenario). As often occurs, her fears became a reality and he became violent towards her. He attacked her, not only with a knife but also a pair of garden secateurs. He then locked her in the house before cycling to a police station, where he confessed about the attack to the first officers he saw. Officers rushed to the home to find this poor lady lying in the hallway, alive but in massive distress. Although serious, her injuries were not deemed life-threatening. An officer from the local CID was allocated the investigation and visited her in hospital to obtain an account of what happened. Most officers today wear body worn video (BWV) cameras that record what the officer can see and hear. That was the case here, so that first account from the victim was recorded on video. Tragically, this lady's condition took a turn for the worse, and she sadly died. We then took over the investigation as this was now a murder. The fact we had an account from the victim was, of course, highly unusual but extremely powerful – and upsetting – evidence.

TYPES OF FORENSIC EVIDENCE

Now we know who might be at a crime scene but *what evidence are those experts looking for?* The key types are:

- DNA
- Fingerprints
- Blood
- Fibres
- Footmarks
- Evidence from firearms, including ballistics

Locard's Exchange Principle

One of the first lessons taught to detectives is Locard's principle of exchange. Dr Edmond Locard (1877–1966) was a French forensic scientist very much ahead of his time, who established that every contact leaves a trace. That principle is the foundation of modern-day forensic science. If I touch an object, parts of me remain there, even if it's at a microscopic level. That exchange can include DNA, fingerprints, blood, fibres, footmarks and ballistic material.

Let's consider each of those in turn.

DNA

Deoxyribonucleic acid is a bit of a mouthful, but thankfully we all know it as DNA. This is what most of us think of when we hear the term 'forensic evidence'. Hugely important in criminal investigations, it plays a key role in solving murders. So, what is DNA? Put simply, it is our body's programming system. It determines who we are, from our size and shape to the colour of our hair and how our body functions. It provides us with an *almost* unique code which defines and identifies us. I say almost, as identical twins will have the same DNA. That code is known as your DNA *profile*.

The most common sources of DNA are blood, skin, saliva, semen and hair. If a criminal leaves DNA at a scene and it is found, this can be used as evidence to link them to the crime. In reality, however, the *finding* can be a difficult process as traces can be microscopic, or in some cases, not present at all.

If two people fight, there's a reasonable chance DNA will be found. This is because they have had physical contact. In other cases, such as a shooting, it can be challenging. If I fired a gun at someone from a distance, I am unlikely to leave any DNA evidence due to there being no physical contact.

The Problem of Cross-Contamination

DNA evidence has its dangers, as someone can inadvertently pick up DNA and move it to another location. This is known as cross-contamination. Investigators have to be mindful of this, especially when we consider their ultimate goal of *securing a safe and proper conviction at court*.

Imagine this. An officer is at a crime scene and, without realising, steps in some of the victim's blood. That same officer, in those same shoes, goes to the home of a suspect to arrest them. The officer walks into the suspect's house and some of the dried blood comes off his shoe and onto the hall carpet. A forensic examination is carried out, during which the blood on the carpet is found. Now we have evidence linking the suspect to the victim which, on the face of it, is damning. But that blood got there via *cross-contamination*.

This is precisely why *full-barrier clothing* is worn at crime scenes. It also reduces the risk of an officer introducing their own DNA into the scene. Where possible, officers who have been to one scene shouldn't go to another.

I've often been asked my opinion of TV murder dramas. If I'm honest, I rarely watch them as they are usually unrealistic, particularly when it comes to crime scenes. The detectives often walk around the body with no protective clothing on, picking up the evidence with a pen. The same pen they were probably chewing on moments earlier. I appreciate that, for the purposes of entertainment, having everyone covered head to toe in paper suits wouldn't be viewer-friendly, but, as an investigator, it is annoying to see.

How is DNA Evidence at the Scene Collected and Used?

If DNA is found at a crime scene, how is that linked to a person?
The first step is to identify a DNA profile from whatever was
recovered, be it blood, semen, sweat, etc. That work is carried
out at a laboratory by forensic scientists.

If a suitable DNA profile is identified, it will be compared
with those known to have been at the scene, which will include
the victim. A search can also be made against the national
DNA database. In the UK, we have one of the world's largest
DNA databases, which holds millions of profiles.

If a match is made and the profile is believed to be from
a suspect, that person will be arrested. In custody, they will
have a new DNA sample taken, usually from a mouth swab.
The mouth swab involves scraping the inside of the person's
cheek to obtain skin particles. This new sample is directly
compared to DNA found at the crime scene. If there is a
match, a forensic scientist will give a statistical evaluation
of the likelihood that the person arrested is the same person
whose DNA was found at the crime scene. This number can
vary, but a good result would be one in a billion, meaning that
for every billion people in the world, only one would have
that DNA profile. With more than seven billion people in the
world, that means our DNA profile is not necessarily unique,
especially in identical twins, but it gives a high likelihood of
a match.

As techniques to identify DNA have progressed, it has
actually created some complications. The techniques are now
so sensitive that we can end up with mixed profiles. That
means the DNA of numerous people can be picked up from

one single sample. If there are more than three contributors, it makes it difficult, or sometimes impossible, to positively identify one single person. Think of it this way. If I held a gun, then passed it to you, and in turn it was passed to three other people, all of us would deposit our own DNA. When the scientist examines the gun, the mixture of our DNA is likely to prevent them from being able to draw out a single profile. I found this to be a regular occurrence that was very frustrating.

In the UK, DNA evidence cannot be used alone to convict a person of an offence. There would need to be some other form of corroboratory evidence in order to satisfy a jury that there hadn't been an innocent, random match. For instance, a person's phone placing them close to the crime, a witness identifying them or CCTV.

Myth Buster: *If you watch TV crime dramas, you probably have the impression that police can get results for DNA very quickly. Wrong! The best turnaround for Scotland Yard investigations, from collecting the DNA to getting the result of tests, is around two days and that is on items submitted for urgent examinations. The process of obtaining a DNA profile is slow, has several steps and cannot be pushed through any faster. For lab submissions not deemed urgent, results will take weeks, if not months. It isn't unusual for a case to go to trial while the MIT is still waiting for results from items submitted to the lab. On any single enquiry, the investigation team will be limited to a certain number of urgent submissions. Forensic science has been one of the services hit by government budget cuts, which is a major factor in why results can take so long. Once a person is charged with murder, there is a limited time they can remain in* *custody before a trial has to take place. There may be reasons for extending this time in custody; however, delayed forensic results due to overworked labs isn't one of them.*

Case File: As a long-serving Scotland Yard detective, you sometimes think you've seen everything. You feel there isn't much more that can shock you. Sadly, there always is. This particular case left me with a feeling of dismay at how a human being can be so cruel to a completely defensive victim.

We were called to a murder in East London, at a home for the elderly. It was the sort of home your parents would go to when they're too old and frail to look after themselves. A place where they can feel safe and relatives can take comfort in the fact their loved one is being cared for. That was the case for one 88-year-old lady who was unable to even get out of bed on her own.

On this particular day, her son came by on one of his regular visits. He was bringing her favourite dinner of fish and chips but what he found was too shocking to comprehend: his mum had been viciously murdered. Not only had she been strangled but also stabbed in the neck, just moments before he arrived. He tried to rouse her, but by that time she was already dead.

A detailed forensic search was made of the room, where we found bloodstains on drawers, indicating the suspect had opened them after the murder in order to take anything of value. So, we thought, the motive was robbery. The suspect must have had the victim's blood

on them, so an early arrest would be crucial in tying
them to the scene.

The one thing that I couldn't understand was why.
Why did they need to kill this lady? Seeing her in that
bed, how weak she looked, there was nothing she
could have done to stop the robber. I doubt she would
even have been able to identify them. Killing her
was needless. Whoever the killer was, they had to be
caught, and quickly. Who knew what else they would
be capable of?

Thankfully, the home had a good CCTV system,
which quickly gave us an image of the suspect. But we
were then presented with a bizarre twist: a member of
staff recognised the suspect as having visited the home
the previous day. Not only that, he had signed himself
into the visitors' book. Surely, we couldn't be that
lucky that he'd use his own name? But he had. We
were able to match the CCTV image with the name he
had used, leaving us in little doubt as to who he was.

The suspect was quickly located to a children's home,
where he was arrested for murder. He was taken to the
police station and interviewed in the company of his
solicitor. He completely denied having any involvement
in the killing, claiming to be elsewhere at the time.

As this was happening, we conducted a search
at the children's home. Quite often, in these sorts
of locations, only the suspect's bedroom is looked
at. But, in this case, all credit to our exhibits officer,
who ensured that all of the communal areas were also
searched. What she found, hidden behind a washing

machine, was a jacket. On a cuff of a sleeve was what appeared to be blood. This was submitted for DNA examination and the blood was confirmed as being from our victim. Although the evidence we already had was good, this forensic evidence was compelling. So much so that the suspect, who was only seventeen at the time, pleaded guilty to murder. He was sentenced to life imprisonment with a minimum recommended sentence of eighteen years. Five days after receiving this sentence, he committed suicide in prison.

Did You Know? *Although rare, a person can have two different DNA profiles, which is known as chimera. This can happen in a number of ways, including a bone marrow transplant, a pregnant mother absorbing cells from a foetus or a foetus absorbing cells from a twin. This has the potential for causing issues at a crime scene, as it could be possible for the recipient of a bone marrow transplant to leave behind the DNA of the donor.*

Fingerprints

Fingerprints have been used in criminal investigations for a long time. The first conviction in the UK using this evidence was in 1902. With the recent discovery of DNA profiling, you may think fingerprints have been superseded. This couldn't be further from the truth. Although DNA may seem like the sexy, younger sibling, the old-fashioned big brother is used more often in criminal cases. For an investigator, finding a good fingerprint at a scene is possibly better than DNA. Unlike DNA, our fingerprints are entirely unique to us. Even identical twins will have different prints.

Another advantage fingerprints have over DNA is that cross-contamination is not an issue. Positive match results are also quicker to obtain than when using DNA. Fingerprints can be matched to a suspect in a matter of hours, whereas DNA will take much longer. That time difference can be crucial in an investigation. The sooner a suspect is arrested, the more chance we have of capturing compelling evidence from them.

What Is the Difference Between a Fingermark and a Fingerprint?

Notice a slight difference in the terminology I use. Those from Scotland Yard refer to anything found at a scene as a *fingermark*. *Fingerprints*, on the other hand, are the impressions of a human finger that are physically taken from a person. Classically, that would be done by using black ink on the hands, which are then pressed onto white paper. In cases of murder and terrorism, suspects still have their fingerprints taken this way. In most other cases an electronic scan is made of the hands, which is less accurate than the old ink and paper method. The advantage of the electronic system is that the prints can be compared quickly with the criminal record database. This assists in identifying the person in custody. If they are lying about who they are, their fingerprints will give them away.

How Are Fingermarks Formed?

If we touch an object, we leave behind oil and sweat, which may leave an impression of our skin pattern. These patterns, unique to us, are found on our fingers, palms and the sides of the hands (the part we would do a karate chop with). How likely this is to happen will depend on the surface. A smooth surface, such as a door handle, would be better for showing fingermarks than a rougher surface, such as a brick wall. The mark doesn't need to be of the whole finger or palm for them to be matched to a person. A small section may be enough. These are known as *partial marks*.

A question that often comes up is, *is it possible to place a time on when a mark was left?* In general, the answer to that is '*no*'. Fingermarks can, in theory, remain for years.

Case File: A mark was found on a wall, not far from a murder victim's body. A search of the database showed the mark as coming from a police officer. All officers provide their fingerprints and DNA when they join, which can be used to eliminate officers from crime scenes. This particular officer worked on the other side of London, with no obvious reason for being at that scene. When we spoke with him, we found out he had visited the address several years earlier in his previous role as a telephone engineer. The mark had remained there all that time.

Case File: A fight in the street led to a man being killed. Nearby vehicles were examined, revealing a fingermark on a car belonging to one of the attackers. The owner was spoken to, and he confirmed that he had washed his car only two days earlier. This meant the mark could only have been made within the previous two days. This is one of the few ways in which a mark can be timed, although it will only provide a window rather than a specific time. Because of this mark, the suspect was forced to admit being present at the killing.

How Are Fingermarks Found and Collected at the Scene?

The two most common types of fingermark at scenes are known as *patent* and *latent*.

Patent marks are visible, usually because something is on the hands when they touch an object, such as mud or dirt. These can be photographed, allowing the captured image to be searched against the police's fingerprint database. The *best* mark that can be found at a murder scene is classified as *patent*. The Holy Grail of fingermarks, it is the one mark that *can* be timed and which is usually damning for a suspect. That is a mark in blood. If a suspect's fingermark is in the victim's blood, they will have some serious explaining to do.

Latent marks, on the other hand, are invisible, requiring special methods to make them visible. *How is this done?* Even after all these years, one of the main methods is still the use of aluminium powder and a brush. By dusting an area, the powder will cling to the oil and sweat left behind, bringing out the detail of a fingermark. This can then be photographed or have tape placed on it, which lifts the mark from the surface. The modern-day crime scene examiner will also use other chemicals, such as iodine and silver nitrate, to find marks as they change colour in reaction to the oil and sweat. Special light can also be used, such as ultraviolet, to bring out otherwise invisible marks.

Myth Buster: *Scotland Yard detectives do not look for fingermarks. That is the job of the crime scene examiner. Detectives have no training in how to recover marks. The only use they would have for a magnifying glass would be for the crossword.*

Did You Know? *Koala bears have fingerprints almost identical to those of humans. That must cause a few issues for Australian police.*

Blood

You may wonder why I've created a separate section for blood when we have already covered this above in DNA. Well, bloodstains at crime scenes can tell us more than *who* has bled. *Who* blood belongs to is important but *how* a bloodstain was formed can be even more so. The technique used for this is called blood pattern analysis (BPA). Forensic scientists use biology, physics and mathematics to establish how bloodstains occurred. In basic terms, they look at the shape, size, location and distribution of any staining to determine how it was formed. This can assist in revealing the locations of assaults, where people were, the amount of force used, the weapons used and the sequence of events.

If you ever watched the American TV series *Dexter*, you'll have an idea of how that works. The premise of that show is that Dexter, who works as a crime scene examiner, also happens to be a serial killer. Whenever he attends a crime scene, he has the knack of being able to interpret exactly how a person was killed by studying bloodstains. In real life, the interpretation isn't *quite* so simple or indeed accurate. However, his extra-curricular activities may give him a slight advantage!

Types of Bloodstaining

There are three categories of bloodstaining: passive, transferred and projected.

Here are some examples of types of staining:

- **Drop**: You're probably familiar with this type of stain. Imagine the blood on the floor after you have a nosebleed. That circular splatter is made from the blood dropping straight down. If that drop came from someone who was moving, the shape of the bloodstain would indicate the direction of movement. (passive)

- **Pool**: Picture a dead body lying on the floor with blood coming from a head wound and spreading out around the body. That is pooling. (passive)

- **Contact stain**: This happens when blood is transferred from direct contact between two objects. If a suspect has blood on their hand, then touches a door handle, the bloodstain on the door handle would be a *contact stain*. (transferred)

- **Cast-off**: This is when the blood comes off a moving object. An example would be a knife. As the suspect pulls the knife out of a victim and backwards, blood sprays off, casting a pattern. We often see that pattern on walls and ceilings. It looks like lots of small blood droplets. (projected)

- **Impact spatter**: If force is used on blood, the action causes a spattering outward in spots. An example would be someone getting hit with a hammer several times. After the first hit, the hammer begins to impact the bloody wound, causing it to spatter outwards. The size of these spots of blood indicates the amount of force used. The smaller the spots, the greater the amount of force. (projected)

- **Arterial spurt**: If an artery is severed, the heart will push blood out at great speed, in a spurting motion. As the heart pumps, the blood will spurt and stop, spurt and stop. That causes a distinct pattern, a bit like a zigzag. (projected)

The type of staining is important, particularly if blood is found on a suspect or their clothing. If the blood is a result of impact spatter, for example, this would indicate they had been close to the victim when the assault occurred.

How Is Blood Found at the Scene?

Firstly, a visual examination is carried out. Any staining that looks like blood can be tested at the scene. This is called a *presumptive test*, which indicates whether it may be blood or not. If this test is positive, a sample will be taken for submission to a laboratory. Further examinations will be made using lights that show stains that are otherwise invisible. Again, presumptive tests can be carried out on these. Finally, chemicals can be used that identify areas of bloodstaining by applying them to walls and surfaces. The most common is luminol, which reacts with the iron in the blood. This technique is useful if attempts have been made to clean the blood and there are only trace amounts left that aren't visible.

Case File: The murder was in a house in Peckham, South London, which was shared by several people. A man who lived there was stabbed to death. Witnesses saw a suspect running away from the scene. He was wearing a high visibility jacket, so he was easy to spot. He was stopped by police a short way away and arrested on suspicion of murder.

The man was interviewed and, as is normally the case, he made no comment. He did provide a short, written account, known as a prepared statement. In this he claimed to have come across another man attacking the victim and stepped in to stop the fight.

The victim had extensive injuries. At the post-mortem, he was found to have around forty-six stab wounds, including injuries consistent with an attack using scissors. One of the wounds was created with such force that it penetrated the victim's skull.

The suspect's high visibility jacket was examined by a forensic scientist, and the bloodstaining on it told a completely different story to the one he provided in interview. Knowing what you know now about blood distribution, you can imagine the patterns that would have been on that jacket. Needless to say, his story didn't hold sway, and he was found guilty of murder.

Case File: We were called to the scene of a murder. A 16-year-old boy had been killed in a gang fight. I spoke with the senior officer to get an understanding of the incident. As we were talking, I looked down and realised we were standing in blood. That is not good scene management. I followed the blood trail, which carried on for at least 200 yards. I had never seen a trail with quite so much blood. Whoever had bled must have been seriously injured. It transpired not to be a whoever but more of a whatever. In these sorts of murders, involving a large attacking group, they are often described as acting like a pack of animals. In this case, that was true. That poor boy had not only been stabbed but savagely attacked by a dog, who had left the trail of blood. It was the pet of one of the main attackers. We would later use that dog's DNA to link the suspect to the murder. It was a landmark case and the first where dog DNA had been used in a criminal prosecution.

Did You Know? *Blood pattern analysis (BPA) is a useful tool, but the interpretation has to be carried out by a person of sufficient experience and training for it to be accurate and valuable. In Australia, in 1980, two parents were convicted of killing their nine-week-old baby. Their defence was that a dingo had snatched the sleeping baby from a tent. BPA was used in the case against them, which included a bloody handprint on the baby's clothing and bloodstaining in their car boot. However, after several court cases, the parents had their convictions overturned. The bloody handprint turned out to be red sand, and the 'blood' in the boot of the car was proven to be a spilt drink. The case highlighted the importance of using properly qualified experts in the interpretation of BPA, and was made into the film:* A Cry in The Dark, *with Meryl Streep.*

Fibres

All fabric material is made of fibres. They are found in clothes, carpets, bedding, curtains, armchairs, etc. Whether the material is a natural fabric, like wool, or man-made, like nylon, they will shed these fibres: tiny pieces of material that are often invisible to the naked eye.

Those fibres will have their own characteristics, making it possible to match them to the originating material. This can evidence a person's contact with a particular material, which goes back to Locard's Exchange Principle: *every contact leaves a trace (see also* page 40). If I sit on a sofa, fibres from my clothing will remain on that sofa, while I will pick up those produced by the sofa. This exchange of fibres is strong evidence that I sat there.

Fibres are collected using tweezers or with sticky tape that is applied to a surface and lifted (similar to how legs are waxed).

If I was to ask you what a potential danger around this evidence might be, what would you think? If you thought cross-contamination, you'd be spot on. When dealing with such minute forms of evidence, there is always the possibility fibres could be accidentally picked up and moved by investigators as they move around the crime scene. This reinforces the need for full-barrier clothing.

Case File: Probably the most famous case to have used this type of evidence involved Ted Bundy (1946–89). Bundy was a serial killer in America, responsible for at least thirty murders. One of those was 12-year-old Kimberly Leach. Part of the evidence linking Bundy to this murder were fibres found in his vehicle, originating from Kimberly's clothing. Those fibres, combined with other evidence, were used to convict Bundy of that murder. He was also found guilty of numerous other murders and was sentenced to the death penalty, which was carried out on 24 January 1989.

Did You Know? *Fibre transference evidence was also used in the successful prosecution of black British teenager Stephen Lawrence's killers. This evidence came to light after a cold case review (when police re-examine unsolved cases), which was only possible due to advancements in this field of forensic science not available when the crime was first investigated in 1993.*

Footmarks

Every suspect, at every murder, will leave footmarks. The trick is finding them. Sometimes they're obvious; for instance, if they are made in blood. Usually, they are more difficult to identify, particularly when others have walked on the same floor. With murders, it is important to establish *who* has been at the scene so we can rule out any footmarks from police and others attending in a professional capacity. If shoe marks are found, you need to know who made them. It never ceases to amaze me how many people enter a crime scene. Police officers are inherently nosey, so, when there is a murder, there always seems to be an uncontrollable desire to 'have a look'. Add in ambulance crews, and it wouldn't be unusual to have ten or so people trampling around. This creates a lot of work for the investigating team, who would need images of everyone's shoes to compare with any marks found.

Once a crime scene has been established, this potential

destruction of evidence by people walking around it is addressed by the use of a *common approach path*. This is a route that people follow that minimises the potential they will walk over evidence. Stepping plates are also used. These are raised square steps that allow people to walk around the scene without treading on evidence.

How Are Footmarks at the Scene Collected?

If the footmarks are on a flat surface, they are photographed. If there is an indentation, for instance in mud, then a cast is made to create a 3D version of the mark. These are used to compare against footwear taken from suspects. A forensic scientist will give their opinion on any likely match. Their analysis is based upon the tread pattern of the footwear combined with any wearer characteristics. We all walk differently, which affects how shoes wear. Thus, two identical shoes, worn by different people, will have unique wear marks that could match that shoe to a mark found at a crime scene.

This isn't commonly used as evidence, as it is based on the opinion of the scientist, rather than exact science. If someone stepped in blood and created a footmark, the blood on the shoe would be better evidence. Plus, a shoe's tread wears over time. So, the sole of a shoe found six months later could look very different to how it did at the time of the murder.

Did You Know? *Just like fingerprints, the ridge detail on the soles of our feet is unique. This could be used as evidence to place a person at a crime scene if a suspect left a footmark with their bare feet.*

Firearms and Ballistics

The use of guns in London is widespread. Every year there are around 2,000 gun-related offences reported in the capital.[v] So, unsurprisingly, many murders result from people being shot.

When a scene is searched after a shooting, what is it they are looking for? The simplest way to answer that is to break it into three areas:

- The gun
- The discharge from the gun
- The damage caused by the gun

The Gun

If you want to convict a person of a shooting, finding the gun they used is quite helpful! Although you'd imagine a suspect would try very hard not to allow such an incriminating piece of evidence to come to light, this actually happens more than you would expect.

Let's start with a little exercise. Put yourself in the position of a person who has just shot and killed someone. When you fired the gun, unless a silencer was fitted, there is likely to have been a loud bang. (Any gun, by the way, will still make a certain amount of noise, even with a silencer.) That noise is likely to have attracted attention – the attention of people who may call the police.

So, at this point, you've killed someone, you've made noise doing it and the police are probably on their way. Now you need to make your escape. *What do you do with the gun?* If you get caught with it, you're in big trouble. So, you decide to get rid of it. But where and when?

That is a dilemma faced by all murderers in this position. If a murder is planned, the killer may have thought this through. If it was spur-of-the-moment, probably not. Either way, they will all have the same issue: *what to do with the gun?* Some will keep hold of it. Others will look to dump it as soon as possible. Everyone else will fall somewhere in between.

For those that ditch it straight away, they won't get caught with it, but there is a better chance it will be found. If it is, they may be linked to it forensically. On the other hand, the longer you hold on to it, the greater the risk of being stopped by police with it still in your possession. Even if you give it to someone else, there's no guarantee they won't get caught with it, and if they do, will they really not say where it came from? The reality is that suspects don't always make the right decision, and this can result in the recovery of the gun.

What Happens to the Gun When it's Found?

Firstly, the gun will be photographed in the position it was found so there is no doubt as to where exactly it was. Then it has to be made safe to handle. If not, there's every likelihood it could accidentally go off. Only specially trained personnel are allowed to carry this out.

Once safe, it will be carefully packaged while ensuring the forensic evidence isn't compromised. The gun will then be taken to a laboratory, where it will be examined for fingermarks and DNA. After that is completed, it will be examined by a ballistics expert. That examination will include a test firing. When a bullet is fired, marks will be made on it – marks unique to that gun. If there are bullets that have been recovered from the crime scene, this will allow the expert to analyse whether they were likely to have been fired from that gun. However, it isn't always possible to say that with complete certainty as it's based on opinion. If the markings are not clearly the same, the expert may only be able to say there is a *probable* match. If that is the case, the evidence may not be of a sufficient level for prosecution purposes. Checks will then be made to see whether this gun has been used in other shooting incidents. One gun is quite often used in a number of crimes.

Did You Know? *Ballistic matching was first used after seven rival gang members were killed by gunmen working for gangster Al Capone, on 14 February 1929 in Chicago, USA. That incident is better known as the St. Valentine's Day Massacre. A forensic scientist by the name of Calvin Goddard used a specially adapted microscope to compare bullets from the crime scene to those from Tommy guns taken from Capone's gang members.*

Types of Gun

The four most common types of firearm murder investigation teams (MITs) come across are:

- Revolvers – These are like those used by cowboys, with the spinning drum. They usually hold six rounds of ammunition. Once fired, the cartridge remains inside.

- Semi-automatic pistols – The most common type being the 9mm. Once fired, the cartridge case is ejected from the gun.

- Shotguns – Either single- or double-barrelled. They fire small, metal balls, known as shot. Criminals often remove the barrels to make them easier to conceal, commonly known as *sawn-off shotguns*. Their potential damage is frightening. If you perform an internet search of *shotgun* and *watermelon*, you'll see what I mean.

- Sub-machine guns – Yes, amazingly, these are used in the UK. They fire a rapid burst of bullets, with little accuracy. Suspects tend to pull the trigger and spray bullets from side to side. Innocent bystanders are as likely to get hit as the intended target. Cartridge cases are ejected after firing.

Did You Know? *In the year ending 31 March 2020, in England and Wales, there were 27 killings where firearms were used as the murder weapon. Of those, seven were licensed firearms.[vi] According to Home Office figures recorded on 31 March 2020, 586,351 people in England and Wales had a firearm and/or shotgun licence issued to them.[vii]*

The Discharge from the Gun

You may think that's a strange expression: *discharge*. Why not say bullet? Because, when fired, more comes out of a gun than the bullet.

Depending on the gun, five types of evidence may be present at the scene: cartridge cases, bullets, shotgun pellets, wadding and gunshot residue (GSR).

Cartridge Cases

A round of ammunition consists of more than a bullet. A cartridge contains propellant powder, above which is held the bullet. When the trigger is pulled, the cartridge is struck, igniting the propellant. Hot gases cause the bullet to separate and fire out of the barrel.

Depending on the weapon, the cartridge case may or may not be ejected from the gun. As they are manually put into a gun, cartridge cases can provide potential forensic evidence, i.e. fingermarks or DNA.

Bullets

It is bullets that cause the damage. When fired, one of three things is going to happen to a bullet:

1. They'll hit a person without exiting their body.

2. They'll hit a person then exit their body.

3. They won't hit a person.

If the bullet hits a victim without exiting their body, and the person is killed, the bullet will be recovered during the post-mortem.

If the bullet exits the body, it is *likely* to be found at the scene, although this can't be guaranteed.

If the bullet doesn't hit a person, it will keep travelling until it either hits an object or loses momentum. Finding these bullets can prove difficult. It is possible for a bullet fired from a 9mm handgun to travel for more than a mile. If a bullet hits an object, however, it is likely to be damaged. That damage could be fragmentation, or the bullet could be bent into a mushroom shape on impact.

Shotgun Pellets

Shotgun ammunition is different to that used in other guns. Rather than firing a bullet, they fire small metal balls, known as *shot*. Shot can vary in size from small pellets to one large slug. When used in a murder, pellets will remain embedded in the victim rather than exiting the body as bullets can. Pellets have less penetrating power than a bullet, but, collectively, they can cause a lot of damage.

Wadding

A shotgun cartridge will contain propellant and shot, between which is a piece of plastic or fibre, known as wad or wadding. This is likely to be discharged from the gun and is often recovered from scenes. The only forensic value from these is in identifying the type of powder used, which could suggest a link to a gun or a person, if the same type of powder is found elsewhere.

Gunshot Residue (GSR)

As I said above, when a gun is fired, it isn't only the bullet that comes out of the barrel. A small cloud made up of gases and microscopic particles is ejected from the gun. This is known as gunshot residue (GSR). The person firing the gun, and anyone standing nearby, will have GSR settle on them. The problem with GSR is that it doesn't stay on a person for long. As people move around, it starts to fall away and can be lost. If clothes are washed, then all traces of GSR are likely to disappear. There are various types of GSR, which differ according to the propellant used in ammunition. This can help link a suspect to a particular shooting.

The most infamous case involving GSR in the UK was the TV presenter Jill Dando murder of 1999. The man originally convicted had a single particle in a coat pocket, which his defence argued could have come from cross-contamination. His conviction was subsequently overturned, and the case remains unsolved.

In terms of finding GSR particles, what is considered good evidence? Here is a guide, used by some forensic scientists that I've worked with. This shows the relative strength of the evidence depending on the numbers of particles found:

- 1–3 particles – Low
- 4–12 particles – Moderate
- 13–49 particles – High
- 50+ particles – Very high

However, someone standing next to the shooter is just as likely to have GSR on them as a suspect, so the presence of these particles doesn't indicate *who* fired the gun. GSR could also be present on a person who handles a firearm without necessarily firing it. This evidence, therefore, has to be handled with care and not on its own seen as indicating guilt.

The Damage Caused by the Gun

As we know, a task of the crime scene examiners is to build a picture of events. It may not always be possible to know how many bullets were fired, particularly from witness accounts. Bullets won't always be found, and they may also fragment into lots of pieces. So, analysing ballistic damage is important in adding to the understanding of what happened. This could include looking for the number of bullet impact sites where damage is found and if angles of trajectory can be identified.

Finding the damage isn't always easy. Investigators may need to look beyond the crime scene to find it. As I said above, bullets can travel a long way. When found, the damage will be photographed and any bullet fragments recovered.

Case File: A shooting occurred outside a block of flats. At least three firearms were likely to have been used. As one group were fleeing the scene, they were fired upon and damage was caused to their car. Witnesses saw suspects searching for ejected cartridge cases. Even the most naïve of criminals know about the potential forensic evidence from these. Even so, we still recovered several cases from the scene. We also found a silencer.

Luckily, witnesses saw two of the group walking away from the flats. We carried out a search of the route they took and, hidden in a bush, we found a bag containing a pistol. We also found a pair of gloves.

The firearm was test fired, which confirmed it as the one used to kill the victim. The gloves were covered in high levels of GSR, suggesting they were likely to have been worn at the time the gun was fired.

DNA examinations were carried out on the gun, gloves and bag. DNA was found on all three, but unfortunately too much. Remember when I spoke about mixed profiles? Well, at least seven people had handled the gun, and the same number had worn those gloves. This was a gang crime, so that was to be expected. Firearms are often handed around. We managed to identify one person's DNA on the strap of the bag, which led to him being arrested and charged. At court, he was found not guilty of murder but was convicted for possessing the firearm. Although the forensic evidence suggested it was this man who was likely to have fired the fatal shot, there was a lack of other evidence to support this (such as eyewitnesses). On its own, the DNA and GSR evidence were not enough to persuade the jury he was guilty of murder.

THAT'S THE THEORY OF FORENSICS, BUT WHAT HAPPENS IN REAL LIFE?

So, we've looked at the theory, but how does it work in real life? Let's look in more detail at a case we investigated, including the process and the professionals involved.

Case File: It all started with a dog walker finding a body in a bush (it always seemed to be dog walkers). It was a small grassy area in the middle of a South London housing estate. I say 'body', but it would be fairer to say *remains*. What we found was a skeleton with very little skin and no internal organs. Most bones seemed to be present, although the left hand was missing. The body was wrapped in a bedsheet, tied in three places, and underneath they were wearing a T-shirt, trousers and socks but no shoes. A suit jacket had been wrapped around the head. We could see it was a man due to a long beard. No identification was found on the body. There were no CCTV cameras nearby and no witnesses to tell us how the body got there.

The first to enter the scene were the crime scene manager, exhibits officer and photographer. Their first task was to establish a *common approach path* (*see also* page 58). The photographer captured the scene on film to tell the story. No blood was visible, and no weapons were found. The area was covered in sawdust but none was seen on the body itself. So, at that stage, that is all we had: a body, lying in a bush, wrapped in a sheet and clearly dead for some time. We didn't know if this was a murder or whether there was some other explanation for the death. As it transpired, the answer wasn't quite what we were expecting.

In this situation, what facts would you want to establish?
The first questions we were looking to answer were:

- Who is this person?
- What happened?
- When did they die?
- Where did they die?

Until we found those answers, it was going to be difficult to establish *why* that body was there, and *how he died*. With no witnesses, no CCTV and no idea who this person was, we needed the use of forensic experts. Let's have a look at who we sought help from:

Forensic entomologist: This expert came to the scene. Within the hollow of the body, she identified a large amount of beetle waste (beetle poo). To the untrained eye, this looked like soil. If insects have been through multiple life cycles, as these had, it makes it impossible to put an estimate on when the death happened. However, from the type of insect activity that she recorded, she *was* able to say death had occurred elsewhere and therefore this was a deposition site.

Forensic pathologist: As I mentioned earlier in the book, forensic pathologists play an important role in establishing the circumstances of a death. Although they mostly examine bodies in the mortuary, during a special post-mortem, they sometimes examine a body at the scene. On this occasion, he didn't feel that was necessary. He would use photography to get an understanding of the scene. We carefully removed the body, to be transferred to a mortuary. Sawdust was underneath, and above were recently cut trees. As none of the sawdust was on top of the body, it was clear it had been deposited *after* the cutting.

A special post-mortem was conducted, but establishing a cause of death was going to be challenging. There was hardly any skin and nothing remained internally. A fracture was noted to one rib, but it was unclear whether this had occurred before or after death. The left hand was missing, as were some toe bones. Identification from fingerprints was not an option due to the absence of skin and DNA profiling would take some time.

When had death occurred? The pathologist could not be sure, but he estimated around a year ago. He based this on the level of decomposition.

Forensic odontologist: The deceased still had teeth, but without any idea of his identity, we had no dental records for comparison. So, this line of enquiry was a non-starter.

Forensic anthropologist: We submitted the rib to a forensic anthropologist to establish whether the fracture was ante- or post-mortem. Unfortunately, this was inconclusive, although the fracture was minor and would not have contributed to the death.

So, at that stage, we had very little to go on. The only point we were confident of was that victim had died elsewhere.

In the background, we were carrying out extensive enquiries to identify the deceased. We conducted house-to-house enquiries in the area, which meant we visited every address looking for information. This housing estate was huge, so my team and I spent days knocking on every door. We met some very nice people but none who had any useful information.

We used human remains dogs to search for any other site where the body may have been. These dogs are highly trained, and it is possible for them to find buried bodies even after quite a few years. Their skills are honed using pig carcasses. Unfortunately, their search came to nothing.

One fact we did establish was that the tree cutting had been carried out only five days before we found the body, narrowing down when it was placed there. We seized extensive CCTV footage and circulated images of the clothing via the media. Posters were delivered locally. The missing person database was searched. None of these enquiries provided any further answers as to who the man was or how he may have died.

During investigations like this, you sometimes need a lucky

break, and that is what we got. We were two weeks in and no closer to knowing who this man was or why he was in that bush. It was nearing the end of another long day when we received a phone call from local police who had arrested a man in suspicious circumstances. The local authority had sent cleaners to a flat after receiving complaints from neighbours about smells emanating from the residence, which was not far from the deposition site. On arrival, the cleaners had found some bones that appeared to be human fingers. Police were called, and the man was arrested on suspicion of murder. He was then cautioned: 'You do not have to say anything. But it may harm your defence if you do not mention, when questioned, something which you later rely on in court. Anything you do say may be given in evidence.'

His response to that caution was, 'He died naturally. He died of natural causes. Parkinson's disease.'

Of interest, he had changed his name during the process of being brought in for questioning. He had given one name at his flat and another when booked into the police station.

He was interviewed on two occasions with a solicitor present. Throughout both interviews, he mostly exercised his right to silence by answering 'no comment' to the majority of questions put to him. All he would say was that he had no idea why the bones were in his flat, the friend he mentioned had died ten years before and that he had never heard of the name he originally gave to police.

Under these circumstances, we were left with little option other than to bail him. Further enquiries would be needed. What these revealed was that this man was not the lawful tenant of the flat. However, he had been purporting to be him for a very long time. The actual tenant was the person whose name he had originally given to the police.

We were able to trace two sons of the real tenant. We spoke with them, and they told of a strained relationship with their father. They hadn't spoken to him in years.

They provided DNA samples which, along with the finger bones and a femur from the deceased, were submitted for DNA examination. The scientists were able to use familial DNA to show that both the femur and the finger bones belonged to their father.

We looked into the deceased's medical history, which showed he was not a well man. He was suffering from various conditions, including heart disease. He kept regular appointments, so we were able to identify when he was likely to have died, almost to the day. What we were shocked to realise was that this was ten years ago. The reports of the smells had also gone back years, fitting with this timeline. The body had remained in the flat for that whole period. This was a studio flat, with only a kitchen, bathroom and a single room for living and sleeping. It is in that room that the body remained. *For ten years*. Decomposing and crawling with beetles, maggots and flies. All while this man lived, ate and slept in that same room.

Why didn't he tell anyone? Because the flat was in the name of the deceased, and this man feared he would end up homeless if he reported the death. For years, neighbours complained of the smells, but it was only ten years later that the local authority did something about it. They sent a letter to the flat informing the tenant they were coming to clean. Knowing this, he felt he had to dispose of the body.

For those ten years, he took on the identity of the dead

man. He claimed the dead man's pension. Otherwise, he thought people would become suspicious. He didn't want to be dishonest, so he didn't claim his own pension.

The Crown Prosecution Service (CPS) were asked to make a decision on how the man should be dealt with. There was no evidence that this was a murder. The deceased man was not a well person, with a number of ailments that could have killed him. Technically, an offence under the Coroner's Act had been committed as he should have informed people of his friend's death. Their decision was that prosecuting him wasn't in the public interest.

As for the dead man, he got to have a funeral, but one attended by only me and a colleague. All in all, a very sad set of circumstances.

CONCLUSION

So, what have we learned about crime scenes? They can be many things – from a person, to a vehicle, to the place that the suspect dropped their weapon. They are the foundation of a murder investigation, providing you with much of the evidence that you need to begin your journey towards conviction. They are also where the future of the investigation hangs in the balance if good procedure is not followed. If poor decisions are made at the beginning, lawyers can easily poke holes in your case at the finish line. However, detectives don't carry out much of the work at a crime scene. It is during the investigation stage where their skills become essential. So, let's move on to the next section of this book, where the detective takes centre stage.

CHAPTER 3

THE INVESTIGATION

INTRODUCTION

I'm sure you've seen many murder dramas, usually involving a central character and a sidekick. It's often a detective chief inspector or detective inspector, with their trusty detective sergeant in tow. After a few twists and turns, they eventually catch their suspect. All very neat, and all very unrealistic.

The reality is very far away from that fictional world. Murders aren't investigated by one or two people. They are investigated by dozens, all as important as each other in solving a case. If you see one person claiming credit for a high-profile conviction, take it with a huge pinch of salt – no one person is *ever* responsible for a conviction.

In contrast to these stories, it isn't, in general, exciting work. It's about attention to detail, being methodical and having logical strategies in place. Murders aren't solved on one piece of evidence or quickly. Investigations can take years, sometimes without ever finding the killer. Scotland Yard traditionally solve around 90 per cent of murders, which, although impressive, still means some killers don't get caught.

Those that are caught will be defended by top barristers, whose job it is to undermine the work of the investigation team, sowing doubt in the minds of juries. That means murder investigation teams (MITs) are held to the highest standards in everything they do. Any mistakes *will* be found out, then used to potentially help killers walk free. So, where do we start as detectives?

Let's begin by looking at what the first few days of an investigation really look like.

What Is it Like at the Start of an Investigation?

Let me paint a picture of an investigation at the outset. While the work at the scene is happening, the rest of the team will gather together. The likelihood is they would have just started work, preparing themselves for a long day ahead (the first of many long days).

The senior officers will meet to discuss what resources are available to them. From a team of thirty, rarely will everyone be available. Some will be absent due to leave, courses, court trials, sickness or other abstractions. It wasn't unusual to begin a murder investigation with fewer than ten people.

Officers will then be assigned specific roles for the investigation. The roles people perform are rotated, so no officer does the same on every enquiry. Certain roles require specific training, such as family liaison and exhibits. Another consideration is activity on other investigations. At any one time, each MIT is likely to be investigating approximately ten murders. Some investigations will be awaiting court trials, while others will remain unsolved. Every new murder affects those that came before. The more enquiries you have as a team, the less you can give to each of them.

Meeting with the Team

Constant and clear communication is hugely important in murder investigations. Any team, in any walk of life, is a group of individuals, each with their own tasks, but working towards a shared goal. All those moving parts must remain aligned, otherwise they could easily be pulling in different directions. Meetings are an important part of that process. Bringing people together to share information is the best way for everyone to understand where the team is heading and how their work fits in with others.

The first meeting gives the team an understanding of the incident. The first MIT officers at the crime scene provide that information, explaining exactly what has occurred and an outline of what actions have been taken. This will be an opportunity for the team to ask any questions of them. This stage of the investigation is known as *the handover*. This may include photos of the scene or any available CCTV footage, although information is mostly given verbally.

Once the handover has finished, the senior investigating officer (SIO) will instruct the team on who is tasked with particular roles and the early priorities. At the very start of an investigation, those priorities will be lines of enquiry such as managing scenes, the post-mortem, family liaison,

CCTV, interviewing anyone who has been arrested, urgent laboratory submissions and important witnesses. Those are the type of enquiries that will be conducted regardless of the circumstances. We will come on to hypotheses later and how they can steer an investigation; however, they are unlikely to have been formed at this early stage.

At the end of this meeting, all team members will know what their individual task is and will go off in their own directions to start work. I always found this stage quite exhilarating, especially on cases where it wasn't clear who the killer was. You may be thinking to yourself, *blimey, how are we going to solve this one?* But you know, from experience, that things can, and probably will, change quickly. What you know in a week is likely to be far more than you know at that point. It is that anticipation, of what was to come, that I found most exciting.

After that, the team will have at least one meeting a day in order to provide an update on progress made and on what each detective has found out.

Myth Buster: *We've all seen them – the boards that TV detectives use for an investigation. Decorated with photographs of the victim, potential suspects and the crime scene, and covered in arrows and question marks – they are like a mind map of the evidence. Now, I'm not saying that never happens, but it is rare. Each MIT works in an office that just about caters for twenty people. They will have anything from ten to twenty murder investigations, all running simultaneously. If every murder had a board like that, the team wouldn't have space to work. So, when you're thinking about what the investigation looks like, you can leave that detail out.*

The Collective Mind

If you are a fan of *Star Trek*, you will have heard of The Borg. If you're not, you're probably wondering what the hell I'm going on about.

Well, The Borg were one of the most successful species in the *Star Trek* universe. Their strength was a *hive mind*. They had a collective conscience, which means they were all aware of each other's thoughts and thus could work seamlessly as a unit. Yes, I know that's science fiction, but the theory has merit.

A murder team consists of around thirty minds. All with their own individual thoughts, experiences and viewpoints. When it comes to solving murders, good ideas on how an investigation should progress do not only come from senior officers. In many investigations I was involved in, suggestions came out of team meetings, leading to lines of enquiry that solved the murder. Every team member should have a voice, and good leaders must encourage that. There is an old saying, *two minds are better than one*. So, what does that make thirty minds? That said, with so many voices, people don't always agree. Ultimately, the SIO will have the final say in which direction an investigation takes.

PART I

INVESTIGATIVE THINKING

Here, we'll explore investigative thinking. That is, we'll delve into the thought processes of detectives – both creative and systematic – that allow them to develop hypotheses, outline effective strategies and make solid decisions to move the investigation forward.

WHERE DO WE BEGIN?

OK, so a new murder investigation has commenced. *Where do we begin*? Firstly, the team will ask themselves, *what do we know*?

What Do We Know?

In any murder investigation, murder investigation team (MIT) officers will attend the scene early on. Those officers will initiate the investigation, while gathering as much information as possible. At some point, those officers will meet with the investigating MIT, providing a full briefing of what has occurred.

The information available will vary. Some enquiries are more straightforward than others. For instance, in domestic homicides, suspects are frequently arrested early on because police are often called by neighbours to the incident or, on occasion, suspects phone in themselves. Killings involving people with mental health issues can be the same. They are rarely planned and suspects aren't usually trying to hide their involvement. Each investigation will pose its problems, but a lack of information in these categories won't be one of them. You will usually know who the victim is, what caused their death and when and where they died. It may also be obvious who the suspect is. The challenge will often be in showing exactly what happened, *proving* the suspect committed the murder (to a level that would satisfy a court) and understanding *why* the incident happened.

Other cases will prove more challenging, as the last case file in Chapter 2 proved (*see also* page 67). Some may involve the discovery of a dead person, with not much more to go on.

Other sources of information will be sought. Police databases may provide background, including crime reports. Previous incidents involving the victim and potential suspects, if they are known, may provide context as to why a murder has occurred.

Once you are clear on *what you know*, you need to seek answers to the question, *what don't we know?*

What Don't We Know?

A murder investigation is really about *finding answers to the questions you need to ask*. It's as simple as that. Nothing fancy, nothing complicated, just a set of questions you need to find the answers to. Yes, you can flower it up. Some people may even write whole books on the subject! But that is all it comes down to.

The trick is:

1. Knowing what questions to ask
2. Working out how to answer those questions

Knowing What Questions to Ask

Senior investigating officers (SIOs) are taught about the 5WH principle. It's a simple way of setting out questions you need answers to. *What is 5WH?* We had a glimpse of this approach with the case of the body in the bush, where this system helped shape the investigation. It is the use of six prompts to help focus the mind on what information is required. These are:

- Who?
- What?
- Where?
- When?
- Why?
- How?

With these, the SIO can go on to ask the questions needed to solve the murder:

- **Who** is/are the victim and suspect(s)?
- **What** happened?
- **Where** did it happen?
- **When** did it happen?
- **Why** did it happen?
- **How** did it happen?

In some cases, all of those questions will be known. In others, none of them will. With the body in the bush, we started with nothing.

Working Out How to Answer Those Questions

So, we know the questions, *but how do we get the answers?* That is the job of the detectives. Each will have tasks designed to fill in those gaps. But, to do that, a coherent plan is required. In other words, strategies.

Did You Know? *In English law, if two (or more) people commit a crime together, and one goes on to commit another crime, the other person(s) may also be liable for that other crime if they foresaw the other person may possibly have gone on to act like they did. This is known as joint enterprise. So, as an example, if two people commit a robbery, and one seriously assaults the victim who then dies, the other person may be guilty of being an accessory to murder if they foresaw that the other person may commit GBH. They may be found guilty even though they played no part in the killing. It is because of this law that multiple people are often found guilty of a single murder, particularly where gangs are involved.*

INVESTIGATIVE STRATEGIES

There are numerous lines of investigation available, meaning ways in which the team can gather crucial information and evidence in order to solve the case. These might include:

- Family liaison
- Special post–mortem

- Media appeals
- Witnesses
- CCTV
- Phones
- Intelligence
- Arrest of suspects
- Trace, interview and eliminate (potential suspects)
- Interviews of suspects
- Scene examinations and searches
- Submission of items for forensic examination

The officers involved in these enquiries need direction on exactly what path to take.

For the CCTV officers, *where do they look for footage?*

For the telephone officer, *what numbers do they investigate?*

For the intelligence officer, *who do they research?*

I talked earlier about *big goal, little goals* (*see also* page 15). It is those little goals that need to be identified in order to achieve the big goal: a safe and proper conviction. It will be down to the senior officers to set these, in the form of written strategies. And these strategies will be tailored towards answering those six questions. We'll look at most of these lines of enquiry, in more detail, later on in the chapter. In the meantime, you may be wondering how they answer those questions, especially in cases where little information is known. If all you have is a body, how do you know where to look for those answers?

A useful tool used in murder investigations is the use of hypotheses.

DEVELOPING HYPOTHESES

We've all seen a murder on the news and speculated on what may have happened. *I reckon it was the boyfriend.* That sort of thing. When we do that, we are forming a hypothesis. That is no different to what the investigating team do. However, forming investigative hypotheses doesn't mean speculating wildly on what may have happened. These hypotheses are based on known information and logic.

The more available information, the more specific those hypotheses are. Conversely, if little is known, the hypotheses will be broader. As an example, if a person is murdered and they are known to be a drug dealer, a reasonable hypothesis would be that they were killed as a result of that illegal activity. There may be other hypotheses, but the most obvious one would be the main focus of the investigation. This is known as the *working hypothesis*. However, these have to be fluid. An investigation will go where the evidence takes it, so if fresh information comes to light that contradicts the current hypothesis, a new one will need to be considered.

If a victim has been in a volatile relationship with a history of violence, the most likely hypothesis would be that the partner was responsible. Again, that would be the *working hypothesis*. However, if a person is found murdered and there is no indication as to why, there are likely to be several hypotheses, all as probable as each other. In that instance, they would all need to be worked through, eliminating those that can be. These hypotheses would also be broader, as little information is known. Examples of broad hypotheses might be:

- Murdered by a person known to the victim
- Murdered by a person unknown to the victim

As investigations progress, more information will become known. So, hypotheses can become more specific, be eliminated or other hypotheses formed. However, how hypotheses are actually used is the personal choice of the senior investigator. I tended to use them, while I saw others who did not. There are no hard and fast rules or any guidebooks available. Some may decide to base all of their decision-making on a hypothesis, using it as a driving force for their investigation. Others may keep a more open mind and merely keep it in the back of their thoughts while gathering evidence.

Let's look at a real-life example to illustrate how they can be used in practice.

Case File: There is a saying in murder investigations: *Learn how someone lived and you will learn how they died.*

In *most* murders, there is a link between victim and killer. That link may be loose, but it is normally there if you look hard enough. However, immersing yourself in horrific murder scenes, or the lifestyles of some victims, isn't always an easy thing to do, even for experienced murder detectives.

We were called to the scene of a double murder in Norwood, South London. The scene was a ground-floor, one-bedroom flat. It was an old 1960s block. The front door looked straight out on to a grassed area. Inside, we found one of the most horrific crime scenes I've ever seen. When we walked through the front door, the bedroom was to the left. In there was one victim, who I will call Man A. He was lying on his bed, facing up. His covers appeared half on. The impression this gave me was that he had been asleep prior to the attack. An attack of extreme brutality. He was covered in blood, as was his bedding. There was *cast-off blood* up the walls. This poor man had not only been continually stabbed, but his face was a bloody pulp. It didn't take a lot of detective ability to work out what had caused those injuries. Lying on the bed next to him was a clothes iron, broken and bloody. He had stab wounds all over his body. Too many to count. It was impossible to tell what the man looked like facially, but from his grey hair, he appeared to be at least in his fifties.

When you examine a crime scene, you look for anything that appears out of place, for any sign of what may have taken place. A technique I used was to stand at the door to a room, slowly scanning across. *What can I see? Should that be there? What looks unusual?* What jumped out from this room was lying on the bed. This was a scene of brutal violence, with blood everywhere. But, across the bed were a pair of trousers, completely blood-free. They must have been placed there *after* the attack. Interestingly, both pockets had been turned out. *So, was this a robbery?*

To the right of the bedroom was the living room. On the floor was a mattress, turning this room into a second bedroom. Next to the mattress, face down, was a second man: Man B. He was wearing a T-shirt and jogging bottoms. Through his top you could see stab wounds into his back. To me, it looked like he had been stabbed where he lay. Again, more wounds than could easily be counted. This man looked slightly younger, with long hair and a Mediterranean appearance. Looking for anything unusual, one item screamed out at me. Just feet from the victim in the living room lay a single latex glove. *Why would there be a latex glove near to a murder victim? Could that be from one of the police officers who attended?* If so, that was poor scene management on their part. *Or was it from a suspect?* If it was, that told of preplanning. This was a suspect who was aware of forensic science. Either way, we needed to get to the bottom of why it was there.

The attack in the living room looked less ferocious. That threw up immediate questions. *Was that significant? Was the attack more personal on Man A, or had he simply put up more of a fight?* Something else stood out: some blood on the floor that gave me a glimpse into this man's final seconds of life. There were drag marks in blood, showing he had pulled himself along before succumbing to his injuries.

What did the number of injuries tell us? Having more than sixty stab wounds is unusual, some of the most I had seen. Even twenty stab wounds are more than we see in most murders. To me this suggested a number of possibilities. In my career, I had seen several murders with similar injuries. They all tended to involve either severe mental illness, a crime of passion or a drug-fuelled attack. *Surely it had to be one of these?*

I always tried to put myself into the position of

the victim. It helped me get a better understanding
of the scene. A picture of their last moments. I found
this scene chilling. Man A was apparently asleep
when attacked. *Did he have a chance to wake up? Was he
disturbed by noise but unable to get out of bed fast enough?*
Either way, those last moments of his life would have
been terrifying. And then the other man; dragging
himself along the floor with stab wounds in his back.
*Was he being stabbed while desperately pulling himself across
the floor? Was he trying to call someone for help?* Both
murders were utterly awful.

There was one other discovery, something that gave
us a glimpse into the past. There were no lights on inside
the flat, but we found the reason for that: no electricity.
There was a key meter which had run out of credit.
We went to a local shop and topped this up. When the
power was switched back on, we were presented with a
picture of the scene at the time of the murders. As soon
as the power was back, a television came to life in the
living room. The volume on high. That room's light also
came on. *So, was Man B awake before it happened?* On the
other hand, no light came on in the bedroom. *Did this
add to the idea of Man A being asleep?*

The victims were taken to the mortuary for post-
mortem examinations. *How could this help us piece
together what happened to these two men?*

Man A had been stabbed more than sixty times,
to his face, neck, chest and back. He also had defence
injuries to his hands and arms. *So, he had put up a fight.*
If he was asleep at the start, he certainly wasn't for long.

He also had severe blunt force trauma injuries to his face and head. *That must have been the iron.*

Man B's injuries told of a different story. He had stab wounds to his chest and neck, one of which severed his carotid artery – the artery that runs down the side of your neck, carrying blood to your brain. This was in addition to the stab wounds on his back and confirmed the image I had of a man being attacked, falling to the floor, then being stabbed again while lying face down.

As this was going on, we were carrying out various enquiries to establish what may have happened. Unfortunately, there was no CCTV in the vicinity of the murder. No witnesses saw or heard anything. The family of Man A described the two as being purely flatmates. Their only mutual acquaintance was a work colleague of Man A, who introduced him to Man B as a potential lodger.

With little to go on, some broad hypotheses were required to keep the investigation focused and help us to conduct enquiries that would identify the suspects, no matter the true circumstances.

So, what hypotheses would be considered for this scenario?

At this stage, we considered three, all of which had to be pursued simultaneously:

1. The murders were carried out by one or others *known to Man A*.

2. The murders were carried out by one or others *known to Man B*.

3. The murders were carried out by one or others *unknown to both*.

These hypotheses covered any scenario likely to develop as the investigation progressed. When pursuing hypotheses one and two, it would be key to understand the lives of both men. To achieve this, family, friends and work colleagues would be interviewed to build up *victimology*, which is an exercise in seeking a thorough understanding of a person's life. In addition, the content of their phones, social media accounts and computers had to be examined. Their home was thoroughly searched, phone records obtained to understand who they had been in contact with. The use of intelligence would also play an important part in building a picture of their lives.

If hypothesis three were true, it would likely be the result of a break-in gone wrong. In that case, we needed to look at all burglaries in the area, as well as local burglars who were known to use violence.

As you can imagine, following up all three hypotheses, at the same time, is a huge task. As we progressed, there were aspects of each victim's life that suggested a potential motive.

On the face of it, Man A's life was unremarkable. He worked hard, mostly keeping to himself. There was no obvious reason as to why somebody would want to harm him. When we searched his phone, he had some messages that could possibly have led to a motive, although it was unlikely. However, with no other indication of why he would be targeted for murder, we had to follow these up.

Man B was a drug user who associated with other drug users. This led to a hypothesis that it was his lifestyle that had led to the murders. We interviewed those he most closely associated with, all of whom denied any knowledge of the attack. We then spoke with a cousin of the victim, who lived in America. He told us Man B had mentioned a falling-out with two friends, which stemmed from him making an advance on one of their girlfriends. When we had spoken with those friends, neither told us of this falling-out. We analysed phone records, which suggested Man B had met the two friends a day before the murder. CCTV was traced from that location and showed them together on the same road. Another fact not mentioned by these friends. They were arrested but maintained that they had nothing to do with the murder. Their DNA was taken and they were bailed from the police station.

Hypothesis three, at this stage, looked less likely. There was no sign of forced entry to the flat, and nothing appeared to have been stolen. Although those trouser pockets had been turned out, there were valuables that hadn't been taken. Phones were openly on charge and cash was found in drawers. There were also no recent burglaries in that area and certainly none where violence had been used. This allowed us to put hypothesis three on hold and focus on one and two.

With more information available, the other hypotheses could become more specific:

1. The murders were carried out as a result of Man A's phone contact.

2. The murders were carried out as a result of Man B's falling-out with his friends.

This allowed for non-relevant lines of enquiry to be put on hold, while focusing on aspects that would go to prove or disprove these new hypotheses.

Having hypotheses and actually being able to prove them are different matters. As a team, we favoured hypothesis two, the falling-out with friends. It just made more sense. But we were struggling to get the evidence to back those suspicions up. I vividly remember us being in our office late one night with everyone's photographs on a board, one of the few times we actually did this. We had a timeline of what we knew and a large map showing locations of people at different times. We were all bouncing ideas around, trying to think of an angle we may have missed – we were sure we were on the right track but we just couldn't confirm it. The frustration among us was palpable.

In the background, forensic examinations were taking place. The problem with a scene such as the one we found is that there's a huge number of potential forensic submissions. There were dozens of swabs for blood and DNA, and they couldn't all be examined at once. These have to be prioritised in terms of those most likely to yield results. Forensic scientists then slowly work their way through them, which can take weeks, even months.

Many of those forensic swabs came from the post-mortems. Sometimes, in investigations, small things can happen that completely change a case. At Man A's post-mortem, we had a very experienced crime scene manager (CSM). The pathologist is responsible for taking the swabs and usually decides which to take. At this procedure, however, the CSM noticed some blood on a toe: a round drop, similar to a nosebleed. He pointed this out and persuaded the pathologist to swab it. His rationale was that, if the victim was lying down, *why would he have a drop of blood on him?* That turned out to be one of the shrewdest decisions I've ever witnessed in an investigation. The blood spot turned out to match DNA taken from one of Man B's friends. Just thinking about it now, it still amazes me. Man A was covered in blood, with some of the worst injuries I've ever seen. To notice that one drop, and how it differed from the rest, was outstanding.

Just like London buses, once a break in the case happens, more often come along. Swabs from the arms of Man B contained DNA taken from the other friend. That same friend's DNA was also inside the latex glove found at the scene. This DNA, combined with other evidence, was enough to charge them with murder. At trial, they admitted being present but blamed each other for the killings. The jury was not convinced, finding both guilty of murder.

I will talk later about the reasons people kill, but in this instance, the incident with the girlfriend triggered emotions like anger or disrespect. Those emotions,

fuelled by drugs, led these two to take the lives of those
men – the man in bed had nothing whatsoever to do
with that.

This result was achieved by firstly following broad hypotheses
while the information was limited, and then becoming more
specific as more details came to light. One of the things an
investigator has to be careful of is making assumptions. These
can often come from what is known as a *gut feeling* or sometimes
referred to as a *copper's nose*. As officers, we all like to think we
have good instincts, and most probably do. But as often as
those instincts may be right, there are times when they are
wrong so the danger is following those instincts at the expense
of the evidence. We will look at *confirmation bias* in the next
section about decision-making. Recognising that possibility
when forming hypotheses is crucial. Making a hypothesis too
specific too early, without having the information to justify
it, can seriously jeopardise an investigation if you turn out to
be wrong. Following the leads that stem from that hypothesis,
while ignoring others, is likely to result in the loss of evidence.
So, if we have a gut feeling, we listen to it, but we must
understand that we may be wrong.

Creating a Hypothesis in Practice

Just as an exercise to get you thinking, consider this scenario.
A 17-year-old girl has been reported missing by her family.
She left home to see a friend and never arrived. She hasn't
been heard from for nearly thirty-six hours, and none of her
friends know where she is. Her phone is switched off, and
there has been no activity on her bank account. Presented

with these facts, what hypotheses would you consider as appropriate? Remember, at the early stages of an investigation, they will need to be quite broad, with the potential to develop as the investigation progresses. If I was the senior investigating officer (SIO) for an incident like this, I would consider five hypotheses as reasonable in these circumstances. I would also start with scenarios of her being alive, then look at those if she was dead.

As I said, given the circumstances, I would consider five hypotheses:

1. The girl is alive and at a location of her own free will (she perhaps ran away).

2. The girl is alive and at a location against her will (kidnapped/abducted).

3. The girl has been murdered by one or others known to her.

4. The girl has been murdered by one or others unknown to her.

5. The girl has come to harm in some other way and will be in a hospital or at some unknown location (illness/accident/suicide).

Until more information is available, all five hypotheses would be considered and explored. You cannot assume she is dead, as this may prevent her from being found safe and well. Equally, you cannot assume she is alive, as important evidence may be lost if this became a murder enquiry. Finally, harm can come to a person in other ways.

Five active hypotheses may seem a lot, but, in practice, the work for each will overlap. Let's look at some likely lines of enquiry that would support these hypotheses:

- **Phones**: Information sought will include calls and texts, as well as where the girl's phone had been used. This is relevant for all five hypotheses.

- **CCTV**: We would look for footage of where she was last seen, and attempt to track her movements. Again, this is relevant for all five hypotheses.

- **Witnesses**: This could include friends, family, work colleagues and neighbours. All of these people may hold information relevant to each hypothesis.

- **Forensics**: This could be less relevant until we identify potential crime scenes. However, the girl's DNA is likely to be sought from her home, probably from a toothbrush. This will enable identification, should she be found dead and other methods aren't available. If she has been killed but her body is not found, then her DNA may be needed for comparison to samples from crime scenes.

- **Intelligence**: Building a picture of her life is important in all five hypotheses (victimology). This includes understanding who she associates with, the places she frequents, how she travels around, any issues she may have in her life, her relationships with her family and whether she has ever gone missing before.

- **Media appeals**: Asking the public for information or sightings will assist in all hypotheses.

The enquiry team will then seek to narrow down the hypotheses or formulate more specific ones.

Now, suppose the worst was to happen and her body was found. One of the first questions that needs to be answered is: *how did she die?* If there is evidence that she was murdered, that immediately eliminates three of the hypotheses, leaving only two:

1. The girl has been murdered by one or others known to her.

2. The girl has been murdered by one or others unknown to her.

So, although the team may still have little information, they will carry out enquiries that cover both these eventualities. No time would be wasted and no evidence lost. The team will then come back to those six questions:

- **Who** is/are the victim and suspect(s)?
- **What** happened?
- **Where** did it happen?
- **When** did it happen?
- **Why** did it happen?
- **How** did it happen?

You can now see how investigations begin. Even with little information, the team can progress enquiries in a focused, methodical manner. Starting broadly at first, they then become more specific as more information is obtained. With all that in mind, the next time you see a news report of a murder, consider the types of hypotheses the investigation team will be working towards.

INVESTIGATIVE DECISION-MAKING

Any murder investigation involves a series of decisions, all of which are open to the most intense scrutiny. Months later, highly experienced barristers, with the benefit of hindsight, will judge decisions you had to make, often when you had limited information and you were under time pressure. They can also come with huge risk attached. Without wishing to sound overly dramatic, some decisions can be a matter of life and death. They concern the most dangerous individuals in society. These are people who have killed and would do so again. If poor decisions are made, they can end in catastrophic results for police officers, members of the public and witnesses.

These factors make good decision-making an essential skill for senior investigators. However, no matter how skilled a person is at decision-making, poor choices still occur. I have made them myself. Whenever I made a decision that turned out to be wrong, or saw others do the same, I looked at *why*. *What was it that led to that bad decision*? This has led me to believe there are five common reasons for poor decision-making.

Why Do We Make Bad Decisions?

1. **A lack of focus on the objective**: Not being clear on what outcome is being sought.

2. **Having too little information or seeking too much**: Not having enough information to make an informed decision; or wanting to gather so much information that you end up delaying the decision or, worse, not making one at all.

3. **Confirmation bias**: Having a predefined choice that clouds your judgement, leading you to search for corroborative information or interpret information in a biased way.

4. **Too many or too few options**: Having a narrow set of choices or too many to choose from, creating *choice overload*.

5. **Not considering the consequences**: Failing to consider what could go wrong if you make a certain decision.

Did You Know? *A log of the important decisions is maintained in all murder investigations by the senior investigating officer (SIO) and Investigating Officer (IO). These are recorded in a specially designed book with self-carbonating pages, where each decision is timed, dated and signed. The defendant's lawyers will have access to this book, meaning all decisions are carefully audited and transparent. Each entry will also include a detailed rationale of how that decision was arrived at. This ensures the integrity of the decision-making process within Scotland Yard murder investigations.*

How to Make Better Decisions

In thinking about *why* bad decisions are made, I considered what methods we could use to make better choices. I didn't want to stand in the witness box of the Old Bailey, trying to justify a bad call. To prevent that, I developed a system for decision-making that addressed the reasons these poor choices were made. When I had a decision to make, I would work through each of the five stages below. Handily, they formed an easy-to-remember acronym: DI COP.

1. **D**efined goal: You need to be clear about what your aims are. Without a clear objective, *how can you expect to make the right decision*? In murder investigations, *securing a safe and proper conviction at court* needs to be at the forefront of your thinking.

2. **I**nformation: Consider and seek the information you *need* to make an informed decision. In any decision-making process, there will be things that you *need* to know and things that would be *helpful* to know. You should always prioritise seeking out the information that you *need* to know. This ensures you focus your resources and don't waste time gathering information without a clear purpose. As an example, when a decision is required on whether a suspect should be arrested, you *need* to know what information exists that indicates they may have committed the offence. Without that, how can you be satisfied that reasonable suspicion exists? It would be *helpful* to know where they were on the day of the killing, what their offending history is, how much contact they have had with the victim, and whether they changed their behaviour in any way after the murder, etc. However, it's possible to make the correct decision without those details. Plus, if that information isn't readily available, with the time it takes to find it out, you'll likely start losing evidence if you pursue it before arrest.

3. **C**onfirmation bias: In order to avoid this trap, you need to be conscious of it as a problem. You must ensure you have an open mind and don't jump to

conclusions. I have seen information being sought to *confirm* a decision so many times, rather than looking for information to help *make* a decision (I've been guilty of it myself). A classic example of this in murder investigations is where a suspect has been identified, with the team seemingly fixated on them at the expense of any other evidence. The most famous case where this occurred is probably the investigation into the murder of Rachel Nickell, who, in 1992, was brutally murdered whilst walking on Wimbledon Common with her young son. The investigators were convinced that a man by the name of Colin Stagg was the killer, going as far as using an undercover officer to try to obtain a confession from him. They charged him with the murder, but the trial collapsed at court, and rightly so, as he was innocent. Some years later, the real killer was caught, and admitted the crime. As confirmation bias goes, this is an extreme example of what can go wrong.

4. **O**ptions: Decision-making should never be binary. If you find yourself deciding between only two choices, you've gone wrong somewhere. You are ignoring other options. I always forced myself to think of a third option, which quite often presented the better choice. There may be more than three, but that has to be the minimum, and try not to have more than five, especially if options are being created just for the sake of having them. Having too many options can cause its own problems, with the decision-maker

suffering from choice overload. There has been a lot of academic research that has proven this theory.

5. **P**repare to be wrong: Imagine you have made a decision. *What if that option turns out to be wrong?* Try to look at the repercussions for each decision in this way, as it tends to focus the mind. Contingencies should also be considered to address any consequences you want to avoid. As an example, a suspect has been identified for murder but police can't locate him. They make a decision to release a previously-taken photograph of him in the media to appeal for help from the public in finding him. They then get a call which results in him being found and arrested. Great work, yes? But then they have to put the case together against him, including the use of identification parades. A witness picks him out, which proves to be important evidence at the trial. His defence then use the fact his face was all over the news to undermine the identification. They accuse the witness of picking out the person they saw on TV, as opposed to who they saw committing a murder. If that decision to release the image goes on to undermine the case at court, it doesn't look like such a great choice, does it? It is thinking forward to what could go wrong that prevents these sorts of issues.

So, how does that process work in practice? Let's look at a real-life example.

Case File: We were the on-call murder investigation team (MIT) when we were called to the scene of a murder. There had been a large fight involving around ten men from two rival gangs. It was the sort of scene that I would describe as chaotic. That is no criticism of the officers there as there was an awful lot going on. Multiple suspects, numerous scenes and several important witnesses.

I quickly had to get my head around exactly what had gone on, which started with obtaining a briefing from the inspector in charge. One of the first things we discussed was a witness that was with some of his officers. It transpired he was a friend of the victim who was likely to have been at the scene when the fighting was taking place. The inspector asked me *should we treat him as a witness or arrest him as being involved in the fight*? I had been at the scene for barely two minutes and was being asked to make a decision that could have huge ramifications later if I got it wrong. By now I had developed the DI COP method of decision-making, so I ran through that process in my head. As you'll see, when I explain my thought process, it may not necessarily follow that particular order.

The first thing that occurred to me was that I would need *more information* before I could make any sort of decision. I knew this man may have been there at the fight, but *what had he done? Had he committed any offences*? If so, *what*? Also, *was he being cooperative? Did he have any injuries*? Most importantly, *what had he said about what happened, and, in particular, what had he said in relation to the murder*? I told the officers to get me that information before I decided what would happen to him.

That last question was important when considering what my *defined goal* was, i.e. *to secure a safe and proper conviction at court* for the murder. Yes, there may have been some other offences committed, but with no other apparent victims, those offences would be minor compared to the killing, which had to be the priority. If he had information about the murder, that was the most important consideration.

I was also conscious of *confirmation bias*. We were investigating a gang crime, so there was a danger an assumption could be made about this man. If he was a member of a gang or, at the very least, an associate, views could be formed of him that could affect decision-making. I needed to ensure I didn't jump to any conclusions about him.

I then considered *options*. The immediate ones, as presented to me, were to arrest him or treat him as a witness. *How would each of those assist me in my goal?*

1. Arrest him for offences connected with the fight: This would allow us to secure any evidence on the man, i.e. his phone, clothing and forensic samples. But, in *preparing to be wrong*, once arrested, it would be difficult to get an account from him as to how his friend died. After all, that was the priority. It could also alienate him and we could lose an important witness.

2. Treat him as a witness to the murder: This would allow us to establish what had happened. He may help us identify suspects, leading to early arrests and securing of evidence. His account could be vital at any subsequent trial. But, in terms of consequences, we wouldn't have the power to take his clothing, phone and swabs for forensics. And, *what if he had committed offences*? If he had, the defence may accuse us of making promises about how he would be dealt with in return for providing a statement. If police are seen to obtain evidence through inducement, that can seriously undermine the witness's credibility.

As always, there must be other options. I had to consider what they may be. Firstly, my priority was the murder. The arrest for minor offences option seemed the least likely to help with our goal. So, treating him as a witness was favourable. But *what about those negative consequences*?

This thought process helped me form a third and more favourable option.

3. Treat him as a witness but with contingencies in place: This would mean: (a) seeking his cooperation to obtain his phone, clothing and forensic swabs, and (b) ensuring no promises were made in relation to any offences he may have committed and recording this fact. In terms of consequences, the largest would be around prosecution of any minor offences the man may have committed. By speaking to him about what went on, but not under caution, we could damage the case for those offences. But I considered it a matter of public interest that the murder took priority.

So, *how did this play out*? The officers came back to me and said the man was willing to cooperate. He was present at the incident and saw what happened. There was no evidence at that stage of him having committed any crimes. He was willing to go with officers to the police station and allow us to download data from his phone and take any forensics we needed as well as his clothing. He also provided a statement, although, if I'm honest, it was only half the truth. He refused to name those involved, even though we were sure he knew. However, his account was still important in terms of providing us with the background to what happened and some of the details of the attack.

My decision-making process was recorded, with a full explanation of my rationale. This was then disclosed to the defence and, as is often the case, was unchallenged. In my experience, when I recorded this process, with the rationale fully explained, more often than not I wouldn't be asked to justify my decision at court.

UNDERSTANDING MOTIVE

In murder, motive is an important issue. It is also the most complicated. In my research for this book, many of those surveyed wanted to know *why do people kill*? I'm sure it is something you would also like to know more about so in this section we will explore that most fascinating of subjects. We will look at the importance motive plays within a murder investigation, before going on to look at the reasons people kill.

What Is Motive?

Motive is what causes a person to carry out a particular act. Another way to think of it is motivation. If I go on a diet to lose weight, the diet is the *act*, but losing weight is the motivation or *motive*.

One reason to establish motive is for the bereaved family. For them, the answer as to *why* is huge. *Why was their loved one killed*? If they are to make any sense of their loss, this information can be vital. It can also be useful in assisting the investigation, as we discuss below.

Unfortunately, establishing a motive isn't always simple. To *know* what motivated someone to kill, you would need to understand what was going through their mind at the time. *How do you do this*? Well, they could tell you, but they usually don't. Plus, if they did, would they be lying? *Could you truly believe them*? For obvious reasons, therefore, this isn't always achievable.

The most reliable evidence of motive is from sources other than the suspect. That could include witness accounts, words written or said by the suspect before the act, CCTV, intelligence or history between the suspect and victim.

How Can Understanding Motive Help the Investigation?

In cases where it is unclear *who* carried out a killing, establishing a *potential motive* can lead to identification of suspects. If the victim is heavily in debt, *who are they in debt to*? If the victim has been receiving threats, *who were those threats from*?

Case File: It was a warm Sunday afternoon in June, one of the hottest days of the year. I was watching my son playing in a football tournament when I received a call. Little did I know at the time that this would lead to an investigation that would stay with me forever.

We were the team covering murders that week in South London. I was told there had been a fire, although nobody had died at that point. I left the football and made my way into work. Colleagues and I travelled from Lewisham to Tooting. I have to be honest and say that, at that time, I hadn't appreciated the impact this crime would have. I'd been to so many scenes in my career that they ceased to affect me emotionally. However, that all changed when we arrived and saw the devastation caused. This mid-terraced, 1920s-style house, in a quiet side road, was completely gutted.

Health and safety rules prevented me from going inside, which I was grateful for. There is something deeply disturbing about a house fire. As I looked inside this blackened wreck, I could see evidence of the family who lived there. Charred pictures on the walls and family coats hanging by the door. The fire must have been terrible, ripping through the whole house. It is one thing being told about a crime, but it is something else seeing it with your own eyes.

We were told there were five people in the house: a mother and her four grown children. It transpired that petrol had been poured through the letter box and set ablaze. It seems it was only by some miracle, and a passing member of the public, that the whole family had not perished.

At that stage, we hoped nobody would lose their lives, but the reports coming from the hospital were not good. All the family members had varying degrees of injury, but two of the sisters, one aged twenty-one and the other only fifteen, were in a serious condition.

There is a certain type of morbid humour detectives share. It's part of our coping mechanism. If someone from the outside overheard our conversations, they may think we are unfeeling or warped in some way. That couldn't be further from the truth. We care deeply. But to get through what we see, there has to be some light relief. You couldn't cope if you wallowed in the tragedy. Today felt different, though. None of us were in the mood for jokes. Everyone had a serious air about them. I could see it in my colleagues' faces. They were sharing the same thoughts as me. Seeing that burned-out house brought home the horror of what that family went through; what they were still going through. I can't think of anything more terrifying than waking to your house being on fire. There seemed a steely determination among all of us that, no matter how difficult, we were going to catch whoever did this.

Investigations aren't normally taken on by a MIT unless someone has died. On occasion, other units may expect us to take on an enquiry before a death. The problem with that approach is people often survive the unexpected. MITs struggle to deal with the current level of murders, so taking on more investigations just isn't sustainable. That does sometimes cause friction between the different departments. There was no such issue here. We all agreed that we wanted to take this case, regardless of whether everyone survived. Whoever did this needed to be brought to justice and we knew the best chance of that happening would be for us to carry out the investigation.

One of the first things we did was to send two family liaison officers (FLOs) to the hospital. Now, whatever I write, no matter the words I choose, I could never get across how hard that was. Those two officers spent days there, sitting with the mother.

Tragically, she lost both daughters. Their injuries were just too severe. Our officers were with the mother at the time of each death. Later in this chapter, I will explain the role of the FLO in more detail. For now, first and foremost, they are investigators. They were there to obtain information from the family in order to assist the investigation. They would help us to understand how they lived, so we might understand how they died. In these circumstances, given the trauma they had gone through and were still experiencing, that is so difficult. You must balance the needs of the family with the needs of the investigation.

So, why did this happen?

With little to go on at that early stage, we had two broad, working hypotheses:

1. Somebody from within the household was the target.

2. This was a case of mistaken identity and they were not the intended targets.

Let's consider each hypothesis in turn:

1. **Somebody from within the household was the target**: *Who were this family?* Extensive victimology was conducted on all family members. This showed them as being the most 'normal' people you could wish to meet. The children were either at school, university or work. Mum was a hard-working person too. They had no criminal history and no contact with the police. None of them were in a relationship that would suggest a motive for hurting them. There was no drug use. No debt. In fact, there was absolutely nothing that would give rise to such an attack. So, we concentrated the majority of our efforts on hypothesis two.

2. **This was a case of mistaken identity and they were not the intended targets**: If this were true, we needed to identify who the *real* targets were. The obvious place to start was the neighbours. We'd begin with those either side, then work our way out. Nothing. *What about houses that look similar?*

No. *What about houses in different streets with the same number?* No. *OK, has anything similar occurred in the area?* No. *What about gangs? Have there been local incidents?* Actually, yes. There were gang tensions, which we followed up. We even carried out arrests and executed search warrants. However, none of these led anywhere.

We had media appeals, spoke to everyone for streets around, collected vast amounts of CCTV footage and visited every petrol station for miles. Everything we did hit a brick wall. We couldn't find any reason as to why this happened.

Sometime later, our FLOs passed us information given to them by the family. In what was almost a throwaway comment, they told us of a boy that the younger sister had been seeing but who she'd broken up with. He had become upset by this.

However unlikely, it was the only lead we had with a possible motive. The decision was made to arrest this 14-year-old boy on suspicion of murder. We went to his home and found him in his bedroom. Whenever I arrest a person for murder, I make sure I'm looking them straight in the eye. If there is going to be something that gives them away, it's usually then. I saw no reaction from him. No look of fear or dread; no sense that he had been caught. *Maybe we were wrong?* At the police station, he was interviewed, denying any involvement with the attack. We had no real evidence, so he was bailed and given a date to come back in the future.

Whenever a person is arrested, a thorough search is conducted of their home. These can take days, as was the case here. In the meantime, we arranged for the family to stay at a local hotel. I drove some of them there, including his mum, dad and a male cousin.

We finished our search, seizing various items, including a petrol can and computers. It can take weeks to look through computers, but due to the circumstances of this case, we had the laboratory working overtime for us. One afternoon, we received a phone call from a lab engineer, telling us of a discovery on this boy's computer. The day before the attack, he carried out an internet search of '*how to burn someone's house down*'. To say we were surprised is an understatement. Even though he was the only person with an apparent motive, he was still just a child. None of us had ever come across a case where anyone of that age had been responsible for two murders. At almost exactly the same time, we were made aware that he and his family were due to fly out to Pakistan. We didn't waste a minute, driving to his house as quickly as possible. We found him there, bags packed, ready to go. He was rearrested, this time without getting bail. In fact, he wasn't released again. He was charged with both murders and convicted in court.

Our investigations revealed he had engaged the help of others, including the cousin I drove to the hotel who was also convicted of both murders.

There was no forensic evidence linking that boy to the fire, no CCTV footage and no intelligence to say it was him. The case was solved working backwards from his arrest. The computer evidence was the starting point, leading to phone evidence, CCTV images from near his house and forensics from his home. Without an exploration of that tenuous motive, I doubt the convictions would have been achieved.

After the case's conclusion, the girls' mother wanted to thank our team. She came to our office one lunchtime with nibbles and cake and made a point of thanking us all individually. I found the strength and dignity that lady showed truly humbling, and I will remember that handshake forever.

When Is Motive Not as Important?

Having said all that, I'm now going to contradict myself. You see, as important as a motive *can* be, it isn't *always*. In fact, in many murder investigations, the motive is never established.

You may be thinking, *is that a problem*? In all honesty, no. In reality, when a jury is considering a case, they will *not* be asked to look at *motive*. To explain this, think back to what constitutes murder. It is when you *unlawfully kill a person, with the intention to kill or cause really serious harm*. So, as you can see, the *why* doesn't come into that definition. It is all about the act, the death and the intent. Those are the points a jury will be basing their verdict on. *Why* the murder happened does not affect that process.

In an ideal world, the prosecution would want to show motive, as it creates a more persuasive case. Juries want to know *why* a murder happened. They are being asked to make an incredibly difficult decision, and I think it's just human nature to want to understand the reason behind such violent behaviour. I'm sure showing motive increases the chances of a successful prosecution, but it is quite hard to quantify.

Also, any motive needs to be proven, which can be difficult as we know from our discussion above. Often, motive comes as intelligence, which can't be put before a jury. To be used at trial in this way, the intelligence needs to be turned into evidence. That can only be done through witness testimony or documentary proof. Often, we have to accept that we cannot achieve this. Sitting through a trial, knowing *why* the murder happened, but accepting that the jury cannot be told, can be extremely frustrating.

The Murder Motive Categories

If I asked you to list some motives for murder, *how many could you come up with*? I would imagine quite a few.

If you research *motives for murder*, you will find numerous theories from academics, psychologists and law enforcement officers.

My experience of investigating killers, rapists and terrorists for more than half my thirty-year career tells me that the motive for killing falls into one of three categories. *What qualifies me to say this?* Spending time with these criminals, talking to them, looking deep into their lives, investigating their actions and seeking accounts from those closest to them.

These categories of motive are:

- **Push of emotion**: Where a person kills as the result of triggered emotion.

- **Pull of emotion**: Where a person kills in the pursuit of experiencing emotion.

- **Gain**: Where a person kills for a beneficial gain to them or others.

The exception to this is killings involving mental illness, a subject I will cover later in the book in Chapter 4, The Trial (*see also* page 293).

Murder is a *mens rea* offence. This means a killer has to make a *conscious decision* to *kill* or *cause really serious harm*. This is a decision, I think, made due to one of these three states of mind. Let's look at each one in more detail.

Push of Emotion

Where a person kills as the result of triggered emotion.

We all feel emotions. They result from chemicals being released in our brain, as a response to some form of *trigger*. Sometimes these have a positive effect on us, other times negative. On occasion, the response to this *trigger* can be so intense, it causes us to act in ways we wouldn't normally. We've all been there, but for most of us, it doesn't lead to acts of violence. If we get angry with someone, we may say something we later regret, but that is usually the worst-case scenario. However, as a detective, I saw the result of people not being able to control their emotions, be it anger, lust, jealousy, humiliation or the desire for revenge. Feelings so strong that they drove them to kill.

Case File: When I was called into the Detective Chief Inspector's office, I knew what was coming. We had worked together for long enough for me to read the signs. When he was about to ask me to do something upsetting, his face always gave him away.

A three-year-old boy had been killed while staying with relatives. His uncle had been arrested for his murder. When I joined the MIT, a separate team investigated child deaths. Budget cuts meant that team were disbanded, so their work now came to us. This was our team's first child death. Two of us would need to attend the post-mortem. This was what the DCI was going to ask me to do. I had been to many of these in the past, but only adults. Before I sat down, I already knew what my answer would be: *Yes, of course.* My first consideration was selecting which DC would come with me. I went back to our office, running through the team members in my mind. *Who is available? Who has the experience? Who will cope with what I will be asking them to do?* None of us had signed up for this. Child deaths were not our area, until now.

When I asked my colleague, I wasn't surprised by her answer. I knew she would say yes. *Are you sure you're OK with this?* She was positive.

We travelled to Great Ormond Street Hospital in London, where the post-mortem was to take place. As with most hospitals, the morgue is hidden away. A place that has to exist but one which nobody wants to be reminded of. We eventually found it, although not easily.

When we walked in, we met with the pathologist who was to carry out the examination. As is normal procedure, I gave him an account of what had occurred based on the information available. The boy had been staying the night at his aunt and uncle's house. The aunt, who had been working nights, claimed she came home to find him ill, so called an ambulance. However, when paramedics arrived, they judged the boy to have been dead for some time, contradicting her story. It seemed apparent that the boy had died while in his uncle's care. How he died, however, wasn't clear.

We then donned our full-barrier clothing and entered the examination area. Lying there, unclothed, was that poor little boy. No more than a baby. I'm not normally an emotional person, but on this occasion, I had to take a deep breath just to compose myself. I could see from my colleague's expression that she was feeling the same. There are some sights in life you just can't unsee.

The examination began. Early on, the injuries hadn't seemed excessive but then the pathologist stopped what he was doing. He told me that he didn't believe the injuries were consistent with the account I had given that the boy became ill in his bed and died there. He believed they were more consistent with having been hit by a car travelling at thirty miles per hour. That, or having been dropped from a first-floor window.

Doubting myself, I made a call to officers at the

crime scene and explained the situation. I needed to make sure the boy hadn't fallen from a window. I was assured there was no chance of that, but, even so, the pathologist still doubted me. The internal injuries this boy had were truly shocking. Seeing how much he had suffered was heartbreaking. *How could a person do this? What would drive them to end a young child's life in such a cruel way?*

As is often the case, all became clear later on. The truth of what happened played out at the trial. The uncle had indeed inflicted those brutal injuries on his nephew. Not by dropping him from a height, but by hitting him with his hands and feet. *The reason?* The boy had wet the bed. He inflicted injuries reminiscent of a car accident on a three-year-old, all because he had wet himself.

Why? He had felt emotion *(anger)* in response to a trigger *(his nephew wetting the bed)*, pushing him to murder that poor, innocent young boy.

Pull of Emotion

Where a person kills in the pursuit of experiencing emotion.

As we discussed, emotion is a response to a stimulus. It's a process we go through every day. As humans, we thrive on emotion. In fact, we actively seek it. We watch comedies in order to feel happy. The scarier the horror film, the more we enjoy it.

Some of us seek more intense forms of emotion. Take adrenaline junkies. They throw themselves out of planes or hurtle down mountains at breakneck speed, all to feel emotion. They're chasing a high so intense that they're willing to risk their lives to feel it.

The problem comes when the activities carried out to experience that emotion endanger someone else.

Think of bullies. They inflict pain on another person, either physically or emotionally, to feel better about themselves. If you take that to the extreme, that's what some murderers are doing: inflicting severe pain on others in order to feel positive emotion.

The classic example is domestic abuse. These perpetrators are often masking their inadequacies by seeking control over their partner. They commit cruel acts to give themselves a sense of power. Sadly, this too often leads to the death of their victim. In my experience, most domestic murders fall into this category. Of course, there will be instances where a domestic murder stems from a more spontaneous push of emotion, a flash of anger or jealousy, but I would say that most occur because of an emotional need (a pull) to control the victim over a sustained period. Thus, these types of killings aren't usually spur-of-the-moment. You may be surprised I say that and think most domestic murders stem from a *push of emotion*. If you do, I understand why and will explain shortly the reason I think a lot of people would have the same thought.

Sexual predators are another example. They are feeding their lustful desires by carrying out sexual assaults. Just like adrenaline junkies, those desires often need to be fed with increasingly serious assaults, sometimes leading to murder.

And then there is the worst kind of killer: the ones who do it for pure enjoyment.

Case File: As a murder detective, I would have liked to have investigated a serial killer case, but I didn't get the opportunity. Those cases present the greatest of challenges to investigators. You aren't just investigating one murder, but several, all of which need to be linked. Thankfully, these are very rare.

One such case occurred during my time on the MIT, which I played no part in. This killer was responsible for at least four deaths and the rapes of numerous men. He carried out these murders to gain sexual gratification, killing his victims by overdosing them with a drug called GHB (aka 'date rape' drug). His actions were classic *pull of emotion*. He had no regard for the men he killed, only a need to fuel his desires. He then disposed of his victims without a thought for their dignity or the feelings of their families, dumping their bodies in a graveyard, each time placing a bottle of GHB in their hand in an attempt to cover up his crimes.

Did You Know? *In the UK, there is no official definition of what constitutes a serial killer, although numerous attempts have been made to provide one. In legal terms, it doesn't exist as a concept. If a person committed multiple murders, they would not have any separate definition attached to them. Each murder would count as its own charge and conviction. The FBI's definition of a serial killer is 'the unlawful killing of two or more victims by the same offender(s), in separate events', although this is primarily used as a method of identifying when the FBI would step in to assist local law enforcement with a case. As a homicide detective, I find the fixation with serial* *killers understandable, yet misplaced. The reality is that people, especially women, are in much more danger from those closest to them. In the year ending 31 March 2020, in England and Wales, there were 131 murders of females where the identity of the suspect was known. Of those, 47 per cent were killed by a partner or ex-partner; just 18 per cent were killed by people they didn't know, none of whom was a serial killer.[viii]*

Gain

Where a person kills for a beneficial gain to them or others.

In the previous two mindsets, emotion played a key role. In this third category of motive, emotion is not the driving force behind a person's decision to *kill or cause really serious harm*. A person may be feeling emotion when they form that intent, but it is not the *reason why* they go on to kill.

In these instances, the person is hoping to gain something for themselves or others. In their mind, they need to *kill or seriously harm* the victim to achieve that gain.

I want that, but to get it, I need to hurt you first.

When I talk about gain, I'm not just talking about money, although that is clearly a popular motivation when we think about robbery. But gain is a much broader category than that. The gain doesn't necessarily need to be something tangible. Examples could be terrorists looking to further a cause, a prospective gang member killing as part of their initiation or a person looking to enhance their reputation to engender fear. They all want *something* that they are willing to kill for in order to acquire it.

Case File: In my days of dealing with terrorists, I encountered quite a few one-to-one. Some of the acts these people planned were shocking. I interviewed one suspect over the course of two weeks. It was an intense fortnight, with a lot of time spent together, building up a good rapport. In between questioning, we would joke around and talk about everyday things. According to his solicitor, this suspect missed my company on the days he wasn't interviewed.

Why was I interviewing him? He was part of an Islamic terrorist cell that was planning various terrorist attacks in the UK, with the aim of killing as many people as possible. This included the planting of a bomb at a certain point on the London Underground system to cause mass flooding; a plan to derail two busy passenger trains to cause a head-on crash; the blowing up of a tall building so it would collapse in on itself and the making of a 'dirty bomb' for which he and his co-conspirators had calculated not only how many people would die, but also the numbers that would go on to develop cancer and the rate of resultant defective births. To him, these were all justifiable levels of atrocity because he felt so strongly about what he would *gain* for his group's cause.

You may ask yourself: *How could you laugh and joke with him*? Someone prepared to do some of the worst things imaginable to other human beings. I will discuss interviewing in more detail later, but a fundamental part of talking to people in this situation is making them want to talk back to you. Whatever personal feelings I had for a suspect, no matter what they had done, needed to be put aside. If I had any hope of them speaking to me, I needed to focus on my own goals: to encourage them to reveal information that could assist in recovering harmful material such as weapons, explosives or chemicals; to provide an account of their actions and their intentions; and, ultimately, to acquire evidence of any crimes.

However, those lighter moments also allowed me a glimpse into this suspect as a human being. What I saw was, on the face of it, a normal guy. Apart from our religious beliefs, we had fairly similar backgrounds. We were both working class, growing up on council estates with similar educations and from good family homes. We both liked football, which we could talk about for hours. But, at some point, our lives took drastically different directions. What made him choose to do what he did, I will never know. I could never get this out of him. What exactly he thought his religious cause would gain from those terrible acts, I have no idea. Having seen first-hand the death and destruction terrorism brings, I cannot see what it achieves other than pain and misery for so many.

Does That Theory Work?

Can there be only three categories for motive?

To help answer that, let's look at a type of killing committed regularly in London: *gang murders*. It's probably the most common type of murder I investigated. *But what are the reasons behind it?* And *how do they relate to the three categories of motive?*

There are numerous reasons for these murders, including:

- Disputes over drug-dealing territories – gain

- Feelings of hatred for their rivals – push of emotion

- Enhancing gang reputation – gain

- Revenge for previous incidents – push of emotion

- Retaliation for disrespect shown in music videos – push of emotion

- The sense of power derived from the attack – pull of emotion

- Initiation into a gang – gain

- The thrill of killing – pull of emotion

- Robbery – gain

- To establish dominance in an area – gain

Whatever the reasoning, the overall motivation will always come back to *push of emotion, pull of emotion* or *gain*. The same is true of any murder. *Why don't you try it yourself?* Think of any scenario that may lead someone to kill. Other than when mental illness is the cause, the motive will always fall into one of these three categories. As you go through the case files in this book, have motive in mind and consider which one is at play.

The truth is, I believe that we overcomplicate the question of why people kill. Ultimately, killing a person is just an act. A terrible act with terrible consequences, but an act all the same. And, as human beings, we are motivated to act by just three reasons: *what we are feeling*, *what we want to feel* and *the benefit we desire*.

The Effect of Drink and Drugs on Motive

If a person kills while under the influence of alcohol or drugs, *how does that affect the motives for murder*? In reality, it doesn't. What this may do is cause a person to become more emotional, to reduce their inhibitions or cause them to make poor decisions. In which case, they may be more likely to kill, but that doesn't change the motive behind it. An angry drunk is still being pushed by emotion. A drunk rapist who acts because of lowered inhibitions is still being pulled by emotion. And a high drug addict who kills a person in a robbery is still acting for gain.

The exception to this would be where a person is so intoxicated they were unable to form the intent of *really serious harm* or *to kill*. If that fact can be proven by a defendant, they may not be guilty of murder, as it removes the *mens rea* element that is required to prove the offence.

The Psychology of a Killer

So, they are the reasons for *why* people kill but you may be asking yourself, *how is motive affected by the psychological make-up of a killer*? Does personality type, a personality disorder, a person's upbringing or a traumatic life event affect that decision-making process? Do those factors cause a person to have more of a propensity towards violence, thus making them more likely to kill?

Well, I'm probably going to disappoint you with my answer. The truth is, I can't say. I can guess, but my answer would be no more well informed than yours. I'm not a professional psychologist, I'm not even an amateur one. Whether any of those factors are relevant to the murders we investigate rarely becomes known. When they are, it will usually stem from a partial defence of *manslaughter by diminished responsibility*. In those instances, we try and get as much background on a defendant as possible to allow the psychiatrists to make an informed decision on state of mind at the time of killing. That would generally include information from those who had treated the killer for any mental health issues, past contact with police and background from those closest to them, such as friends and family. Rarely will we be able to get that information from the killer themselves. They seldom talk in interview, and, when they do, it will be to explain away what happened, not confess to it. So, as murder investigators, we are not exposed to any deeper reasons behind a person's decision to take a life.

When a case comes to court, other than for the above partial defence, the fact a person had some deep-rooted issue that may make them more likely to use violence is very unlikely to be raised. Firstly, the prosecution would not be allowed to use that as evidence against a defendant. A person's previous offending history *may* be admissible if it is relevant to the case. For instance, if the murder was the result of a stabbing and the killer had previously been arrested for possessing a knife. In that instance, the previous conviction would be seen as evidence of *bad character* and could therefore be put before the jury. But imagine if the defendant had a recognised condition such as antisocial personality disorder (ASPD). The fact a person has ASPD may make them more likely to act aggressively, but it wouldn't be allowed as evidence against them and rightly so. There are many people with that condition who don't go on to hurt others, so that diagnosis shouldn't be held against them.

Then consider the defence. Unless it is in respect of a plea to *manslaughter by diminished responsibility*, or mitigation as to an act of murder, *why would they raise an issue such as a personality disorder or a past traumatic life event?* It wouldn't be in their interest to do so. If I was on trial for a murder, which I denied doing, raising a personality disorder – one that could be construed as making me more prone to emotional and violent outbursts – is hardly going to help my cause.

It is for those reasons that factors that *might* make a person more likely to use violence are rarely raised at court. In turn, they are unlikely to form part of the MIT investigation strategy, although on occasion it may be helpful. Take the case with the boy burning down his ex-girlfriend's house (*see also* page 112). Most teenage boys get turned down by girls at some point. What they don't do is allow those feelings of rejection to drive them to kill. *Was that boy suffering from some form of personality disorder?* It would certainly go some way to explaining his extreme reaction. Although, as I say, it wouldn't have made a difference to the facts of the trial. But it may have helped that poor mum at least try and gain some understanding as to why her two daughters were murdered in that way.

When would these factors be more likely to come to light? Well, in all honesty, it would be far beyond the point of police involvement. If a killer is ever likely to fully admit their actions, along with the reasoning and background behind them, it would be after conviction and to a doctor in prison or hospital. It is for those reasons that detectives on MITs are not able to provide the answers to questions people may have on killer psychology. Those can only be answered by others with the experience to do so.

Did You Know? *Efforts are made to record the apparent circumstances of a murder, although that isn't always possible. In the year ending 31 March 2020, of 695 murders recorded in England and Wales, 49 per cent were categorised as a result of an argument, revenge or loss of temper (push of emotion). Only 6.5 per cent were recorded as being in the furtherance of theft or gain (gain).[ix] There is no category of circumstances that would indicate pull of emotion. Why? I suspect that is because, for that to be ascertained, an honest admission is required from the suspect (a rare event), but it also points to a more deep-rooted issue. I believe many of those recorded as loss of temper are in fact due to pull of emotion, particularly in domestic murders. It is much easier to put the killing down to a single explosion of emotion rather than a history of controlling behaviour, ending in an all too predictable result. I believe that stems from a problem we have in society where domestic violence is concerned. Look at it this way. If a kid is bullied constantly at school, which leads to violence, resulting in that kid's death, the narrative around the incident is 'child bullied at school is killed by evil tormentors'.*

Now, replace the bullies with a husband and the kid with a wife. I guarantee the narrative will become 'husband kills wife in a fit of rage due to her… (making him jealous/answering him back/burning the dinner)'. That husband has almost certainly been bullying and controlling the wife over a sustained period, but the killing will be attributed to one 'triggering event'. Worse still, there will even be some blame apportioned to the wife, even if it's at a subconscious level (she dared to make him jealous/answer him back/burn the dinner).

The headline about the school bully would never refer to how the kid wore glasses/spoke with a lisp/was a bit different. In that scenario, the narrative will always be about how evil the bullies are. Why this is goes deeper than my understanding. I suspect it comes from the fact the organisations who record, report on and investigate these matters are, or were, male-dominated institutions. Whatever the reason, until it is properly addressed, more lives will sadly be lost.

Myth Buster: *I mentioned serial killers a little earlier and how I haven't dealt with any personally. Very few murder detectives have. The reason for this is that, in the UK, they are extremely rare. During my twelve years investigating murder, there were only two confirmed serial killers identified in London, responsible for seven known deaths between them. In that same time, many more than a thousand other killings occurred. When murders connected to serial killers do happen, the huge amount of attention they get probably distorts the reality. That, and the fact that the media likes to convince you that there is a serial killer lurking in every town and city in order to create drama and boost their ratings. Thankfully, they are not.*

NOT ALL DEATHS THAT MITS ARE CALLED TO ARE MURDERS

We've been talking about murders almost exclusively in this chapter, but the truth is that MITs will be called to many suspicious deaths, not all of which are murders. They will probably attend more deaths that *aren't* murders than are. However, these will be treated as crimes until murder is ruled out. Quite often, a post-mortem is needed to eliminate foul play. Certain deaths can look suspicious, particularly when alcohol is involved. Heavy drinkers often fall over, causing head injuries. It can sometimes be difficult to distinguish murder from one of these deaths until the pathologist undertakes an internal examination. If a death is deemed non-suspicious or inconclusive, the investigation will be carried out by local detectives rather than a MIT.

Case File: Early one Sunday morning we were called to a suspicious death in West London. When we arrived, we found a dead man with the worst head injuries I'd ever seen.

He was lying across the pavement, his head near a parked car and his feet a few inches from a garden fence. He didn't appear to have any other injuries. There were no witnesses to what happened and no CCTV to help us. *Was it murder?* I walked around the scene, taking in everything I could see. It was a quiet side road on a warm summer morning. An area I was unfamiliar with but which seemed fairly affluent. It certainly wasn't a typical location for a murder. And on a Sunday morning? I know there aren't any rules as to when a person can commit murder, but this was definitely unusual. The spread of the man's head injuries suggested severe force, greater than I could ever generate. *Surely people would have heard a violent assault?* No, this didn't feel like murder to me, although I had been wrong in the past.

I discussed it with MIT colleagues, who were as flummoxed as me. Local police always expectantly look to MITs for answers, like we have some special powers of deduction in these mysterious cases. Alas, this is not always true. Certainly not on this occasion. I could only think of two hypotheses as to how these injuries had occurred, neither of which seemed that likely:

1. It was the result of an assault.

2. It was the result of a road accident.

I very much doubted the first, so I pursued the second. I arranged for traffic officers to attend, but there was no evidence of a crash. Plus, the matter from the head injury was on the pavement side of the parked cars. *How could that happen in a collision?*

We must have been quite a sight for any passers-by: half a dozen detectives, all perplexed and without a clue as to what had gone on. I'm not sure if I was actually scratching my head, although I wouldn't be surprised.

Then we all had an epiphany. As we were standing around, a plane came roaring over the top of us. We were on the flight path to Heathrow Airport, at the point when planes lower their landing gear. *It couldn't be, could it?*

We looked through this man's pockets and found his mobile phone, which was in French. We also found a coin from an African country. It was all pointing to him having fallen from a plane coming into land.

It turned out that was indeed what had happened. He had stowed himself on board a plane from Africa and fallen from the hold just before landing, although he was almost certainly dead long before this happened.

He had landed in between a fence and a car, with inches on either side. He was also only a few metres from houses. At that time on a Sunday morning, he could have landed on people sleeping in their beds and caused serious injury or death. It was a miracle that there wasn't more damage caused.

At the post-mortem, he was found to have broken virtually every bone in his body, which wasn't apparent from looking at him. As this wasn't a murder, the investigation into who this man was remained with local officers. Luckily, they were able to identify him and inform his family back home.

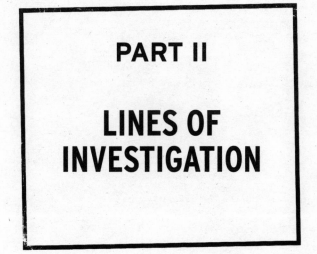

PART II

LINES OF INVESTIGATION

Here, we'll focus on the main lines of investigation that murder investigation teams (MITs) will pursue. This will also illuminate some of the key actors, processes and evidence types – from interviewing eyewitnesses to attending the post-mortem. The topics we'll cover are:

- Family liaison
- Special post-mortems
- Media appeals
- Witnesses
- CCTV
- Phones
- Intelligence
- Trace, interview and eliminate
- Criminal profiling

FAMILY LIAISON

I imagine you have lost someone close to you. Most of us have. Losing a loved one is probably the hardest experience in life, no matter the circumstances. If it's by murder, it is likely to be even more difficult. I say *likely* because I don't *know*. I met countless bereaved families and witnessed their grief, but, as much as I tried to empathise, I could never *know* what they were going through. Nobody truly can, unless you have been through it yourself. To lose somebody through illness or accident is one thing, but to have a life snatched away due to someone's deliberate actions is something else.

There is a reason I started this section by looking at this role. I've spoken a lot about goals. For the investigating team, a main one will always be helping the victim's relatives. The obvious way of doing that is to get justice for them by convicting those responsible. Beyond that, it is also about making the process as painless as possible. However, the criminal justice system isn't designed with victims in mind. There are numerous measures to protect offenders but little for victims and even less for their families. They will have so much to contend with once they become embroiled in the process of a murder investigation:

- They won't see the victim until after the post-mortem, which can take days.

- They will be asked to make a formal identification. If facial injuries are severe, there is a chance they won't be able to see them at all.

- It will take at least a month before the funeral can happen, sometimes much longer.

- Police actions can seem intrusive.

- The family may be hounded by reporters.

- A trial can take a long time to come to court. Before the pandemic it was at least six months from the point of a person being charged until the start of the trial. Since then, cases have been taking up to two years.

- If the family give evidence, the defence barristers do not always act with care, compassion or understanding towards them. I have seen parents of victims being given an extremely hard time, with no consideration of what they are going through, and being used to dig up dirt about the victim's past. You would hope they'd go easier on a bereaved relative, but sadly that isn't always the case. I saw one barrister accuse a victim's father of being involved in his son's drug dealing. There was nothing to suggest this was true; it was a narrative this lawyer had created to help his client's case. He was particularly accusatory and aggressive with this poor man. The judge even warned him to stop, which he just ignored, continuing this unfair line of questioning. After he had given evidence, all I could do was apologise for the way he was treated, even though it was not of our making.

- Finally, and possibly hardest of all, defence barristers are likely to target the character of the victim. They will often paint them in the worst possible light in an attempt to remove any sympathy from the jury, often blaming the victim for their own death while describing the killer as an innocent party. To hear that, on top of everything else, can be too much for some.

You might be wondering: *How do they cope?* In my experience, the answer is usually *with great dignity*. They will go through a range of emotions, some coping better than others, but the way most conduct themselves is truly humbling.

How Can the Family Liaison Officer Help the Investigation?

Now let's consider the role of the family liaison officer (FLO).

What is their role? Think of them as the link between family and the MIT. Their purpose is to facilitate information back and forth. When we consider the adage, *learn how someone lived and you will learn how they died*, the family will usually be key to that.

Let's look first at the information flow *to* the family. The FLO will help the family to cope with that list of difficulties above. They will ensure the family know what to expect as the investigation progresses. It can be an intimate relationship. The FLO will be with them throughout, from the moments after the murder up until the conclusion of the trial. It is sometimes the FLO who will deliver the awful message that their loved one has been killed. The FLO will be completely honest about how difficult the process can be; there is no point in sugar-coating it. There will be occasions when the family feel out of control and in the dark, believing that they have no voice or that their lost relative has been forgotten among everything else. They were certainly feelings often expressed to me by families.

However, when it comes to other aspects of the investigation, the FLO cannot always be so open. There will be details that cannot be given to the family. Sensitive information that has to remain within the MIT. As an example, this might be suspects' names. It would be wrong to share this with the family for several reasons. If that information got out, and the suspects knew they were being investigated, it could seriously jeopardise the recovery of evidence. There may even be occasions where retribution may be sought. There should be an agreement between the senior investigating officer (SIO) and FLO about what information can be shared.

When seeking information *from* the family, it becomes difficult for the FLO. Put yourself in that officer's position. You have just met a bereaved family dealing with the most unimaginable pain. They have, a few moments previously, learned someone close to them has been murdered. A bombshell that will take a very long time to process. While this is all still incredibly fresh, *you* come into their home. There will be a range of emotions being expressed. They will be demanding answers from you. *What happened*? *Who did it*? *Have you caught them*? Questions you probably aren't yet able to answer.

But helping them isn't the only reason you are there. The FLO is, first and foremost, there to investigate. They're not there to provide emotional support for the family, that isn't their role. That *can* happen; I guess it is hard to avoid. You are a detective, and part of the MIT, trying to solve the murder. To do that, you have questions of your own. You need to build a picture of the victim's life to establish victimology. You have to know about their love life, friends and enemies. You need to find out what car they drove and what phone they used. *Did they use social media*? *Where did they hang out or visit regularly? Where did they work? Were they involved in crime? Did they use drugs?* You will be trying to understand the most intimate details of their life, but you'll have no idea which of them may be crucial to the investigation. Their bedroom will need to be searched and computers seized. All of this while the poor family are going through what is, almost certainly, the lowest point of their lives.

How would you handle that situation? Would you feel able to do it? If you said *no*, you wouldn't be alone. Being a FLO is very much voluntary. No officer would ever be made to do it, and many choose not to.

So, *what training are FLOs given?* Firstly, only experienced detectives would be eligible to perform the role. They then attend a week-long course at Hendon Police College. During that training, they'll be given the tools they need to perform their role, but, in reality, no course can truly prepare them. The real learning comes from doing the job.

What Support Is There for the Bereaved Family?

If the FLO's role isn't technically one of emotional support, *who is there for the family?*

This is mainly provided by a charity called Victim Support (https://www.victimsupport.org.uk/). The Ministry of Justice provide funds for a section of this charity known as the National Homicide Service. This service is specifically for bereaved relatives of victims of murder and manslaughter. They provide practical support, such as helping with funeral arrangements or applying for compensation. They can also arrange for counselling.

Another charity is Support After Murder and Manslaughter (SAMM), which primarily provides emotional support (https://samm.org.uk).

In cases that result from mental illness, a charity called Hundred Families can provide help and advice (http://hundredfamilies.org).

Having seen these charities at work, the difference they make for bereaved families is often life-changing.

When the Relationship with Families Goes Wrong

The relationship between families and police is not *always* a good one. There can be various reasons for this, but I will not try and address these. They are numerous and often very complicated. Thankfully, this is the exception and not the norm. Of the cases I was involved in, there was only one where the relationship broke down beyond repair. In that instance, communication was made via the family's solicitors. The police will do everything possible to maintain a good relationship. If it can't be a *good* relationship, they will try and make it as workable as possible. It is in nobody's interest for it to be otherwise.

When the Relationship with Families Goes Right

In contrast, I could write a book on our positive relationships with bereaved families. Some of the most amazing people I've ever met had lost someone through murder. The way they carried themselves was inspiring, with such decorum and strength. I did often wonder to myself, *could I do the same in that situation?* My honest answer is *I have no idea.* They would have had dark moments, barely holding things together. Feelings of absolute hate and anger for the killers, as well as despair at their predicament. However, from the way they acted, you would almost never have known it. This was especially true at trials. Families were usually there throughout proceedings. Those closest to the victim would be allowed into the main area of the courtroom as opposed to the public gallery.

For many of them, the trial would have been their first opportunity to see the murderers. The people who had ripped their lives apart. *Could I guarantee I wouldn't lose it in that situation?* I don't know. These trials can be on a knife-edge and convictions aren't certain. Anything that could sway the jury against the prosecution's case may damage the chances of getting a positive result. It was a fear we always had, that someone from the family would lash out at some point, but they never did. Even in the face of some truly hurtful and often underhand tactics from the defence barristers, they retained their grace under pressure.

We will come to court trials later, but whenever the jury announced their verdict, the first faces I sought out were those of the family. Having been on this journey with them, to see the relief on their faces after a guilty verdict gave me incredible satisfaction. It was never going to bring their son or daughter back, but knowing justice had been served gave them some comfort at least.

When There's a Suspect in the Family

On some rare occasions, a murder suspect may come from within the bereaved family. If that happens, the FLO will be key to the investigation, which is why it is a role performed by experienced detectives. Any situation like this is very delicate. If a person is suspected of an offence, they shouldn't have questions put to them without first being cautioned. If they're not cautioned, then anything they say is likely to be inadmissible in court but that suspicion may not be enough to justify an arrest. It is on those occasions where decisions have to be watertight, with a detailed rationale.

Let's consider a scenario. Imagine a stepfather is suspected of murdering his stepdaughter, but those suspicions are based on a *hunch* rather than concrete evidence. If the MIT decide to arrest him, which turns out to be wrong, it is likely to have a huge impact on that family. The arrest would probably become public knowledge and even if no charges followed, the stepfather would have that hanging over him, probably for as long as the crime remained unsolved. Even then, if someone else is charged, the stepfather is likely to be brought into the trial by the defence, who will be eager to propose a viable alternative suspect.

On the other hand, if he isn't arrested, everything he says to the FLO will still be looked at by the MIT. If he then says anything incriminating, he could be arrested and charged. However, that decision not to arrest and question him under caution will be scrutinised. At any trial, the defence would do everything possible to exclude any comments he made before the arrest on the grounds he should have been cautioned. This could undermine any attempt to convict him.

As you can see, the decision-making process is critical and complex. Either of those options can potentially have terrible consequences. I often wonder: *Did we always get it right?*

Case File: A father had died from a stab wound to the chest. We found him with the knife still in his torso. It happened in the family home, with no indication of outside involvement. There was no sign of forced entry, a struggle or defensive injuries on the deceased. We were thus convinced somebody within the family had killed him. There were adult children in the household, as well as the mother. They all denied any knowledge, which left us in a difficult position. If we were going to prove who carried out the attack, we would need forensic evidence. To get that, we believed we needed to arrest the suspect, but *who was that*? We felt we had two choices: arrest everyone or arrest no one. With no arrests, we would lose any opportunity to collect forensic evidence.

So, the decision was made to arrest everyone. The rationale was that it was better to arrest the *wrong* person than lose the evidence needed to convict the *right* person. It was only after the father was fully examined that the truth became clear: he'd inflicted the wound himself. He had committed suicide by pushing a knife into his own heart. *How did we know*? When someone does this, they often stab several times before they summon up the willpower to push the knife through. This leaves tell-tale marks around the point of entry. So, the family were released and apologies made. *Were we wrong in what we did*? Absolutely. *Could we have done anything differently*? Yes, we could. In hindsight, there were other options we could have chosen. Options that would have prevented us from adding significantly to that family's grief.

As we discussed in our section on decision-making (*see also* page 102), if you find yourself choosing between just two options, the process is flawed. There are always other choices, you just need to give thought to what they are. This case happened before I developed the technique of DI COP (defined goal, information, confirmation bias, options, plan to be wrong).

To their absolute credit, they were understanding of the predicament we found ourselves in.

SPECIAL POST-MORTEMS

The main purpose of a post-mortem is to establish a cause of death. Post-mortems generally occur after a suspicious, sudden or unnatural death. They are conducted by pathologists: doctors specially trained in the examination of body tissue to determine disease.

In cases where homicide is suspected, the post-mortem will be conducted by a Home Office-approved forensic pathologist. The procedure for this is more thorough than a standard post-mortem and is known as a special post-mortem (SPM). They will normally be carried out within twenty-four to forty-eight hours of the body being discovered. The timing is generally down to availability of a suitably qualified pathologist.

How Can the Special Post-Mortem Help the Investigation?

The cause of death: First and foremost, a post-mortem helps to establish a cause of death. Remember, for a killing to be classed as murder, death needs to have been a direct result of an assault. For that reason, the pathologist has to look for all possible causes, including any natural ones. So, they will also seek to identify any underlying illnesses and, if they exist, whether they contributed to death.

When I talk about *cause*, it means *what* killed the person. A typical cause could be *gunshot wound to the head*. Another could be *stab wound to the chest*. A pathologist would not define the cause as something like *murder, suicide* or *accident*. Any comment on how that cause came about would come under *circumstances of death*.

The circumstances of death: The pathologist will be seeking clues as to the circumstances of how a person died. For instance, if a victim has defensive injuries, this may indicate a struggle.

What are defensive injuries? Typically, they are cuts or bruises to the victim's arms or hands. Picture someone being kicked to the head. Instinctively, they would pull their arms up to protect themselves, which would lead to bruising. Or, if someone is being attacked with a knife, they would put their hands up to fend off the attack. This is likely to leave wounds to the hands and arms. Conversely, a lack of defensive injuries may portray a different story: one where the attack was so quick that the victim may not have had a chance to defend themselves. They may even have been unconscious or restrained.

The identity of the deceased: If not already established, the post-mortem may help to uncover this. Methods of identification could include dental records, fingerprints, DNA, scars, tattoos and previous medical procedures. Essentially, they could use anything distinctive enough about a person that would prove it was them.

In England, formal identification is usually carried out visually, by a person who knew the deceased well.

The time of death: We will look at this in more detail later in the chapter, but it can be possible for the pathologist to provide an estimate on when death may have occurred. This is a subject that, for obvious reasons, is a sensitive one. If you feel this topic may be distressing, it may be wise to skip to the next section.

Who Is Present at the Special Post-Mortem?

Before we look at the procedure, let's consider who is likely to be there. At post-mortems where a murder is suspected, the following people will be present:

- Forensic pathologist
- Mortuary technician
- Crime scene manager (CSM)
- Photographer
- MIT detective inspector or detective sergeant
- MIT exhibits officer

There may be others, depending on the circumstances of the death.

The First Steps in the Special Post-Mortem

Before any procedure takes place, the MIT officers will provide a briefing to the pathologist, outlining what is known of the circumstances around the death.

At the start of the examination, photographs are taken of the deceased. This will continue throughout all stages of the procedure. It is essential to keep a record of the process and its findings.

An important task will be swabbing for DNA. These swabs are a larger version of the buds we use to clean inside our ears. The targeted areas are typically hands, arms and face. Fingernail clippings will also be taken for traces of blood, skin, hair and fibres from suspects. Any clothing the victim is wearing will be removed.

Before any intrusive procedures are carried out, they will visually examine the body, looking for obvious signs of injury. Certain injuries will aid in identifying the cause of death, but we will come to those later.

If the victim has been shot, an X-ray will likely be taken. This will assist in finding any bullets and their fragments. In some cases, the pathologist will ask for a CT scan, which will also assist in identifying broken bones. If fingerprints have not already been taken, this is likely to happen here to aid in identification.

The Special Post-Mortem Process: Going Under the Knife

The difference between a special post-mortem (SPM) and a regular post-mortem is the level of examination. In an SPM, the pathologist will be looking to identify all injuries, not just those that caused the victim's death. This is because every injury provides evidence as to how that death occurred and could be useful in a trial when convicting a suspect. For instance, a person may have died from a stab to the heart but bruising to other parts of the body would indicate the attack consisted of more than just one stab. Remember, this process is part of the effort to establish *exactly* what happened. Those injuries may not always be visible on the surface. For that reason, most of the skin is peeled back to look at muscle and tissue underneath.

The pathologist, aided by the mortuary technician, will make various incisions to the body. The internal organs must be accessed in order to be analysed. They will make cuts in a 'Y' shape to the front of the body, which allow access to the whole of the chest area. The sternum is then removed by separating it from the ribs, exposing the chest cavity. Each organ is removed and weighed on scales. There is a whiteboard on the wall where the weight of each is recorded. Slices will be made into each organ to establish how healthy they are. They must be examined for injuries *and* disease, as the pathologist will need to eliminate a natural death.

Case File: Three homeless men were living in a brick shed and one had been found dead. There was no sign of a struggle and his friends said he'd just fallen asleep and not woken up. He had a slight head injury, but, as a heavy drinker, these injuries weren't unusual. An SPM was arranged, more as a precaution than anything else. It was a judgement call as to whether we would have one. However, as soon as the pathologist opened the body up, it was clear we were dealing with a murder. The victim had massive internal injuries consistent with being stamped to death. Strangely enough, it turned out to be at the hands (or feet) of one of his friends. In this case, the special post-mortem provided us with crucial evidence that entirely changed the nature of our investigation. These were clues that we could not have accessed in any other way.

To access the brain, an incision is made from ear to ear. The scalp is then cut away using a scalpel. This allows for the front and back of the scalp to be pulled down, exposing the skull. To allow viewings by family, both sections are later pulled back into place. Using an electric circular saw, the mortuary technician will remove the top of the skull. This will expose the brain, allowing for its removal. It is this part that I found hardest. I never got used to it. Think of sitting in the waiting room at the dentist, hearing that drilling sound. It is like that, but a thousand times worse.

As an aside, mortuary technicians, in my experience, are a strange breed. I found them to have an extremely morbid sense of humour with a stomach for things beyond what most people could bear. I suppose doing that job would take a certain personality. During my first ever post-mortem, the technician ate a sandwich. They are, and perhaps have to be, completely immune to the horror of cutting up and delving into a dead body. They seem able to remove all emotion from the situation. All respect to them, though – it certainly isn't a job I could do.

Using a scalpel, the skin is separated from the body. The first time I saw this, I was shocked at what it revealed. Until then, I had never considered what *fat* looked like. It's bright yellow and not pleasant to look at – it made me want to go on a diet immediately.

Various samples will be obtained from the body. These include muscle tissue, which is used to raise a DNA profile. Blood will be taken for toxicology tests, usually to establish the presence of drugs and alcohol, although there are other uses.

All organs will be returned to the body, unless they are required for examination by specialists. They will try to return the body to as normal a state as possible, with incisions sewn up, so the relatives are able to view the victim.

The Second Post-Mortem

If a suspect is being investigated for a murder, they are entitled to ask for a second post-mortem of the victim. This is also carried out by a forensic pathologist and may be performed on the body or from photographs and notes taken at the original procedure. The reason for this is to ensure the findings of the first pathologist are tested. It is a right any charged person has in relation to all the prosecution experts, including any forensic scientists.

Discovering the Cause of Death

As I said earlier, one of the key ways in which a special post-mortem can help the investigation is by shedding light on the cause of death. There may be any number of reasons why a person dies. Let's have a look at four of the more common causes:

- Stab wounds
- Blunt force trauma
- Gunshots
- Asphyxiation

Stab Wounds

I've listed this first as in my career, this was by far the most common method of killing in the murders we investigated. Stab injuries are referred to as *sharp force injuries*. Superficial injuries are referred to as *incised wounds*. Ones that are deeper than they are wide are referred to as *stab wounds*. The pathologist will record where on the body a wound is found, the width of the entry wound, and the depth and injuries caused.

If a weapon is seized during the investigation, it is often taken to the post-mortem. The pathologist may then comment on the likelihood it was used in the murder. The weapon will be sealed to ensure there is no cross-contamination, which could compromise DNA evidence.

Blunt Force Trauma

This is one of the most common causes of death in special post-mortems, partly due to the fact it covers a variety of scenarios. It can include falls from a height, impact from motor vehicles, bomb blasts, as well as being struck by objects such as bats, bricks, hammers and fists.

Gunshots

When a gun is used, a ballistics scientist may be present at the SPM. They assist the pathologist in their findings and provide indications as to the type of firearm that may have been used.

Bullets and shot recovered from the body may help identify the type of firearm they came from.

Asphyxiation

We've all heard of it, but *what does it mean if someone dies of asphyxiation?* It is a lack of oxygen that leads to death. The two most common methods of asphyxiation relevant to murder are:

- Suffocation
- Compression of the neck or strangulation

Suffocation is the failure of oxygen to reach the blood. It can happen in a number of ways, including by smothering, suffocating gases and choking.

Compression of the neck: If enough pressure is applied to the neck, it will prevent oxygen from getting to the lungs. This is more commonly known as strangulation. The three categories of strangulation are:

- Manual strangulation
- Ligature strangulation
- Hanging

Manual strangulation is the placing of pressure on the neck by a person, usually with their hands.

Ligature strangulation relates to anything applied to the neck; for instance, a belt that is used to cut off the airway. Both of these can leave injuries to the neck. These can be external (on the skin, in the form of bruising), and internal, such as damage to the hyoid bone or larynx.

Small red spots, the result of haemorrhaging blood vessels, may appear around the eyes or on the forehead. These are known as *petechiae* (pronounce pi-tee-kee-a). This is sometimes the only external sign of manual strangulation.

Hanging is almost exclusively associated with suicide rather than murder. However, a hanging could potentially be used to cover up ligature strangulation.

Discovering the Time of Death

Myth Buster: *One of my earliest disappointments when attending post-mortems was discovering how inaccurate the timing of death is. I, like most of us, was brought up on TV dramas where the pathologist was able to give the police a time of death, down to the hour. In reality, only a window of when death has occurred can be given. The longer after death a post-mortem is conducted, the larger that window becomes. The only way to truly time a death is if it is witnessed.*

As soon as death occurs, predictable processes of change begin. It is these processes that allow the pathologist to give time estimations. The problem is, as predictable as those processes are, they are affected by other variable factors, which means that every case is different. These factors might be the temperature of the environment, whether the person had a fever or if the deceased had been doing physical activity prior to death.

Let's consider some of these key changes and how they can provide us with clues that might help the investigation. This isn't my area of specialisation, so I'm relying on the excellent *Time of Death, Decomposition and Identification: An Atlas* by Jay Dix and Michael Graham (CRC Press, 1999) to help inform my descriptions. The three key changes that occur are:

- Rigor mortis
- Livor mortis
- Decomposition

Rigor Mortis

You have probably heard this term before, *but what does it mean in practice?*

It happens after a chemical change in the body's muscles occurs, causing them to become rigid. This process is temperature dependent, with it being slower the colder the environment is. There is a pattern to this process, allowing it to be used in providing an estimation of time of death:

- One to three hours after death: rigor mortis begins to move through the body.

- Ten to twelve hours after death: complete rigor mortis, after which body starts to slowly relax.

- Twenty-four to thirty-six hours after death: rigor mortis will fully leave the body.

Once rigor mortis ends, however, it won't return. Those quite wide ranges show why this is not as accurate as TV pathologists might suggest. Rigor mortis can also help show if a body has been moved after death. If a body is found with an arm stiff in the air, for example, the deceased must have been moved after rigor mortis set in.

Livor Mortis

This is also known as hypostasis or lividity. When the heart stops pumping, gravity will act on the blood, causing it to settle within the body and resulting in discolouration of the skin. It looks similar to bruising, which can confuse people when they see this for the first time.

After around eight to ten hours, the colouration will become fixed. Up until that point, the blood will move and resettle if the body is moved.

- Twenty to sixty minutes after death: discolouration becomes noticeable.

- Eight to ten hours after death: discolouration becomes fixed.

Decomposition

As soon as a person dies, their body begins to decompose, although that process may not become apparent for some time.

The environment plays an important role in decomposition. In warm temperatures, for example, the process will be quicker, with the opposite being true in cold conditions. As is the case in a refrigerator, cold temperatures help to preserve organic materials. If a body is in water, or buried underground, the process will be significantly different to a body lying on top of the ground. To put that into perspective, a body that has been above ground for a week is likely to have similar decomposition to one that has been underwater for two weeks, or a body that has been buried underground for six to eight weeks.

The first sign of decomposition is a green discolouration of the skin, which begins in the abdomen. That process starts at around twenty-four to thirty-six hours after death. Other signs include swelling of the body and slippage of the skin.

Did You Know? *Soon after death, a person's eyeballs flatten due to loss of blood pressure.*

Entomology

Entomology is the study of insects, including their life cycle, which is another option in determining the time of death. We covered this science in Chapter 2: The Crime Scene (*see also* page 23), but as we saw, it is not always straight-forward, especially if death has occurred a long time before.

What Happens After the Special Post-Mortem?

At the end of the special post-mortem, the pathologist will usually give a provisional cause of death. If a cause cannot be established, further examinations are likely, including toxicology tests.

There may also be occasions where particular organs are sent to relevant experts. Most commonly, this would be the brain. That expert will carry out a more detailed examination of the organ, assisting the pathologist in their findings.

Once the pathologist has all the information they require, they will give the cause of death. There may be occasions when this is not possible, particularly in cases where heavy decomposition has occurred. The pathologist may be asked to present their findings to a court. If it is a homicide case, this will be at a criminal court. If a death has occurred in some other way, this may be at a coroner's court.

What Is it Like to Be Involved in a Special Post-Mortem?

I often get asked the question, *do post-mortems bother you*? As I said earlier, removal of the skull took some getting used to, but, on the whole, I've learned to cope with them. It is the odour that can be the hardest thing to deal with.

Case File: The worst experience I had turned out to be a death from natural causes. It was the height of summer and he was a heavy drinker. He was found in an abandoned toilet, living in a state you had to see to believe. As it wasn't clear how he died, we arranged for a special post-mortem (SPM). The undertakers took the body and the next day we attended the mortuary. As soon as I walked through the front door, I gagged – I had honestly never experienced anything like it. Well, that was until the body was opened up. I had to wear a mask while sucking on extra strong mints. With every out-breath, I tried to blow a minty breath up my nose. I have never fainted, but that was probably the closest I've come. Even the pathologist struggled. *Do you know who didn't though?* The mortuary technician. They were happily whistling away while the rest of us were struggling to keep our breakfast down.

Case File: The time I remember being emotionally affected by a post-mortem the most was nothing to do with our own SPM, strangely. We were in a children's hospital, which is where child SPMs were conducted. A colleague and I were standing waiting for our procedure to begin. We were leaning against one of the trolleys. Suddenly we both realised that, lying on it, right next to us, was a dead child. It was a pretty little girl, aged about five. She was wearing a flowery dress, her hair neatly done in pigtails. If I hadn't known better, I would have thought she was just sleeping. It suddenly struck me that, upstairs, there would be two grieving parents, having just lost their angel of a daughter. As a parent, that hit me hard. I don't know if it was because of the way she looked, the fact I wasn't prepared for it or the thought of those poor parents with their world falling apart. That was something I thought about for a long time and the image has stayed with me.

Did You Know? *In the year ending 31 March 2020, there were 695 murders recorded in England and Wales. The methods of killing recorded included the following: Sharp instrument 40 per cent; beating (no weapons) 17 per cent; strangulation/asphyxiation 11 per cent; blunt instrument 7 per cent; shooting 4 per cent; motor vehicle (used deliberately) 3 per cent; burning 2 per cent; poison or drugs 2 per cent; drowning 0.5 per cent.[x] These statistics confirm my own experience, in the fact stabbings are by far the most common form of murder, with knives being the number one weapon.*

MEDIA APPEALS

How Can the Media Help the Investigation?

The media is a useful investigative tool that helps us to obtain information and identify witnesses. It is unlikely police would be able to speak to all witnesses at the time of the incident. Some may not wait around, while others could have been just passing by and would have left by the time the police turn up. There will also be information circulating about a murder that an appeal might be able to tap into. It is rare that nobody knows who the suspects are. Their friends and family will quite often be fully aware. The use of media is the best way to appeal to these people.

In the past, that would be via newspapers or TV. My favourite method as a young detective was local newspapers as they were read by people in the area of a crime. The way we consume news has changed, however, especially for younger generations. Social media plays an increasingly important role in how investigators get their messages to potential witnesses.

Scotland Yard have a department whose sole job it is to handle these media appeals. They are leant on heavily by those in MITs. When appeals are made, they go out across the whole range of news outlets, hoping to capture every demographic.

What Information Is Shared?

The answer to this is, generally, the least amount necessary. If you release too much information, it can alert suspects to what you know. It can also influence witnesses. You want them to tell you what *they* saw of the incident, not what they read in the media. The idea of news releases is to *get* information, not to *give* it. The message will be:

1. This event happened.
2. This is where it happened.
3. This is when it happened.
4. Do you have any information?
5. If so, this is how you can pass it to us.

The information is likely to be seen by those who committed the murder. Phone downloads show suspects often research the crimes they have committed. It stands to reason. If you committed a murder, you would want to know how much information the police have.

The messages put out by police also aim to provide reassurance to the public. For example, if a murder has happened near to where you live, it would be nice to know it was an isolated incident.

You will sometimes see a suspect's image being circulated by police. This is not a decision that is taken lightly, for two reasons. Firstly, it may alert the suspect. They will be in no doubt that the police are looking for them, which could mean they will get rid of evidence or leave the area. Secondly, that image may be seen by witnesses. If they were then to take part in attempts to identify the suspect, the release of the image would be seen as contaminating their evidence. The defence are likely to say that the witness is only picking out their client as they saw that released image in the media.

How Are People Persuaded to Give Information?

If you were to follow a murder on the news, you'd likely see changes over time in the type of information put out by the police.

The initial releases will have limited detail. They are likely to mention the location, a time and give a general indication of what has happened. They won't name the victim at this stage. This is because formal identification is unlikely to have taken place and because the family may need time and privacy to process what has happened before it's shared with the rest of the world. The name of the victim isn't normally released until the family have agreed that this can happen. The exception to this is when a suspect is charged and appears at court. The victim's name forms part of the charge, in this case, so it is in the public domain. These initial releases will also have an appeal for information, usually to a general police phone number and Crimestoppers UK.

As more information becomes known, more will be released. A direct appeal from the senior investigating officer (SIO) is usually included. Once a MIT has been allocated to the investigation, a dedicated *incident room* phone number will be added. This is a direct line to that team. The victim's family will be asked to provide a photograph of the deceased that they are happy to release to the media. This has two main purposes. Firstly, it may jog people's memories and prompt them to give information. It will also put a face to the victim to humanise the crime. Psychologically, people are more likely to help if they see the victim as a person, not just a name and age.

If unsolved, there may be further releases, including appeals from the victim's family. This can be extremely emotive, tugging on people's consciences and making them more likely to help.

Sometimes, the SIO may make a direct appeal to the suspect or people close to them via the media. Believe it or not, suspects do occasionally give themselves up, so this is worth a try. Plus, family members have been known to turn people in if they feel it is the right thing to do.

Finally, a reward may be offered. This is usually around £20,000 and will be for a specific purpose, i.e. information leading to *arrest* or information leading to a *charge* or *conviction*. This money comes from the police's budget. A reward will usually come later in an investigation. It is preferable for a witness to come forward without this inducement. If a suspect is charged, the defence will be told of any reward. A tactic often used in court by the suspect's team is to accuse the witness of providing a statement *purely because of the money*; an attempt to undermine their credibility.

> **Case File**: A suspect had been identified in a murder (I'll tell you how we came to identify him later on in the book). He knew police were looking for him, so he went on the run. He was single, had no home and wasn't using a phone. A co-defendant had been charged and was awaiting trial. If we didn't locate this man in time, it was likely to have a serious impact. This is an issue with separate trials: defendants tend to blame each other. This gives both a greater chance of being found not guilty. He was missing for six months. We obtained authority to offer a £20,000 reward for information leading to his arrest. We used the media to make appeals to the public, which included *Crimewatch UK* and news outlets in the areas he was believed to be in. At the same time, we paid regular visits to all of his associates, executing warrants at places we believed he was staying. We sent messages to every phone contact, making them aware of the reward and reminding people of the law around harbouring a wanted criminal. We needed to make it as difficult as possible for him to evade arrest.
>
> A couple of weeks before the trial, we were starting to fear he wouldn't be arrested in time. Then, to our

relief, a member of the public phoned in and told us where he was. Officers attended and arrested him. It turned out that this man's friends had forced a woman to let him stay at her place. The police's hunt for him had made him too hot to handle. He wasn't safe at any of his associates' homes. That woman, who will appear in a later section, had phoned the police herself. The two men stood trial together and both were convicted of murder. Without the reward and appeals, I have no doubt he would have remained at large. Who knows, they may both have got away with murder.

WITNESSES

Witnesses are probably the most important element to a murder investigation and definitely the most difficult. The problem is they're human, which makes them completely unpredictable. Throw in the fact they have just witnessed a murder, a traumatic event for any person, then add their concerns about giving evidence at court. They will have worries about being perceived as a *snitch*, fears of repercussions and, often, distrust of the police. It is a wonder murder investigation teams are able to persuade anybody to give evidence at court.

How Can Witnesses Help the Investigation?

Witness is actually a broad term. The pathologist is a witness, as are police officers, scientists and anybody who adds evidence to a case. But, in the truest sense of the word, witnesses are those who have witnessed an event. They may be referred to as *eyewitnesses*, or in the MIT, they are known as *significant witnesses*.

They are the ones who will best portray the story to the jury. Without them, a case would be hollow; it would have no life. Murders are awful events. They are violent, distressing and utterly terrifying for anybody who was there. If you want a jury to convict a defendant, knowing they will be sending a person to prison for a long time, you need to bring that emotion from the crime scene into the courtroom. I've sat through trials where the majority of evidence comes from other sources, such as CCTV, phones and forensics. This information may be compelling, but from a human point of view, it just isn't the same. You need the jury to have a sense of what it was like to *be* there; how *terrible* it was in the moment. When they look at the defendant, you want them to think, *how could you*? If you can achieve that emotional engagement rather than present a dispassionate set of facts, you stand a better chance of a conviction. A top barrister I worked with spoke about *moments* during a trial. Moments where you could hear that proverbial pin drop. When the hairs on the back of your neck stood up and the jury were open-mouthed. It's those *moments* that gain a conviction. Moments of emotion best provided by people who were *there*. Those that felt that terror and can bring it into the courtroom.

The problem is you have no idea if your witness is going to provide that or do the opposite and derail your trial. Many times, I saw a witness change their account from that of their statement, even though they would have read that statement just before going in to give evidence. There can be numerous reasons for this, including nerves, the pressure of giving evidence, misremembering or sometimes deliberately changing their story. Until they start speaking in the witness box, you have no idea which way they may head.

Case File: A murder was organised from prison using a mobile phone that had been smuggled in. The ringleader shared plans with other inmates. Two came forward and agreed to be witnesses. When one was giving evidence, he told the court about the confession. He was detailed about what the defendant told him, coming across as believable. That was up until the point he was cross-examined by the defence. The witness also used the smuggled-in phone to make numerous calls to his girlfriend and mother. We were aware of this, but it wasn't a concern. Mobile phones in prisons get passed around. They're a sought-after commodity and people pay good money to use them. This detail wasn't relevant to the case, so we had no reason to bring it up with him. Now, when it comes to prosecution witnesses, they can't be coached. The barrister can't prepare a witness for what is to come or how to answer a particular question. Unlike contact between defence lawyers and a defendant, all interaction between the prosecution and their witnesses is subject to scrutiny. If the court found out a prosecution witness had been given any kind of instruction on how to answer questions, that evidence would be excluded.

The defence barrister began his cross-examination by asking about these calls. The witness, to our astonishment, flatly denied making them. This was an unexpected gift for that defence barrister, who then went to town with it. To say he laboured the point would be an understatement. He went through every call, becoming more sarcastic with each question he asked the witness. *It was somebody else calling your mother, was it? Does she have many other offspring on your wing? Is some other inmate seeing your girlfriend behind your back?* Each time, our witness blankly refused to acknowledge he had made the calls despite clear evidence to the contrary. By the end, the jury were openly laughing. One of our *star* witnesses being mocked by those who would decide the case. Forget the truths he told beforehand, his credibility was shot to pieces. When I asked why he had lied, he said he didn't want to get into trouble for using a smuggled-in phone. That was never going to happen. Nobody cared about him using the phone. That defence barrister's client got off with murder and no doubt this farce had something to do with it. We managed to convict the ringleader, although it was no thanks to this witness's evidence.

On the other hand, some of the best witnesses we had came completely out of the blue. A softly spoken lady who we thought wouldn't say boo to a goose put a defence barrister in his place and gave the greatest evidence I had ever heard. An old-time criminal, swanning into court without a care in the world, had the jury eating out of his hand due to the warm and honest way he came across. A good witness is worth their weight in gold – the issue is knowing which sort they will be.

Witnesses aren't just essential in court, they can add so much to an enquiry. They can help answer all of the important questions that we outlined earlier:

- **Who** is/are the victim/suspect(s)?
- **What** happened?
- **Where** did it happen?
- **When** did it happen?
- **Why** did it happen?
- **How** did it happen?

It is unlikely that a single witness will be able to answer all of those questions. The MIT will be looking to build a picture of what happened, with each witness adding a piece of the puzzle. The combination of their evidence, taken together, is what makes a case.

How Are Witnesses Dealt with by the Police and MITs?

When a person sees all or part of a murder, it is vital a full account is obtained. They will be interviewed on video or have it audibly recorded. An officer will convert that interview into a written statement, which is then signed by the witness. There are some exceptions to this, which we will come on to later.

How soon after the incident would a statement be taken? There is no hard and fast rule. Each witness will be different, and a judgement will need to be made. *If I've just witnessed a family member being murdered, am I likely to be in the right frame of mind to provide a statement?* Probably not. *If I was getting money from the bank and saw someone getting stabbed and killed, would I feel differently?* Probably, yes.

Will a person be compelled to be a witness? In general terms, no, although there may be occasions where this happens. Police will mostly respect a person's decision. In my experience, a witness would most often decide not to provide testimony out of fear. It was a situation I fully understood, particularly when they lived in the area the incident happened. The reality is that repercussions against witnesses are not very common. However, the fear of it happening is very real. But a summons to court can be given if their evidence is important enough to a case. This is not a decision that is taken lightly, as it can present issues. If you drag a person to court, there is no guarantee they will cooperate; they could actually do more harm than good. A witness who has been forced into giving evidence can turn hostile. They may refuse to answer questions, give monosyllabic answers and, occasionally, change their account completely. In our upcoming section on CCTV, I'll talk about a case file involving a shooting, where the suspects used a motorcycle to chase the occupants of a car before killing a passenger. In that case, we obtained a statement from another person in the car. In his statement, he described seeing the bike pillion passenger with the gun in his hand. By the time of the trial, he decided he no longer wanted to give evidence so was summoned to court. Once there, he changed his account, denying ever seeing a gun. As I say, a witness who is *made* to give evidence against their wishes can cause more issues than if they were not called at all.

What Is a Witness Statement?

What constitutes a statement in law is different to what many believe. Countless times I was told by witnesses, *I already gave a statement to the police.* What they actually mean is that they gave a verbal account, which may or may not have been written down. An actual *statement* is something different altogether: a written account on a specific form, at the top of which is a *declaration*. This declaration is where the witness acknowledges that if anything they have said is false, they may get into trouble. It reads like this:

This statement is true to the best of my knowledge and belief, and I make it knowing, if it is tendered in evidence, I shall be liable to prosecution if I have wilfully stated in it anything which I know to be false, or do not believe to be true.

The witness will sign the declaration to say they understand it and also sign the bottom of each page. Only after doing this can a witness make a *statement*.

Will All Witnesses Make Written Statements?

The majority of witnesses will make a statement that is written or typed out, which they then sign. However, not all witnesses will provide their account in this way. In law, there are two categories of witness who have been specifically recognised as requiring additional help at court when providing testimony. They are classified as:

- Vulnerable witnesses

- Intimidated witnesses

The extra help that is made available to them is known as *special measures*. We will look at what that constitutes in detail in Chapter 4: The Trial, but briefly it includes such things as being screened from the defendants and providing evidence remotely. If police believe a witness is either vulnerable or intimidated, then their account would be taken on video rather than in writing. This prevents them from having to recount their testimony at trial as the video can be played in court. They will still be cross-examined on that testimony, but they won't have to provide the bulk of their evidence in person. However, it would be for the trial judge to decide whether that is allowed.

Let's look at how we categorise these witnesses:

Vulnerable Witnesses

- This applies to all child witnesses under the age of eighteen.

- It is also any witness whose quality of evidence is likely to be diminished if:

  - they have a significant impairment of intelligence or social functioning;

  - they have a physical disability or suffer from a physical disorder; or

  - they suffer from a mental disorder.

Intimidated Witnesses

- The quality of the evidence they give is likely to be diminished through fear or distress.

- They might be witness to a gang or gun crime, domestic violence or a hate crime.

- This might relate to the age of the witness, i.e. elderly.

- This might relate to the domestic or employment circumstances of the witness.

- This might relate to the religious beliefs or political opinions of the witness.

- This might relate to the behaviour of the accused, or people connected with the accused, towards the witness.

What Does the Witness Interview Look Like?

It is actually quite difficult to answer this question precisely, as it can vary. But, in general terms, here are some of the options:

Where will it take place? An interview *could* be at a police station. If not, it would normally be carried out at someone's home. Police have mobile equipment, allowing them to undertake a video or audio interview pretty much anywhere. I have interviewed witnesses at their work, school and even in hotel rooms.

Who would be present? If the witness is vulnerable, a person classed as an *appropriate adult* will be present for welfare reasons and to assist with any communication difficulties. For a child, that's usually a parent. An interpreter would be used if the witness (or adult) has poor English. Occasionally, a solicitor will be present, but only if the witness may have committed an offence.

How is it conducted? This is a big topic, but I will keep it as concise as possible.

Interviews with witnesses are broken into sections and the first is known as *free recall*. The witness is asked to give their account, with little or no interruption. Some witnesses will be excellent at this, giving lots of detail. Others, not so much.

In the next phase, the detectives will encourage more recall, before going into more probing questions. They will be looking for *fine grain detail*, a term used for the minutiae of an account. Witnesses will mostly concentrate on *what happened*. The *actions* people carried out: *I saw him stab the boy.* What they probably won't give is a detailed description of the knife, if it was in the left or right hand and the kind of stabbing motion used. It is the detective's task to draw that detail out.

How do they do that? One method is called *cognitive interviewing*, a technique that aids in memory retrieval. It is quite intense and aims to take the witness back to the incident in their mind. They will be encouraged to remember as much detail as possible. My experience of this is pretty mixed. Its success depends on several factors, including the skill of the interviewer, the recollection abilities of the witness, their willingness to fully cooperate and how long after the event it is attempted.

Time elapsed is important for all witnesses. Over time we will begin to forget the detail of everything that we experience.

What Will They Be Asked?

The aim of the interview is to draw out as much relevant information as possible. What the witness thinks is relevant is often quite different to what we need, so this is where the skill of the detective is important.

For those who give identification evidence, there are set areas to cover. They are guidelines from a stated case at the Court of Appeal (*R v Turnbull*). A handy mnemonic has been created to help officers remember the key points: ADVOKATE. There are many mnemonics in law. It's almost as if they think police officers couldn't remember anything without them:

A – Amount of time under observation: How long the witness was watching the incident, or the amount of time they were looking at a suspect.

D – Distance: How far away was the witness from the incident or person?

V – Visibility: This would include whether it was dark at the time and how well lit the area was.

O – Obstructions: Was there anything in between the witness and what/who they saw?

K – Known or seen before: If the witness saw a person, do they know them or have they seen them before? If so, they will be asked details of how, where, when, etc.

A – Any reason to remember: Was there anything about the person that was memorable or made them stand out?

T – Time lapse: How long has it been since the witness saw the incident or person?

E – Errors: Any discrepancies in descriptions given by the witness in the first and subsequent accounts.

What if a Witness Is Lying?

Sometimes, evidence contradicts what a witness is saying. That does not necessarily mean a witness isn't telling the truth. It can be difficult for people to recall events exactly. What is in their mind may be different to what they saw. An incident may be upsetting, especially if violent. They may have focused on one part of events, meaning the rest is a bit hazy. Witnesses will usually try their hardest to remember. They will give an account to the best of their ability, but nearly all witnesses will get some aspects of what happened wrong.

So, if you know a witness is likely to get things wrong, sometimes through no fault of their own, *how can you tell when they are lying*? There are usually three areas in which a person telling lies can get tripped up:

- Firstly, we look at whether their account fits with other known evidence and, if not, how different it is. Small differences may indicate misremembering; large ones indicate potential lies. CCTV is often used for this. For instance, a witness may claim they were in the toilet when an incident happened at a bar, so they didn't see anything, but cameras show them standing near to where it took place.

- The next indication would be changes in a person's account. When witnesses are interviewed, they are asked to go over the same event several times. If the detail changes, this may indicate lies are being told.

- Finally, a person making things up is likely to get caught out when the interviewer asks for *fine grain detail*. When people lie, they rarely think about the detail. When questions are asked to draw that detail out, they are likely to become vague. To an experienced interviewer, that vagueness is a good indication that witness may be lying.

What Do I Mean by Lying?

Well, there are two types of lies. Firstly, there is the saying of something you know to be untrue. This is the commonly recognised definition. However, holding information back on purpose can also be lying. This is something I found more common than the telling of untruths.

Case File: In a case file in Chapter 2, on forensic evidence (*see also* page 40), I recounted an investigation where a suspect was linked to a firearm via DNA. That incident related to a party that was being held at an apartment in Greenwich, South East London. A woman had rented the place for the night via the internet, neglecting to tell the owner about her intended birthday celebrations.

Guests started to arrive at around midnight, all of whom could be seen on the block's CCTV system. The party was being held on a high floor, so people used the lift to reach it. The birthday girl was a person with questionable associates, including various gang members. About an hour or so after the first guests arrived, members of a prominent North London gang began to show up. There were probably around twelve of them and about thirty guests in total. All would have been fine but for the fact members of a rival gang were

soon to turn up, with a history of violence between
the two. Four from the second group went up to the
flat, smiling and joking. They had no idea who they
were about to bump into. The account that follows is
the best we could piece together using forensics and
descriptions from those at the party.

The second group knocked at the door, which was
opened by the birthday girl. The group walked into
the apartment, which had a long hall leading to the
living room. At the end of the hall, the two groups
came together.

A man from the second group pulled out a gun and
fired it into the party. This shot missed all the people,
but went through a television at the back of the room
before lodging in the wall. One of his intended targets
also had a gun, but he had a better aim, so when he
fired back, he hit the first shooter twice. His three
friends carried him from the apartment and downstairs,
back to their cars.

Not finished there, members of the first gang chased
them out, firing more shots at the four as they were
trying to get away. Not only that, but they had two
other guns. So, at least three guns at a birthday party.
We even found a silencer discarded.

The four managed to get away, although the man
who was shot died shortly after. Police were called
there by distressed neighbours, who had been woken
in the night by the sound of gunshots. Unfortunately,
none of the shooters were arrested at the time. We
were able to identify and speak to the majority of guests

but, of those, how many do you think said they saw anybody fire a gun? None, not even the friends of the person killed. The layout of the flat meant everybody would have been close to the shootings. It would have been impossible for nobody to see anything. Most of those who claimed not to were obviously lying. In the police we have an expression for when this happens: everyone at the party would be described as *upstairs collecting fares*. There are usually three potential reasons for this: fear of reprisals, the unwritten rule of not 'being a grass' and distrust of the police.

Unsurprisingly, nobody was convicted of that murder. The only conviction was of the male whose DNA was on the bag containing the firearm.

Identification Parades

Myth Buster: *Now, I bet when you think of ID parades, you are imagining something similar to the* film The Usual Suspects. *A line-up of men, the suspect among them, and a witness being asked to walk up and down to make an identification. In fact, that is exactly how we used to carry out identification parades. However, a few years back that all changed. It went from the witness looking at real-life people to watching them on a video clip.*

Why? As with most changes in the police, it came down to saving money. In the past, we had a pool of people paid to act as stooges. Stooges are the others in the parade, standing next to the suspect, who are supposed to be similar in appearance. With video, a stooge only had to be paid for their time once. Their image can then be used as many times as required. The problem with this method is that a witness is more likely to recognise a person in the flesh. It means that identification parades are now less likely to help an investigation. It is incredibly difficult for a witness, who may have seen a person for only a matter of seconds, to pick them out days or even weeks later. They are *sometimes* successful though and I always took my hat off to those people.

The last thing witnesses need is their task being made harder. On one particular case, I fear we were guilty of that as a team.

Case File: A witness saw men carrying out a stabbing. A group were arrested, but they were unlikely to have been the killers. They had been arrested very early on in the investigation before we had taken it on. As we progressed, the evidence seemed to point away from this group. Before we released them, we held identification procedures using our witness. The rationale was that, if she didn't pick them out, we could be more confident it wasn't them. In my opinion, that decision was a mistake – a massive one. She did what many witnesses do and picked out who she thought *could* have been the suspects. Those she identified were actually stooges. We then identified a second group, whom we were certain were the *actual* killers. But by showing the witness the first group, we had seriously compromised the subsequent identification procedures for this second group. By now she had seen too many faces. Plus, in her mind, she had already picked out the people she thought were involved in the murder. Unsurprisingly, she didn't pick them out, even though we were sure we had the right people. That case hinged on identification, as there was little other evidence. We had no forensic evidence linking the suspects to the victim and no CCTV at or near the scene. I can't say for sure whether she would have identified the killers if we'd done things differently. However, what we did can't have helped. Of the unsolved cases we investigated, this is the only one I feel may have been our fault. We made a decision with the wrong goal in mind, didn't consider other options and failed to think of the consequences of what could go wrong. I wanted to make sure this particular mistake never happened again and although it was too late for the family of this victim, it gave me the impetus to develop a better way of making decisions for the future. Thus emerged my DI COP decision-making model of defined goals, information, confirmation bias, options and prepare to be wrong.

Witness Protection

On occasions, a witness may need to go into the witness protection scheme. I can't go into detail around this, for obvious reasons, but it doesn't happen as often as you might expect. For a person to completely remove themselves from their lives, starting afresh somewhere else, is no minor thing. They have to begin again, under a new identity and cut off from everyone they know. As the investigation team, we wouldn't be told where a witness was being placed. If someone is being moved, it would be for their personal safety, so the fewer people who know where they are, the better.

CCTV

Closed-circuit television (CCTV) has become a part of everyday life. We see the cameras everywhere we go. The majority of us pay them no attention. For criminals, however, they can be the difference between getting away with a crime or not. This is even more true for murderers, as murder investigation teams have the experience and resources to go far beyond the work carried out by local detectives. CCTV evidence is now an integral part of all murder investigations. After witnesses, I would argue it is the next most commonly used type of evidence.

Myth Buster: *In the UK, there is no central CCTV system. All cameras run separately, with the vast majority being stand-alone systems. So, on TV, when you see police or security services apparently obtaining live footage from cameras while tracking suspects, that just isn't possible. There are some systems that can be accessed remotely, but these are usually traffic cameras. Obtaining footage from CCTV actually involves a lot of legwork.*

How Can CCTV Help the Investigation?

The best way to look at that question is to break it down into different stages of a crime:

CCTV of the Build-Up to the Murder

Tracking victims and suspects, in the time leading up to the event, will provide the investigation with important information. This might include any relevant behaviour, such as arguments, drunkenness or violence, whether they can be seen together, clear images that could be used for identification purposes, clothing worn, routes taken, any vehicles used or phone usage. Quite often, suspects can be seen using phones. This can then be aligned with phone call records and added to the evidence against them. In some murders, suspects may attempt to hide their faces during the act. However, if you trace them back to earlier that day using CCTV footage, you may find images where their faces are not covered.

Case File: We were investigating a murder where a motorcycle was used by the suspects. They employed various tactics to avoid its identification, which included using black tape to hide the registration number. The thing with vehicles, though, is that at some point they need fuel. That means using petrol stations, where there are usually CCTV systems designed for reading number plates. We were able to find these suspects filling up with petrol *before* the murder while there was no black tape on the registration number. This then led us to the killers.

Case File: This murder was a stabbing, but all of the CCTV footage of the incident was at a distance, which meant no identification could be made. In

London, you can't go too far without walking past a
camera. This allows people to be tracked. By following
someone's direction of travel, you hope they eventually
go to a location with a quality CCTV system. That is
exactly what happened in this case. By following the
suspect's journey backwards, we caught him going into
a shop before the murder. That shop had a CCTV
system that captured his face perfectly. From that
footage, we were able to identify him.

This technique is particularly useful in unplanned murders.
If an incident happens spontaneously, suspects are likely to
have passed any number of cameras beforehand without trying
to avoid detection. Once their image has been captured,
there is little they can do. They can burn clothes, throw away
phones or even get people to create false alibis for them. But,
if they have passed a camera, that CCTV evidence is likely to
convict them.

It is also useful to have good images from CCTV of a victim
before the murder. They can be used in appeals for information
from the public; they are also impactful at court. There is
something quite chilling about watching a victim going about
their business, completely unaware that their life will soon
end. It is footage we also make sure their families are aware
of. Personally, I would never circulate those images publicly
without their permission, or without them having seen it first.
It must be heartbreaking for them to see the last images of their
loved one, but if the importance is explained, they generally
agree to the release.

CCTV of the Murder

Occasionally, MITs will get lucky. *Very* lucky. The killing itself may be captured on CCTV. When it does, the footage becomes the best witness possible. As we discussed earlier, witnesses have a tendency to focus on different parts of an incident, which makes understanding *exactly* what happened, in an objective sense, difficult. If the act is on camera, it eliminates all doubt.

In my experience, the majority of defendants accused of murder admit they were there. Generally, they have to. There will usually be evidence that would make it very difficult to say otherwise. So, given they have to place themselves at the scene, they are then likely to give a version of events that suits their defence. They often put blame on to the victim, claiming *self-defence*, or suggest it was someone other than them who carried out the killing, while they just happened to be there. It can sometimes be difficult to refute those claims. Witnesses can get things wrong, forensics can be interpreted in different ways and the victim isn't able to put their side of the story across. But, if the incident is on CCTV, that is a whole different matter.

There are groups opposed to cameras on our streets, claiming them to be an infringement of privacy. Everyone is entitled to their opinion, but from an investigator's point of view, I would advocate for more, not fewer. But for CCTV, there would be many more unconvicted murderers walking our streets.

Case File: One Monday morning, we took over a case from another MIT which had carried out the investigation over the weekend. This isn't always an ideal situation, as it is almost like starting the enquiry again. The incident happened in Deptford, South East London. A group of men had been together in the street before two went off to get a minicab home. Those two returned back shortly after to speak with someone in the group before heading off again. In the meantime, one man in the group had received a phone call to say one of those in the cab had been disrespectful about a dead friend. This clearly made him angry, so he confronted the two in the cab. He was armed with a small rubber mallet, which he used to threaten the man who had been 'disrespectful'. Unfortunately, the other men were armed with knives. They chased the man with the mallet and stabbed him multiple times, killing him.

Confrontation murders are all too common. They usually come down to *respect*. Probably the single most stupid reason to lose your life. The victim was a prominent 'drill' artist and part of a well-known South London gang that was regularly involved in murders, both as the perpetrators and victims.

As is normal in these situations, we were given a full briefing of what had occurred and what enquiries the team had carried out. One of the most important pieces of evidence was dashcam video from the minicab. This showed the two suspects walking towards the car before getting in. In a stroke of luck, an officer on our team recognised one of the suspects. He had dealt with him a number of times in the past. This allowed us to make the decision to arrest him. There was one issue though: he was already wanted by police and had no fixed address. He was going to prove tricky to find.

The second man wasn't recognisable, although we had intelligence as to who he may have been. One thing that did stand out was his jacket. A detective constable on our team recognised the make from a maple leaf logo and it turned out to be a £600 jacket. A decision was made to arrest a second person, who was believed to be this man. He *did* have a home, which we went to. By the time we got there, he had cleared out his belongings and seemed to have gone on the run. As always, we carried out a search of his home, looking for anything that could link him to the crime. Usually that would be forensic evidence, but on this occasion, it was something altogether different. We found a shop label for a £600 maple leaf logo jacket. *Bingo!* As soon as we found that, we knew we had identified the right person.

Now, when you own high-cost designer clothing, you will be one of only a few to buy such an item. You would also have bought from one of a low number of outlets that stock them. With so few of this particular jacket having been sold, we were able to identify the exact time and place this one was bought. This shop had a top-quality CCTV system, which showed the man we were looking for walking into the shop and buying the jacket.

So, we could identify these two men and we had fantastic evidence placing them in the minicab. The problem, however, is that we still had no footage of the attack itself. There were witnesses who had heard what happened, or who had seen it from afar, but there was no evidence to say what either of these two men did. And, just to complicate matters, there were three other men who may also have been involved. If we were going to prove murder, we needed evidence of what happened in the actual killing.

Identifying potential CCTV evidence isn't complicated. It is a matter of walking around the area and looking for cameras. That is exactly what we did in this case. The best way to do that is to start at the scene and work outwards. At the scene, we noticed a single camera, high up on a pole. *But who owned it?* There were no markings, it didn't belong to the local authority and it wasn't attached to any business. We made numerous phone calls without getting any closer to whose it was. *Why were we so keen to identify it?* Because it was pointing directly at where part of the attack happened. If it was working and had actually recorded footage at that time, this camera could be a game changer. Our CCTV officer spent several frustrating days investigating before she got to the bottom of it. This area was a long alleyway that ran down the side of a railway bridge. Apparently, there had been issues with cyclists, so a camera was put up to monitor this. We eventually obtained the footage and, *wow*, it captured almost all of the murder. What it showed was so good, we could see exactly who did what.

When we investigate murders, there is a personal

distance from the killing itself. We weren't there, so we can't appreciate what it was really like. We may see the aftermath and be given accounts by witnesses, but it's difficult to truly understand what went on. That is until you see footage as gathered in this case. What it showed was four men brutally attacking our victim. All four had knives, including foot-long machetes. All four used the knifes to either stab or slash the victim. Whatever he may have done to provoke them, he didn't deserve that. He didn't stand a chance. After the initial attack, he stumbled away, getting about fifty yards before collapsing. *Were they finished with him*? No. They followed him up the road, setting upon him again as he lay dying on the floor.

Earlier, I spoke about *moments* in court, usually provided by witness testimony. On some occasions, this can be provided by CCTV. When a jury sees footage like this, they will be transported into that crime scene and the final minutes of the victim's life. This is when the hairs on the back of your neck stand up.

Both suspects were eventually arrested. The man with the expensive jacket was found in the back of a car at the Port of Dover trying to smuggle himself out of the country. In the previous section, when we discussed identification (*see also* page 184), I explained how difficult it was for witnesses to pick suspects out. In this case, thankfully, the minicab driver was able to do exactly that. The expensive jacket was never found, but it didn't really matter. We had proved beyond doubt it was him wearing it. At trial, this man claimed self-defence, which was ludicrous given the callous and vicious nature of the killing.

The second man claimed it wasn't him. His defence team tried hard to discredit the evidence given by the officer who identified him, but the jury were not swayed.

Both men were convicted of murder. Neither would have been but for the CCTV footage.

CCTV of the Scene After the Murder

This primarily concerns capturing how suspects left the scene, which may reveal where they went to, if they discarded any evidence or how they got away. There are many ways for a murderer to flee the scene: on foot, in a vehicle, on a bike or by public transport. Without CCTV, it would be difficult to know which method was used.

Case File: We had a shooting where CCTV captured a suspect fleeing the scene. His route was tracked using numerous cameras. He was eventually seen going into a building site. There, cameras showed him bending down as if hiding something. As a result, the area was searched. What we found was the gun used in the killing. The suspect had tried to hide it under rubble. Without CCTV, it is unlikely that weapon would ever have been recovered. Needless to say, he was convicted of the murder, largely down to that footage. The CCTV officer responsible for this particular piece of detective work received a commendation for his efforts, and rightly so.

CCTV of Suspects' Homes

Cameras near the homes of suspects are a useful source of evidence. For example, they can show what they were wearing before an incident. Murderers are often fully aware of forensics. They know if they attack someone, they are likely to have that person's DNA on them, so they *will* dispose of clothing. What they can't dispose of, however, is footage showing them in those clothes earlier in the day.

Myth Buster: *The ability to zoom in on footage and clean up a blurred image to miraculously reveal a car registration number is not available to us, despite what legal dramas and detective shows might suggest. This misconception is common, even among those in the police and other legal professions. There may be advanced software available somewhere, but, if it exists, those at Scotland Yard never get to see it. Yes, they can zoom in, and slightly improve an image, but nowhere near to the extent seen on TV.*

What Are the Sources of CCTV?

When we talk about CCTV, you probably think of the cameras on buildings. That is certainly where most footage is obtained. The vast majority of businesses have CCTV systems. Over the years the cost has come down, allowing even the smallest of businesses to afford it. The quality is generally extremely good and usually high definition.

With advancements in technology, however, we also have cameras in many other places. I previously mentioned dashcam footage, which is becoming more popular and is usually of excellent quality. Some even record while the vehicle isn't being used.

Other forms of transport are a good source too, particularly buses. If any person involved in a murder has been on a bus, there is usually a very clear record of their journey. They also have external cameras that are fitted in case of accident – a great source of evidence in investigations. Many times, we had buses passing our crime scenes, giving us extra footage, or sometimes the only footage.

Many people now also have doorbells with embedded cameras. They not only capture the image of anyone using the doorbell, but many are motion sensitive so they also capture anyone moving past the house. The quality isn't often that great, but it can assist investigations.

Although not strictly CCTV, there are another set of cameras dotted around the country that have become increasingly important to murder investigations: ANPR cameras. Automatic number plate recognition cameras read registration numbers, sometimes also capturing an image of the vehicle. The data can be used for several purposes, some less obvious than others. Primarily they show the location of a vehicle at a precise time, but they can also be used in conjunction with telephone evidence. If locations in which a phone is used correlate with ANPR activations, this can be strong evidence linking a phone to the user of a vehicle. This is particularly helpful if a phone is unregistered. We'll explore the use of phones in more depth in the next section.

Another source of video evidence, used in virtually every investigation, is police body-worn videos (BWVs). Virtually all police officers now use them. This allows others to see incidents from the officer's point of view, leaving no doubt as to what occurred. I think most police officers consider them to be a useful tool. They provide protection for the officers, proving what they saw and undermining false allegations about what they may have said or done.

How Do We Decide Where to Look for CCTV?

A strategy will be produced by one of the senior officers. Part of that strategy will include:

1. Locations of where CCTV will be sought
2. The time parameters of the required footage

Time parameters will vary according to the incident. It would be something similar to two hours before and one hour after the murder, although it could be much longer.

How Is CCTV Evidence Collected?

At the beginning of this section, we discussed the fact that CCTV cameras are not centrally linked. Officers will, literally, walk the streets looking for them. When identified, each camera will be individually accessed. Some footage will be stored on a hard drive, others in cloud storage.

This can be a huge and time-consuming task. Depending on the type of crime, the area where cameras are being sought can be large. Think back to the section on motive (*see also* page 110), where I told you about the case of the sisters who were tragically killed in a fire at their home. We knew a car was used, but nothing of the make and model. We sought CCTV footage around the house, about a mile in each direction, so you can imagine how many cameras that entailed. Plus, we believed the suspects used a petrol station to obtain the propellant but had no idea which one. That meant we needed to collect footage from a huge area of London, all of which needed to be viewed.

In most murder investigations there are likely to be hundreds of cameras of interest. It can take weeks to collect footage, which can cause issues. The amount of time a hard drive stores recorded footage also varies. It can be anything from twenty-four hours to a number of months. The problem is, until a particular system is looked at, it is impossible to know how long it will be and whether you are likely to soon lose the recordings. Quite often, the footage is already gone, particularly if a murder took time to be discovered.

Case File: A lady was discovered dead in her flat. She was killed a number of weeks earlier, remaining undiscovered all that time. When we took on the investigation, most CCTV footage had already been lost. Cameras that would almost certainly have provided us with evidence had recorded over themselves. The crime remains unsolved, with the lack of CCTV being a major contributing factor.

That is why the seizing of CCTV images is a race against time. Losing footage, especially on cameras that would have shown important events, is one of a MIT's biggest frustrations. It is largely to do with the better quality of footage nowadays. In the past, poor-quality footage, often time-lapsed, was stored for much longer as the files weren't very large. Today's high-definition footage requires much more storage space, resulting in less being held at any one time.

When officers collect footage, they have to be sure that the timings are correct. CCTV systems often display incorrect times. Officers will compare system timing to the *speaking clock*. In the UK, if you dial 123, a recorded message gives the correct time. That may sound like a funny way of doing things, but it is proven to be the best method evidentially. For instance, if the system shows it is eight minutes fast according to the speaking clock, they can calculate the true time when they watch any of the footage. This can be critical if timings become important. In some cases, the exact seconds could be relevant.

How Is the Footage Viewed?

It is a long, laborious process. Officers will watch hours and hours of footage, while keeping a log of what they see, including any movement and descriptions of people. Thankfully, I never did too much of that. Sitting and watching a screen of the same street corner, possibly for days on end, just wasn't for me. Some officers love it and are excellent at it – they get my utmost respect.

The aim is to capture all the relevant pieces of footage so they can be played at court.

Did You Know? *Although I said I would like to see more CCTV cameras in the UK, we are actually the country with the third highest number. The top ten countries in the world based on CCTV cameras per 100 population are: USA 15.28, China 14.36, UK 7.5, Germany 6.27, Netherlands 5.8, Australia 4, Japan 2.72, France 2.46 and South Korea 1.99.[xi]*

PHONES

I'll let you into a little secret (although it is less of a secret if you ever worked with me). In murder investigations, phones are my favourite type of evidence. By the end of this section, you will hopefully see why. Those who have worked with me will probably tell you I was a little bit *too* obsessed by them. The usual protocol in investigations is for a detective constable to be designated a phones officer, with responsibility for that evidence, but for jobs where I was the detective sergeant case officer, I would perform this role in addition to my other duties. It was a combination of how much I enjoyed doing it and my inner control freak. In fact, I was responsible for the majority of phone evidence discussed in this book. As I say, not what usually happens on a MIT, but it worked well for us as a team (and made me happy!).

Early on in my career, mobile phones were almost non-existent. Over time, they have become more popular, to the point where virtually everyone has one, from young children through to the elderly. They are part of our everyday lives. That means they are also part of criminals' everyday lives. This makes them a fantastic source of evidence for police. For killings that are spontaneous, obtaining phone evidence is usually straightforward. If they are premeditated, however, things may be a bit trickier for the MIT but not impossible.

Criminals are fully aware of the potential benefit of phone evidence to police investigators, so they will often attempt to distance themselves from handsets and numbers. Even the least sophisticated of criminals know about *burner phones*. These are cheap handsets with unregistered SIM cards, meaning the call provider doesn't know who is using them as the user doesn't need to prove their identity. Some criminals will change these burners on a regular basis to make it harder for police to know what number they are using.

Despite all these efforts, phone evidence still plays a huge role in modern-day murder investigations. As much as these criminals try to hide their usage, the fact remains that they still need to make calls. So, even if they have a burner, those calls can still be traced back to them. They will call friends, family and girlfriends and boyfriends. Nearly always they will be arrested with a phone on them. Even if it's a new burner, there will be links from that to previous phones.

How Can Phones Help the Investigation?

When we look at phones, and how they can assist an enquiry, we need to consider them in two ways:

1. How a phone is used
2. What handsets have stored on them

How a Phone is Used

Call providers such as T-Mobile, Vodafone, O2, etc. are businesses. They make money from people using their networks. In order for them to charge their customers, they must keep accurate records of all usage. Under UK law, police are able to apply for information from those providers, as long as certain criteria are satisfied, such as a requirement for national security or the investigation of crime. The information they provide is known as a call data record (CDR). It includes calls made and received, messages sent and received, data usage and cell sites used. Cell sites is the term used for phone masts, meaning that we can roughly place a person making a phone call in a particular area by identifying the phone mast that their phone used. The phone companies can also identify handsets used by their unique serial number (IMEI) – international mobile equipment identity. However, these records won't show any content of messages through WhatsApp, Snapchat, etc. This information is encrypted and can only be obtained from the handsets used to send and receive these messages. As you might imagine, these messages can provide fantastic evidence if police are able to retrieve them.

As well as CDRs, police can also apply for details of who the phone is registered to, how it is paid for, how any credit is added to the account and various types of personal information. An application must be made, fully justifying why the information is needed. The authority required for this is from a superintendent for CDRs and an inspector for the personal information. Once obtained, the CDRs will help the investigation by showing:

- any contact between the victim and suspect;

- association between suspects;

- location of phone usage, i.e. cell sites used; and

- change in usage after the murder

Let's look at each of these in turn to see how useful they could be to an investigation.

Contact Between Victims and Suspects

When a person is killed, the MIT will look at the victim's phone usage. Many murders are solved this way. Most murders aren't planned. Some are, but the majority happen spontaneously. That means if there is any association between victim and suspect, it is likely to show up in call records. Even when burner phones are used, association can still be established by Scotland Yard's highly trained intelligence analysts.

Case File: It was early morning, in a quiet side street in Peckham, South London. When we arrived, I saw the burnt-out car. It was completely gutted. The fire, which must have been intense, had been put out the night before, so there was no residual heat coming from it. This allowed me to get close enough to look inside, although what I saw was horrific. In the front passenger seat was a body so badly burned that we could only make out it was a man who was not very tall. *It must be murder, but how had they died?* Witnesses had seen people near the car with a petrol can. They were almost certainly looking to destroy forensic evidence. At that stage, we had no idea who this person was.

If you think back to the *five building blocks*, one priority was to identify the victim. *But how? What did we know about the car?* In the police, we often refer to *pool cars*. These vehicles are shared between groups of youths, often for criminal purposes. Intelligence suggested this was that type of car, used by members of a local gang. This would make it difficult to identify who was using the car, especially as any forensic evidence, such as fingermarks or DNA, was probably destroyed in the fire. *What about the body itself?* The special post-mortem was going to be important in this. Dental records, DNA or fingerprints would be needed. A personal identification was out of the question. Nobody would ever be able to recognise them, they were too badly burned. *But would the pathologist be able to identify how they died?* We certainly hoped so, but the damage the fire caused could make this difficult.

While at the scene, we were passed information about a possible identity for the victim. Not far from where we were, a mother had reported her 16-year-old son as missing. He was due to appear in court the previous day but had failed to turn up. Looking at our victim, *it could have been him.*

We arranged for a forensic scientist to attend, who specialised in fires. He confirmed petrol had been used as an accelerant, having been poured inside the car. A fact most people don't know is that when petrol is set alight, it isn't the liquid that ignites but the vapours. Those vapours can engulf the person starting the fire in flames, leaving burn injuries, or at the very least singed clothing or hair.

At the post-mortem, it didn't take long to establish the cause of death. He had received a gunshot wound to the back of the head. The bullet had passed through his brain, lodging inside the front of his skull. Amazingly, the pathologist was able to obtain a palm print from the victim, despite the extensive burns, and we were able to confirm he was indeed the missing 16-year-old. *So, who had killed him and why?*

To get those answers, we had to return to that saying, *learn how a person lived and you will learn how they died.* A question may have jumped out at you: *Why was he due at court?* We asked ourselves the same thing.

This boy had no criminal record. Unfortunately, he fell into a trap we had seen too often. He lived in an area where gangs were prevalent. These gangs survive by preying on and exploiting children. They use them to sell and hide drugs, as well as hide and move firearms, as was the case here. The reason for his arrest was that he had been taken by car, with three members of a prominent local gang, to purchase a firearm in a town outside of London. *Why was he with them?* His role was to travel back alone on a train, carrying the firearm. That meant *he* took all the risk of being arrested, while *they* drove back home without having to worry about being caught with the gun. Well, that was the plan. Unfortunately for them, police had received intelligence about the exchange, resulting in them all being arrested. Police jumped on them after the gun had been bought. They were all charged with firearms offences and sent to court. Due to his age, this boy was the only one to be given court bail. Sadly, that decision was to cost him his life.

The gang began to put pressure on the boy to accept full ownership of the gun. In their minds, if he said it was his, they could get off their charges. He was offered money to do this and seemed to be going along with the plan. At one court hearing, he even submitted a handwritten note claiming full responsibility. What this gang didn't know, however, was the strength of evidence against them. There was no way their plan would work. The purchase of the gun was captured on surveillance video, showing all of their involvement.

At some point, the boy decided against the gang's proposal. Instead, he entered a plea of not guilty. So, the gang decided to hatch a new plot, one that involved killing the boy, execution-style. Once dead, they could blame him for the crime. Again, it would have been a futile effort given the weight of evidence against them.

Arranging a murder from prison may seem like a difficult thing to do. Unfortunately, it's not. Think back to the case file of the jury laughing at a witness's lies about using his burner phone in prison (*see also* page 172). It was that mobile phone this killing was arranged on.

OK, so you may now be asking yourself, *how do we know that court case is the reason he was killed?* Firstly, the *pool car*. The gang using that car was the same gang he was arrested with. *That cannot be a coincidence.* Then we had the phone evidence.

The boy's family told us he left a relative's house about twenty-four hours before the fire occurred. This was the night before the firearms trial was due to begin. He left the house around 9pm after receiving a phone call. *Who was that call from?* Answering that question seemed to be the absolute priority. We followed the usual procedure, gaining a superintendent's authority to obtain the boy's call data. This gave us the number that called him. It also showed no further usage of his phone after that phone call. *This was the last person to speak with him.* As you would expect with a boy this age, his phone was normally in constant use. *So, had he been killed shortly after leaving his relative's house?* But, if that was the case, *had his body been in the car for a whole twenty-four hours before being set alight? Surely someone would have seen him?* Apparently not. Everything we turned up – phone records, witness accounts and forensics – all pointed to him having been shot and killed in that car shortly after leaving the house. This made that last calling number crucial. *Whoever that was, they must have lured him to where he was killed.* What we discovered about that number was something I hadn't come across before.

It was unregistered, which isn't unusual, but what stood out to me was that the burner phone was set up three weeks before the murder, with every call on it either to or from our victim. The phone had clearly been set up purely to murder this boy. So, there was only one thing left to do: *identify the user and we'd identify the murderer.* Which is exactly what we did. *How did we do that?*

Firstly, we looked at every member of that gang, trying to identify phone numbers for them. We then overlaid their phone usage with the calls made on the burner phone, looking for any made in the same locations. It was a slow process, but, eventually, we identified a phone that was repeatedly using the same

cell sites at roughly the same times as the burner phone.
We were able to attribute that number to someone
associated with the gang; we also proved he bought the
SIM card for the burner phone and added credit.

He was charged with conspiracy to murder. At
court he admitted to:

- buying the phone;
- buying the SIM card;
- activating the SIM;
- adding the credit;
- making the calls to the victim; and
- making the call to the victim to lure him to where
  he was shot.

The only thing he wouldn't admit to was the murder. He
claimed they were going to rob him rather than kill him.
Worryingly, this person was also a police informant, a
fact that was disclosed at trial. It had to be because he was
providing information to the police about this murder:
false information. I don't know whether his fellow gang
members were aware of his status, and using him to feed
incorrect information to the investigation, or whether he
was doing it of his own volition. Either way, it showed
he had a history of telling lies.

In his evidence, he told the court that, ten minutes
before the murder, he gave the phone to someone else.
Someone he refused to name. This was a story that the
jury believed, finding him not guilty.

To this day, I cannot fathom how they came to
that decision. He had been charged with *conspiracy*

to murder, so we didn't have to prove he pulled the trigger. If setting up the phone and luring the victim to where he was killed isn't a conspiracy, I don't know what is. However, we were able to prove who set fire to the car. When arrested, that person had a burn on his arm, singed hairs and traces of petrol on a jacket. We were unable to show that he was involved in the shooting itself, however. An issue we had was that he lived close to the scene, so his phone being in the area of the murder wasn't any help. Due to the fire, we had no forensic evidence linking him to the shooting. Witnesses were unable to pick him out. He was convicted of conspiracy to pervert the course of justice.

We were never able to prove who it was that killed the boy.

The ringleader, who arranged the murder, was one of those originally arrested with the victim for firearms offences. He was found guilty of conspiracy to murder. He was also found guilty of the first firearms offence, as was most everyone else involved.

So, this boy's death achieved absolutely nothing for that group, other than one being convicted of conspiracy to murder. A killing motivated by *gain*, where there was none. A complete waste of a young life. In situations like this, I often see blame being apportioned to the parents. Unfortunately, it isn't that simple usually. I agree that parents have a responsibility when it comes to how their children behave, but not every wayward child is down to bad parenting. This boy's mother and father were great parents, to him and his siblings. As children turn into young adults, they have other, outside influences. That is particularly true for some raised in more deprived areas, such as this boy. He wasn't the first, and certainly won't be the last, young person to be preyed upon by gangs. The exploitation of children is a huge issue in our society. This young boy is just one example of how that can end in tragedy.

The trial for this case ran at the Old Bailey for several months, ending in July. Towards the end of the year, I was in my office when I received a phone call from the boy's father. He was outside, having travelled on public transport to get to me. I went down to meet him, where he handed me a Christmas present, thanking me for everything I had done in his son's case. I know it may only seem a small gesture but, to me, it meant so much. It was one of the hardest-to-prove cases I had been involved in. I invested a lot of time and emotion into it. I was just sorry I couldn't bring the actual killer to justice.

Association Between Suspects

It won't shock you to hear that suspects often lie. They will often say whatever helps them get away with murder, including denying knowledge of others involved in the case. Frequently, contact on phones can be used to refute that. If you have made numerous calls to a person you claim not to know, there is a good chance you're not telling the truth about other things.

In addition to this, contact can also be a sign of preplanning.

If there are a number of defendants, their phone usage can often show patterns consistent with a conspiracy. For instance, we might see calls between them over a period of months, with a sharp increase in contact just before the murder. On its own, there may be other explanations, but when taken together with other evidence, those calls can be telling.

> **Case File**: A drug dealer was killed during a robbery. A group of men had arranged a deal, but they never intended to buy the drugs. Instead, they aimed to steal the drugs at knifepoint. There were five suspects, one of whom was in phone contact with the intended victim.
>
> We examined the call data and identified a pattern. In the days leading up to the incident, one suspect made numerous calls to the victim. After each call, he would then contact the other suspects. Those calls clearly related to the arranged drug deal and provided good evidence of a conspiracy.
>
> On the day of the robbery, the same thing happened: a call to the victim followed by contact between the group. Maps were produced to show the locations of their phones. Using cell sites, we could show them coming together after the call to the victim and then travelling to the location of the drug deal. Unfortunately, the robbery went wrong, resulting in the dealer receiving a fatal stab wound. Phones were pivotal to the prosecution, evidencing a conspiracy between the suspects and the fact they were present at the killing.

Location of Phone Usage, i.e. Cell Sites Used

Myth Buster: *That common scene that you always see in crime dramas where they keep a person talking to trace the call is completely unrealistic. If a call is made from a landline, tracing the location is simple and the length of call doesn't matter. However, a call from a mobile phone cannot be traced to an exact location, no matter how long it lasts. All that can be gleaned is the general area in which the phone is being used.*

Mobile phones communicate using radio waves. Those radio transmissions go to and from a cell site. Our conversation is then transmitted via the network to whoever we are talking to. All done in the blink of an eye.

Picture a phone mast as a triangle. Each of the three sides has its own transmitter, covering 120 degrees. So, between all three sides they cover a whole circle. When police use these masts to establish the location of a phone, they will be told which side of the triangle the signal was using. That's it. No fancy triangulation. No flashing dot over an exact location. They will only get a sector that could cover hundreds of metres. *Not quite as sexy or impressive as it seems in films, is it?*

But that doesn't mean the information isn't of assistance. In fact, it *can* be massively helpful. What can also be shown is movement. Imagine you are using your phone in your car, hands-free of course. You start a call as you're leaving, continuing the conversation until you reach your destination. As you were driving along, your phone would have been changing masts, each time moving to the one with the strongest signal. You would have been oblivious to this, as it would not affect your conversation (unless you moved into an area with poor or no signal), but it can demonstrate to police where someone has travelled and how quickly.

When police apply for call records, they are told where a call started and where it ended. What they won't be told is what masts are used in between, as this information is not recorded. That movement can be excellent evidence, as long as the distance travelled is significant. It's not so helpful if a suspect commits an offence close to an area they regularly frequent, however, such as where they live. Here are a couple of examples that demonstrate this.

Case File: In the investigation where we made a mistake with the identification procedure, showing the witness the stooges before she had a chance to assess video of the suspects, I explained how we had a good idea who the suspects were but lacked solid evidence. We had identified their mobile phones; we were even able to say they were using cell sites covering the scene at the time of the murder. The problem we had was that the 120-degree sector from that mast also included where they lived. The information wasn't accurate enough to distinguish between the scene and their homes, which made cell site evidence worthless.

Case File: There was a large fight between two gangs, one from South East London, the other from South West London. A member of the South East London gang died from head injuries caused by bats. Scene CCTV was poor and we had no witnesses who could identify anybody. We were able to attribute phones to most of the group, however. Call data records were obtained showing their phones coming together in South West London then travelling to the scene of the murder. The call records also showed them travelling back together. Once those phones were attributed to a person, they struggled to deny being there. At their trial, they admitted presence at the murder – the phone evidence left them little option to do otherwise. At that point the trial became about actions at the scene, rather than them being there.

Change in Usage After the Murder

A hypothetical scenario for you. You have just committed a murder; in your pocket was your mobile phone. You are aware police may be able to use that as evidence, to show your presence at the scene and possibly to connect you to the victim. *What do you do with that phone?*

You have two main options. You can carry on using the phone as normal or dispose of the handset. (Yes, there will be other options in your decision-making, as per DI COP, *see also* page 103, but we will concentrate on the two obvious ones.)

It's a tough choice, isn't it? If you carry on using the phone, you won't be drawing attention to yourself but you run the risk of it being used as evidence. If you dispose of the handset, you may be successful in distancing yourself from it, but suddenly not using your phone can look suspicious.

In my experience, murderers tend to take the *disposal* option. The term used for that is *dropping the phone*. The problem with that choice is you are highlighting your involvement in the crime. This is especially true if you had been using the phone for some time and then you stop using it right after a murder. *It doesn't take a lot of imagination to work out why, does it?* It is exactly this behaviour that police will be looking out for, especially in gang murders.

> **Case File**: In Charlton, South East London, there is a large supermarket distribution centre. The employees work in shifts, all coming out at the same time. On this particular afternoon, our victim left to go home. An ex-gang member, he was trying to distance himself from that lifestyle. He no longer mixed with his old associates, mostly stayed at home and managed to secure a job. The problem for those from this life is that it tends to catch up with them.
>
> Outside the gates happened to be around five members of an opposing gang, one of whom he had previously assaulted. He had stabbed this rival in the buttocks with a barbecue skewer. This sort of assault was intended to humiliate and was not easily forgotten. Within seconds of seeing him, they attacked. He was stabbed, beaten and hit with bottles before the killers made off in several cars. This was all witnessed by his horrified colleagues.
>
> As well as finding out *who* these suspects were, we would also need to understand *why* they were there in the first place. My initial thoughts were, *was this a planned killing? Were they lying in wait to attack him?* The location was out of the way, and there didn't seem any

obvious reason for them being there, so it felt unlikely that it was a coincidence.

Luckily, we had a helping hand in establishing the *who*. During the fight, one of his attackers lost a neck chain. One of those thick gold ones with a distinctive pendant. A chain we later realised was his pride and joy. If you think back to Locard's Exchange Principle (*see also* page 40), *every contact leaves a trace*. Well, if you wear a neck chain constantly, you'll leave plenty of trace. We were able to identify him from the DNA left on that chain, leading to his arrest and charge for murder.

As investigations go, that part was relatively simple: he had given us the opening we needed. The difficulty came with identifying the others involved. In my experience, the best way to do that is to look at phone usage. That is especially true of spontaneous events. If a crime isn't planned, suspects won't be thinking about their contact *before* the incident. They may try and dispose of phones, post-killing, but by then it may be too late. Calls, texts and other messages may already have been sent and there is nothing they can do about them. So, with one suspect identified, we set about looking at his phone records. *Who was he in contact with before? Were they planning this in advance? What happened after the murder?* The answer to that last question became an important element in this case. A short time after the killing, this man stopped using his phone. A predictable action but usually a futile one. As we've seen earlier, previous usage is already recorded and, by dropping the phone, you're just highlighting your involvement.

This man's phone records led us to several others. They were identified by cell site locations. By comparing his phone's movements with his associates, we could see who he was with at the time of the killing. They were put on identification parades, with one associate being picked out by a witness. That associate's phone was in the area of the killing and, similarly, he stopped using it just after the murder took place. One of the facts that stood out for us here was his previous phone usage. In the prior month, his phone had been used in 15,000 separate events (calls and texts) – a huge number. It turns out that he was using it as a *drugs line*.

A third man was also identified via his phone, which mirrored the movement of neck chain man. We also had CCTV footage from outside his home. This showed neck chain man arriving just before the murder, then them leaving together.

As an additional piece of evidence, we seized neck chain man's phone. When we searched it, we found a WhatsApp message sent from him to the man who he picked up. In the message, he said he was on his way and in the company of the man with the drugs phone. All great evidence, and all based on phones.

Phones also helped us with *why* they were there at the time. Opposite the scene is a small row of houses. Living in one of these was a drug dealer, who had been contacted by one of the gang members. They travelled there to buy drugs from him, so we were able to establish that this wasn't a planned attack. It was unfortunately a case of *wrong place, wrong time*.

At trial, the jury found all three guilty of murder. Nice and simple, or so I thought. The drugs line man appealed against his conviction. This is nothing unusual, as they always appeal. But, for the first time in my career, it seemed an appeal may succeed. Back in the section on witnesses (*see also* page 180), I told you about a case called *R v Turnbull*. That revolved around identification evidence and certain questions a witness must be asked. Other rulings came from that case, including duties imposed upon the trial judge. These were rulings our judge had failed to comply with. So, through no fault of our own, it appeared one of the convictions might be overturned. However, when the Court of Appeal gave its findings, they rejected the appeal. *Why*? The judges said there was other compelling evidence, specifically quoting the *dropping* of his phone. Going from 15,000 calls and texts in a month to zero, straight after a murder, provided only one sensible explanation: his involvement in the killing.

If he hadn't dropped that phone, he might have won his appeal against conviction.

What Handsets Have Stored on Them

The second angle that we look at when considering how a phone can help the investigation is what evidence might be stored on the phone itself. For those criminals who haven't disposed of their phones, police will be looking to seize them for this purpose. Generally, there are two types of handset: burner phones and smartphones.

Attempts will be made to download the content from phones in order to see what information they hold. Burner phones are usually pretty simple. They don't tend to be password protected and those with security are relatively easy to crack. This allows police to see everything on the phone, including messages and pictures. Burner phones tend to be 2G, so they don't have internet access.

Smartphones are a different proposition. They are nearly always passcode protected. If police don't have that passcode, gaining access can be difficult. Suspects are always asked for their PINs, but rarely provide them.

If a smartphone is accessed, they can provide a vast amount of data. Searching them can be time-consuming, but the potential return in evidence is huge. This could include messages, internet history, photos, videos, app usage, GPS locations, emails and social media activity. Think about everything you have on your phone and what it could tell someone about your life. That is why accessing suspects' phones is so important.

Did You Know? *If suspects refuse to provide the passcode to their phones, they are committing an offence. In murder cases, failure to cooperate can lead to a conviction with up to two years in prison.*

Case File: I said earlier I would explain how we identified the suspect who we'd offered a £20,000 reward for. Let's call him Suspect A.

He made his living from robbing drug dealers. He and his companions would arrange a drug deal, then steal from their prospective supplier. Robbing from drug dealers isn't like sticking up an off-licence. Dealers know they are part of a dangerous industry, so they come prepared. That means those who rob or attack them have to be ready to use extreme levels of violence.

This particular group were just that sort. They had access to all kinds of firearms, with a history of using them. On this particular occasion, they arranged to buy drugs from a dealer in Woolwich, South East London. They first met each other near the town centre, before travelling in three cars to the dealer's flat. The dealer clearly had no idea what he was getting himself into. He was with a friend, so he perhaps felt safe – a big mistake.

At the flat, the plan soon kicked into action. A knife was pulled out by Suspect A, who demanded the drugs be handed over. But, as is so often the case, the dealer wasn't going to give up his stash so easily. A fight ensued, during which the dealer received a fatal stab wound. They then fled, leaving the dealer dying on the floor but his friend unharmed. The friend, concerned about being arrested for selling drugs, decided to run from the flat rather than call for help. It is unlikely the dealer would have survived his injuries, but his friend's lack of action ensured he wouldn't. The friend did call for help eventually, but sometime later and a couple of miles from the scene.

Police arrived at the flat at least an hour after the murder to find the victim dead on the kitchen floor. We attended the scene, beginning the usual steps that you are now aware of. The crime scene manager and exhibits officer got to the stage where they were ready to move the body. As they did so, however, they saw a mobile phone underneath him. *It must be the victim's phone, right*? That's what we first thought. But no, Suspect A had dropped his phone in the struggle. If they were to hold classes for aspiring murderers, I think an early lesson would be *don't leave your mobile phone at the scene*.

Oh, to have been a fly on the wall on their retreat from the murder. As they were driving away, *can you imagine the conversation as he realised what he had done*? We've all had that feeling when we know we've made a big mistake. You feel it in the pit of your stomach. I can't begin to imagine what this man was feeling when it dawned on him. Ironically, they would have had plenty of time to go back and retrieve the phone given that the friend had taken so long to call the murder in.

When Are Phones Pivotal to an Investigation?

The use of phone evidence, in some cases, can be central to the investigation. Take a missing person, for instance. This is a case where a person hasn't been seen for some time and there is real concern for their welfare. When we discussed hypotheses, phone usage was key to most scenarios.

If the phone is being used, it is an indicator of them being alive (although not always, as we will see later in this section). Police will obtain live updates as to the phone's location and to whom calls are being made. Any numbers that are in contact with the person will be the subject of further investigation.

If phone usage has stopped, the missing person may have switched it off. Alternatively, harm may have come to them. Either way, the last area the phone was used will be where a search is likely to begin. As I've said, any cell sites used will only indicate a general area, so it won't be a simple process. It is likely other work will be needed in that area to help with locating their movements, such as gathering CCTV footage.

Case File: We were the homicide assessment team car this particular Saturday, when we were contacted by local police from Bexley, South East London. As well as murders, MITs may also be asked to assist in missing person cases where there is a real concern for someone's safety. This was just such a case. When people are reported missing, they will be classified as low-, medium- or high-risk. There are various factors that dictate that grading, but, suffice to say, it would only be high-risk cases that come to MITs.

As soon as I heard the details of this case, for various reasons, I became concerned. A mum and her two boys, aged eight and four, had been missing for about two weeks. This isn't unheard of, and there can be various plausible reasons for a mum taking her children away, especially if they are in a violent relationship. Right from the start, however, this case felt different. It was a concerned relative who reported them missing. Officers attended their home and spoke with the husband, who said his wife had gone to stay with friends. However, after that initial interaction, nobody was able to contact the husband – he just disappeared. The mum going away was judged to be out of character, and her phone had stopped being used, which seemed unusual. She was also suffering from a debilitating condition which made it difficult for her to get about, adding to the reasons for concern. Her family had received some text messages from her phone telling them she was going away, but *were they actually from her?*

I wasn't alone in my concern. The feeling among the team was the same – we feared the worst. But, if we *were* right, it meant two young children had been killed. We started to look into their lives to get answers to our two main priorities:

- Find the mum and children.
- Find the dad.

When people go missing, the police will look for *signs of life*. This can include phone usage, social media usage, financial transactions or sightings. There were none. Until a body is found, you cling to hope but with every passing hour, and with every negative response to our enquiries, that hope was fading.

Within a very short space of time, that hope had disappeared completely.

As a matter of course, we carried out a search of the family home. They lived in a bungalow, with the two boys sharing a room. The house looked as if they had decorators in. Fresh, white paint in places, a stepladder and sheets on walls. It was December and a small Christmas tree was in the hall. The children's bedroom was fairly sparse but with the kinds of toys you would expect to see. A soft toy dog was on the floor, possibly a favourite plaything for a four-year-old. On the face of it, nothing looked out of the ordinary. That was until we saw what was *under* that white paint. Blood, a lot of blood. It was in the kitchen and, most distressingly, in the children's bedroom – I can't think of anything worse than that scene.

I mentioned previously how I try and put myself in the victim's shoes at the time of a murder to get a feel for what happened; to try and understand how they were killed. Doing that here was just awful. Two young boys, in the place they should feel most safe. In their beds, surrounded by their toys, with the people they trusted most in this world. But that trust was shattered by their father. We will never know for sure how much they knew of what was happening, I just hope it wasn't a lot.

We knew now that the worst had happened, *but where were they*? *Where was the dad*? My hunch was he might have taken his own life. It happens far too often: a father killing his family and then himself. But if he had done that, *where was his body*? *Surely it would be at the house*?

After the discovery of blood, we began a search for the mum and children. We didn't have to look very far. With the use of dogs trained in the recovery of human remains, we found all three victims: they had been buried in the rear garden, all three in the same shallow grave.

I won't go into detail about their injuries as it upsets me even thinking about it. They were horrific and painted a picture of the most violent ending for all three of them. *How could a person do that to his family?* If we had any chance of answering that question, we had to catch him.

We carried out financial checks, which showed he had withdrawn about £400 from their bank account. *So, had he gone on the run?* We looked into his phone records, which set us on the path to finding him.

He had called a friend, who he then visited. He persuaded her to book a flight for him from Heathrow to Ghana, via Amsterdam. We obtained CCTV footage from the UK and Holland, which confirmed he had taken the flights. So, he was now in Ghana, the place of his birth. *How the hell were we going to find him there?*

The media pick and choose the crimes they give publicity to, depending on their newsworthiness. In some cases, a murder may only get a few lines in the local news. In this case, every news outlet wanted to run the story. The mum had been an actress, an angle that added to press interest. I have to be honest, that did make things harder for us. Some newspapers decided to form their own narrative around the investigation. They wrongly reported there were issues with how the investigation was being conducted and went as far as to describe it as 'bungled'. That was hard to read for those of us who were giving everything we could for the case. I won't lie, seeing headlines like that hurts your professional pride, especially when you know there is no truth to them. It also presented a challenge to our relationship with the bereaved family. On the one hand, we were assuring them we were doing everything possible, while on the other, they were reading disparaging headlines about our work. Thankfully they chose to ignore them and our relationship remained a good one. However, the publicity did actually prove helpful later on.

I was the officer tasked with locating him, a job I knew wasn't going to be easy. My first responsibility was to obtain an arrest warrant for him, which involved me attending court and giving the facts of the case. Once we had that, we could start international procedures needed to lawfully extradite him back to the UK.

I made contact with somebody from the British Embassy in Ghana and given the circumstances, they were more than keen to help. But Ghana is a country almost the size of the UK, so *where do we start*? That was when the publicity came into play. We released the fact he was in Ghana to the media and within a couple of days, we received information from British people there who had spotted the suspect at a resort area.

By now, Christmas had come and gone. It was now New Year. Before I go on, I'd like you to have a think about that man. He has just killed his wife and children, and he had fled to the country of his birth. He almost certainly knew the police were looking for him. *What do you think he would do*? My initial thoughts were that he went back to his country of birth to die. Either that or he had decided to hide and to evade arrest. What I wouldn't have expected, though, was that he'd be partying, which, on New Year's Eve, is exactly what he was doing.

At least we now had an idea of where he was. All I had to do was get the Ghanaian police to go to the resort and apprehend him. *Easier said than done.* I'm not saying they didn't want to help, but they seemed determined to do so in their own time.

The problem was, I wasn't the only person trying to find him. A BBC News crew had decided to do the same, except they had one distinct advantage. For Scotland Yard to send detectives to a foreign country, we have to jump through certain legal hoops. Hoops that don't exist for journalists. They were regularly reporting their progress, gradually getting closer to where we knew the suspect was. This added to the need to capture him as soon as possible. Plus, in my mind, there was still the possibility of him committing suicide. For all of us, that would have been the worst outcome: he needed to answer for his crimes.

I was getting good information from members of the public in Ghana, so I was confident of where this man was. The frustration was getting police to him in time. It wasn't as simple as getting officers from that area to arrest him, as they had to come from the capital, Accra, which was several hours away. I had no idea why officers couldn't be sent from a local police station, but they insisted it had to be done this way. With the help of my contact at the embassy, I was eventually able to get police officers to travel to where the suspect was. But, from the BBC News reports, I knew their crew was just as close. The last thing we needed was a reporter turning up at the suspect's location, putting a microphone under his nose and asking him questions about the murders. This could have prompted his disappearance or suicide, would be incredibly difficult for the bereaved family to see and it would have fed into the media narrative around our handling of the case.

What actually happened, in this race against time, was somewhat unexpected. The local community in the village got wind of what was happening and took it upon themselves to capture the man. While I was getting live updates from someone close by, these locals chased him from the village to a beach area. I was trying to relay this back to the travelling police but couldn't get through. Then my phone rang: it was my contact at the embassy. He told me police had caught the suspect, who was now in custody. Finally, we had him and before the news crew had arrived. I later learned that those locals who had chased him to the beach then directed the police to where he was. That really demonstrated the power of social media. Their help proved crucial and the arrest would have been much harder to achieve without the use of social media.

Over the following days, we secured his extradition back to the UK. In these circumstances, the Crown Prosecution Service (CPS) has to authorise his charge before this can be achieved. However, this meant that we couldn't seek answers from him as to why he killed his family as, once someone is charged, they cannot be questioned about their offence. We essentially skipped straight to court preparation. We were in a fortunate position, however, that extradition was extremely quick and he was back in the UK within days rather than months.

How did we piece together the case against him for his impending trial? Well, there was little question he had committed the murders, but *when?* *What was the timeline of events?* For that, we used phone evidence. We established the mum was still alive two days prior to being reported missing. At around 4pm that afternoon, she made a phone call to a witness, who confirmed they had spoken. The following morning, at around 10am, messages were sent from her phone to family members, saying she had taken the kids away. However, the cell site used was close to their home, which undermines this. These messages hadn't come from her; they were sent by the husband in an attempt to cover up what he had done. This showed the murders had occurred sometime between 4pm and 10am, two days before she was reported missing.

Cell site information was also used to show the suspect's movements after the killings.

The picture that we built up using this phone evidence formed the basis of the prosecution. Ultimately, he pleaded guilty to all three murders, receiving a whole life sentence.

Why did he do it? We don't know for sure and

may never know, although there was a suggestion
the mum was going to leave him. That led to familiar
headlines in the press, with a narrative similar to 'man
kills wife and kids because she was going to leave him
and take his kids away'. For me, this is lazy and all too
predictable. It also shifts some of the blame from him to
her (she prompted this by daring to take his kids away).
I know that isn't what these reporters meant, but it
is still there at some subconscious level. For me, the
real reason, and how the headlines should have read,
was 'controlling monster kills wife and kids because
he couldn't cope with no longer having that control'.
That, I believe, was the real reason he killed his family,
but that isn't how these types of killings are reported.

Vehicle Telematics

There is one more piece of evidence I want to highlight in
this section. Our mobile phones are not the only source of this
information. Most modern-day cars are fitted with technology
that uses mobile phone equipment. This might also include *in
car Wi-Fi or GPS*. These cars are fitted with SIM cards similar
to those in our phones and police can access that information
in the same way they obtain call data. And, as with phones,
information can be downloaded directly from the car itself.

INTELLIGENCE

So far, we have looked at lines of enquiry that provide *evidence*
in a case. Evidence is what will be considered by a court. It is

what will be used to achieve a conviction. When police seek charges by sending a file to the Crown Prosecution Service, they will base their decision solely on evidence. They cannot consider intelligence in this process. But, when it comes to solving murders, intelligence can be absolutely vital to reaching a successful outcome.

How Can Intelligence Help the Investigation?

The best way to describe *intelligence* is information that tells the team *where they need to look for evidence*. But, if that information doesn't lead to evidence, it cannot be used by the prosecution in court.

For example, intelligence relating to a murder could include:

- Victimology
- Names/nicknames of suspects
- Names of potential witnesses
- Where evidence may have been disposed of (weapons/clothing, etc.)
- Reasons for a murder
- Locations of wanted suspects

The list is potentially endless, but this is the kind of information that will be passed to a MIT.

Where Does the Intelligence Come From?

The source of intelligence can essentially be broken into two categories: *police initiated* and *publicly volunteered*. Here are some of the methods of obtaining information from these two sources:

Police Initiated

Witnesses: Many people will be spoken to within the investigation, not all of whom will provide evidential statements. Some will provide information on an intelligence basis only. The main reason for this is a reluctance to make a formal statement. A person may be comfortable providing information to an officer, but wouldn't want to attend court and give it as evidence. If this happens, whatever they have said will be treated as intelligence. This can still be hugely important to the investigation and may guide it in a certain direction, the hope being that intelligence can be turned into evidence in some other way, such as forensics, CCTV or a more willing witness.

Informants: The use of informants by police is nothing new. For as long as there has been police, there have been individuals willing to provide information on criminal activity. In the UK, an informant is known as a *covert human intelligence source*, or *CHIS*. A CHIS is usually a person who, through their social, business or criminal activities, is party to information that would assist police. This used to be a murky world, but since it's been properly regulated, it's now carried out far more professionally. In my early career, any officer could manage informants. Having a situation where a police officer has a close working relationship with a criminal can present issues and, in the past, this was open to abuse from both sides. Today, only specially-trained officers are allowed to manage informants. This ensures correct procedures are adhered to and minimises the potential for problems. However, by the nature of this work, there can still be issues. In the previous section on phones, we had a case file involving the murder of a boy who was found in a burnt-out car (*see also* page 204). I explained that one defendant was an informant. Well, what played out during the trial was rather concerning. It became apparent that the informant was the one in control of the relationship with the handler. He was using it to feed false information to the police for the benefit of the gang he was associated with. It did not paint Scotland Yard's informant-handling system in a good light, although procedures changed as a result of that case.

Phone taps: In the UK, police and security services have the power to tap phones. This practice has taken place for years. In order to do so, a warrant is required, usually signed by the Home Secretary. That is the highest-level authority required for any police activity, which demonstrates how seriously the use of this tactic is taken.

What you may not know, however, is that any conversations recorded by UK police cannot be used as evidence in UK courts. It's illegal. If a person is being listened to and admits a murder, that can only be used as intelligence. However, if a phone conversation is recorded in a foreign country where that practice is legal, the recordings can be used as evidence in UK courts. If you think that's daft, I agree.

Bugged houses: Police would not call it bugging a house, but it is the term people are most familiar with. If listening devices are placed in someone's home or car, this is known as intrusive surveillance. Authority for this would be from a high-ranking officer. Any recordings made can be used as evidence. So, if the person who admitted to murder said it in a car with a listening device attached, that could be used against them at their trial.

Police intelligence systems: The police have various systems that hold information on people. I can't go into detail about what these are, as I'm sure you will understand.

Financial records: The financial transactions of victims and suspects can provide a wealth of information. Also, in London, people use bank cards for payment on public transport, which can provide intelligence on their movements. ATM withdrawals and card usage can help build a picture of a person's life, movements and purchase history.

Myth Buster: *On TV, you often see police computer systems throwing up all sorts of useful information at the touch of a button. The reality is quite different. If you are the intelligence officer in an enquiry, you spend a chunk of your time emailing requests to other agencies for information. All of this has to be justified in order to be legal, because the police are subject to the Data Protection Act as much as anyone else. Before an organisation hands over personal information, an officer has to demonstrate that it is required for a purpose such as preventing or detecting crime or national security.*

Publicly Volunteered

Crimestoppers: The charity Crimestoppers UK exists to allow people to provide confidential information anonymously. If that information relates to a murder, it will be passed to the relevant MIT.

The police information room: Whenever MITs make public appeals for information, they provide a phone number. This allows members of the public to call the team directly.

The victim's family: Not everybody is comfortable talking to the police; some see it as *snitching*, they may have an ingrained distrust of the authorities or they feel they will be under threat if they come forward as a witness. They may be more inclined to speak to the family and will therefore pass information on to them about a murder.

How Do We Verify Intelligence?

Any intelligence coming to MITs will be researched and verified. Not all intelligence will be correct. In fact, a lot is either partly or wholly inaccurate. Quite often, the information springs from the *word on the street*, which is notoriously unreliable.

Senior officers on MITs will make a decision whether to act on the information. Those decisions are not always simple. For example, one piece of information could be received that could help crack the case, but it may not be corroborated elsewhere. In that instance, a lot has to be considered before any action is taken:

1. **How accurate that information is**: If there is no supporting evidence, that may be difficult to gauge.

2. **Who provided it**: If they have provided accurate information previously, it may help support the validity of the intelligence.

3. **Who else knows**: Imagine if only the informant

knew this information? If police acted upon it, their safety could be compromised. There is a well-known phrase in criminal circles: *snitches get stitches*. Police informants can be in incredible danger if their involvement is revealed.

Assuming all of these issues have been carefully considered, and senior officers are satisfied with the information and associated risk, police may act on the intelligence.

Case File: A suspect had stabbed and killed the victim. We received intelligence that in the rear garden of a hostel he had burned clothing he was wearing during the murder, but the location given was non-specific. After extensive research, we were able to establish where this was likely to have been. The above considerations were applied to the intelligence and the decision was made to apply for a search warrant. We executed the warrant late at night to maximise the chance of the suspect being present. He wasn't there, unfortunately, but, in the rear garden, we found burned clothes and trainers. One of the trainers wasn't completely destroyed, so we submitted it for DNA examination. In the meantime, the suspect was found and arrested, and a DNA sample taken from him. His DNA profile matched that found in the trainer, and he was subsequently convicted of murder. On its own, the intelligence would not have secured the conviction, but turned into evidence, it was an important element in the case against him.

TRACE, INTERVIEW AND ELIMINATE

To catch a killer, a MIT may require a strategy to help identify potential suspects. A well-established method is known as trace, interview and eliminate, better known as TIE. This practice isn't used in all murder enquiries but may be useful in cases where suspects are unknown.

A group of people are identified, among which could be the killer. A specific criteria can be established to identify this group and anyone who fits this is the subject of investigation. The theory being, you work through the list of people, eliminating those you can, until you identify a likely suspect.

As a simple example, a woman is killed in a park and a witness sees a white man running away from the scene before driving off in a yellow BMW. A strategy could be devised where males within a certain geographical area, who fit the description and have access to a yellow BMW, could be placed on a *TIE list*. They would all be the subject of investigation, to either eliminate them from the list or be raised as a suspect in the killing. In this scenario, there were five men who matched the criteria. Four had alibis, so were taken off the TIE list. The remaining man, who had no alibi, was classed as a suspect and arrested.

In reality it is more complicated, but that is the basic principle.

For TIE to be effective, the criteria need to be well thought out. To assist the senior investigating officer (SIO) in formulating the strategy around this, they may call on the assistance of a criminal profiler.

One fact that needs to be borne in mind, for the killer to be caught using TIE, they would need to appear on the list in the first place. Whether this method is implemented, and how it is carried out, is a decision for the SIO. At Scotland Yard, a person on this list is sometimes referred to as a *person of interest*.

CRIMINAL PROFILING

I know many people find this a fascinating topic, and I'm sure there are cases where this has helped, but, if I'm honest, in the instances we sought this advice, it wasn't helpful. We used profilers in murders where the suspect was unknown and the cases were a little different, i.e. they were not to do with organised crime or gang-related. Of the hundred or so cases I was involved in, we employed the use of profilers three times. I think that is probably a fair reflection of how often they are used in murder investigations. The product we got from them was interesting, but, ultimately, it didn't assist us in solving those cases.

Did You Know? *In the UK, criminal profiling is a function of the National Crime Agency. Those that provide this advice are known as behavioural investigative advisers.*

HOW DO WE MAKE SENSE OF ALL THAT INFORMATION?

At this point, you've been given a lot of detail to process about the various lines of investigation. This is often how it feels when you're in the MIT too.

The investigation will generate a lot of information. Numerous witnesses will have been spoken to, all with their own parts to the story. Throw in CCTV, phone data, intelligence, financial records, ANPR (automatic number plate recognition) and various other strands and it can add up to a mass of material.

So, how do they make sense of it all?

There are two key methods of curating all that information to better make sense of the whole:

- Timelines
- The HOLMES computer system

Timelines

One of the most effective methods of understanding how all of that information fits together is the use of timelines. Laying the information out in chronological order is a fantastic way of building a clear picture of how events happened. It is often the only way. Imagine having statements from twenty different witnesses, all with different things to say, alongside hours of CCTV footage from dozens of cameras. There could also be hundreds of phone calls happening around the same time, with intelligence pouring in. If all of this information can be overlaid with each other in time order, you will be amazed at how clear everything becomes. These can also highlight gaps in the evidence, discrepancies in witness accounts and events of interest.

Who does this work? This is the responsibility of an *intelligence analyst*. They are not police officers but highly-trained civilian staff with access to computer software to help them with the task.

A timeline won't be necessary for all investigations, but it's invaluable for the more complex ones. It will allow the senior officers to look at their strategies, consider hypotheses and, hopefully, make it clearer who the potential suspects are. And, if any are identified, arrests can be made.

The HOLMES Computer System

No, I'm not talking about a fictional detective in a deerstalker. HOLMES stands for Home Office Large Major Enquiry System. It is a computer system used by MITs to record the information generated during an investigation. Each murder will have its own account containing all statements and documents generated. It also records all people, vehicles, addresses and telephone numbers that come into the investigation. This is helpful, as an enquiry can have hundreds of witnesses, all providing various bits of information – each one, potentially, a small part of the puzzle. HOLMES is a way of organising this and minimising the risk of leads being missed.

As I mentioned in our section on who works within MITs (*see also* page 16), there are a number of people whose job it is to manage HOLMES. Included in this will be a detective sergeant (DS), who would be known as the office manager. They lead the small team responsible for HOLMES. There would also be two DCs and at least three members of staff who are not police officers. The environment in which they work is known as the major incident room, or MIR. It is their job to assess every document that comes into an enquiry, to input the information into the system and to identify lines of enquiry that need to be followed up. These enquiries are known as *actions* and each would be allocated to a detective to follow up.

For instance, a statement may name a person as being present at the scene. An action will be created for a statement to be taken from them. The allocated officer will take the statement and then submit it to HOLMES, where it will be attached to the record of that witness.

There may be occasions where murders are linked. If so, the accounts for each enquiry can be joined together on HOLMES, facilitating access to both sets of files for the investigating officers and allowing cross-reference of useful information. Imagine another Yorkshire Ripper case, with murders in different police areas, and how useful this function could be in recognising the connection.

Each murder enquiry on the system will be given an operation name. The names all start with the same letter in a calendar year. So, in 2019 all investigations had a name starting with R, in 2020 the letter S, in 2021 the letter T, and so on.

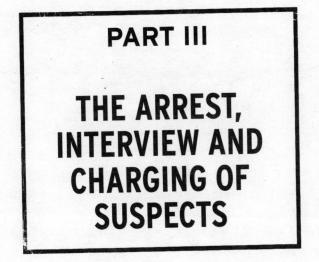

PART III

THE ARREST, INTERVIEW AND CHARGING OF SUSPECTS

The arrest and interview of suspects is, potentially, the beginning of the endgame: the conviction of a murderer. However, it is also a line of investigation as it can provide further intelligence and evidence that will support the case. Below we'll consider how arrests, interviews and the charging of suspects is carried out both in terms of process and legal requirements, but let's take a look first at their value in terms of information gathering.

HOW CAN THE ARREST AND INTERVIEW OF SUSPECTS HELP THE INVESTIGATION?

Police have many powers open to them when investigating crime. Powers such as searching people's homes, taking their clothing and property, obtaining forensic samples such as fingerprints and DNA or questioning them. All powers that can lead to evidence which can either prove or disprove a person's involvement in an offence. But we don't live in a police state where officers can go about doing these things without a level of justification. In order for police to do these things legally, a person will either need to be arrested or, in some instances, have authority granted by a court. So, this phase of an investigation is vitally important, and in more ways than one.

It is critical for the reason I mentioned above, i.e. to obtain potential evidence, but it is also the stage at which it is most likely that the offenders will *get off on a technicality*. For that reason, it requires the strictest adherence to the law and codes of practice that govern police actions. Here, I will be going into the detail of some of those rules so you have an understanding of what can go wrong.

In terms of how interviews can help investigators, it goes beyond what a lot of people might imagine. When talking to others about this subject, they often believe the intention is to get people to confess. Of course, that plays a part in it. If every killer confessed to their crimes during interviews, it would make our job a lot easier, but interviews serve many more purposes than that. For one, not every person interviewed is guilty. In fact, many aren't. The interview is an opportunity to establish someone's innocence as much as their guilt. After all, *every story has two sides*, so it is only right that a person should be able to put across their perspective on events.

THE ARREST OF SUSPECTS

If the goal of *securing a safe and proper conviction at court* is to be achieved, arrests will need to be made. But *how is it decided who to arrest*? Firstly, we will look at the law, then how decisions are made to carry out arrests.

How Is an Arrest Legally Carried Out?

Do You Have Reasonable Suspicion?

First of all, for an arrest to be made, a police officer has to have *reasonable grounds for suspecting* an offence has taken place and *reasonable suspicion* the person is guilty of it. This is a subjective test that essentially boils down to what is in the officer's mind.

Think back to the case file in the section on motive (*see also* page 110) and the decision to arrest the boy for arson. On the face of it, there was not a huge amount of evidence to suggest it was him, but the decision was made on the basis a murder had occurred and he had a potential motive, which gave rise to *reasonable suspicion* he was guilty.

In murder enquiries, *where can that suspicion come from?* This is by no means an exhaustive list, but some of the sources of suspicion may be:

- **Witnesses**: A suspect may be named by a witness as carrying out the murder.

- **Forensic evidence**: DNA or fingerprint evidence may point in a suspect's direction.

- **Intelligence**: Informants may name the suspect.

- **Financial enquiries**: This is particularly true if financial gain was the motive.

- **Trace, investigate and eliminate**: By looking at a group of people the killer is likely to be part of, then systematically eliminating subjects until a potential suspect is identified.

- **Suspect admissions**: Sometimes suspects admit their crimes to other people, who then tell police.

- **CCTV**: The suspect can perhaps be recognised from images at or near the scene.

- **Information from the family**: The victim's families often hold key information or have it given to them.

- **Telephone call data**: This might be phone contact with the victim, the fact they were in the area or the dropping of their phone, etc.

- **Similar offender history**: A particular method may match a suspect's past behaviour; for instance, violent break-ins.

- **Motive**: If someone had reason to carry out a murder.

Is the Arrest Necessary?

OK, so the officer *suspects* the person is guilty of an offence. The officer will now have to *believe* the arrest is *necessary*.

When I say necessary, I mean to say are there other ways of dealing with a person rather than arresting them. For example, could they be summoned to court?

What would make an arrest necessary? Well, remember how the law thinks police officers struggle to recall things? A handy mnemonic has been introduced to help them. If at least one of these reasons exists, the arrest will be deemed necessary.

I – Investigation: It's necessary to allow interviews, searches, DNA swabs, etc.

D – Disappearance: It's necessary to stop the person from disappearing or going on the run.

C – Child: It's necessary to protect a child or other vulnerable person.

O – Obstruction of the highway: It's necessary to prevent this (imagine sit-down protesters in the road).

P – Physical injury: It's necessary to prevent anybody coming to harm (that could include a victim of crime, witnesses or even the suspect themselves).

P – Public decency: It's necessary to prevent this continuing (imagine a naked man running around or a couple having sex in public).

L – Loss or damage to property: It's necessary to stop this from happening.

A – Address: It's necessary because the suspect's address is unknown or doubted, and it may not be possible to contact or find them in order to serve a summons.

N – Name: It's necessary because the suspect's name is unknown or doubted, so it may not be possible to serve a summons on the right person.

With murder cases, arrests would almost always fall under I and D. The suspect will need to be interviewed and searches conducted, and they're likely to go on the run if they know they are suspected of murder. So, in reality, the COPPLAN mnemonic is more relevant to other offences.

What Is Required to Make an Arrest Lawful?

So, a police officer *suspects* a person of murder and *believes* the arrest is necessary. *What will they be required, by law, to tell the suspect?* The arresting officer must tell the person the following:

- The fact they are under arrest
- The grounds for the arrest
- Why the arrest is necessary

How would that sound in reality?

Example: *'I'm arresting you on suspicion of the murder of Bill Smith in the high street on 4 April, as you have been named as being involved. Your arrest is necessary to question you about your involvement.'*

The suspect should then be cautioned using the wording below:

'You do not have to say anything. But it may harm your defence if you do not mention, when questioned, something which you later rely on in court. Anything you do say may be given in evidence.'

Did You Know? *When arresting a person, the use of colloquialisms can be used as long as the person being arrested knows and understands their meaning. So, if a police officer was arresting a long-time criminal who had been arrested many times previously, they could say, 'You're nicked'. The caution would still need to be given in a form that is as close to the official wording as possible, but it doesn't have to be the exact phrasing to be considered legally compliant, as long as the main points are clear. If the suspect is being violent, it would be OK not to caution them at that time, but it should be given as soon as it is practical to do so.*

Case File: I was awoken early one Saturday morning with a text to my phone: *We have a new murder.* We were the on-call MIT for South London, so I was half expecting something to happen that weekend. As was normal, that was all the information I had. I would find out the details when I arrived at Lewisham Police Station, our base. I was met by excited chatter. Considering they were seasoned murder detectives, there had to be something a bit different to this case, and there was.

At around 2am that morning, a car had been found ablaze in Blackheath, South East London, which was only a mile or so from where we worked. The badly burned body of a man had been found in the boot. *Now, that is unusual.* My first thoughts were of organised crime, which seemed the most obvious motive, but, as always when we began a new case, I kept an open mind.

The officers on the homicide assessment team (HAT) car that night had attended the scene and they gave all of us a full briefing on what had happened. The car was found in an alley of houses. Unusually, it was police officers who first discovered it. CCTV in the area had been checked and there was footage of two men walking away from the area the car was in at about the time it is likely to have started. The car wasn't stolen and was registered to an address a few miles from where it was found.

It was confirmed that the car was being used by the brother of the lady who owned it. He told her he was going to a party on the previous night.

We knew we'd need help in identifying whether
it was in fact the brother. He was too badly burned
for the sister to be able to make a visual identification.
However, one piece of evidence convinced us it was
almost certainly him. The family told the family liaison
officers (FLOs) that the brother always wore a large
gold chain. A chain identical to the one we found on
our victim. *It had to be him.* But we needed to know for
sure, so we obtained the brother's dental records and
asked a forensic odontologist to provide analysis. That
evening, it was confirmed via those dental records that
it was indeed him.

So now we knew *who* the victim was but we still
had many questions left unanswered. *Why was he in the
boot of the car? How did he die? Where did he die? Was he
dead before being burned? Who killed him? Why did they
kill him?*

One of the quickest and easiest lines of enquiry
was the car. We ran checks on the registration number
against automatic number plate recognition (ANPR)
cameras. This told us that the car had travelled down to
Brighton the previous evening, a distance of about 65
miles. *Why was he travelling there?*

We also looked at his phone's call data records,
which showed his phone had also been located in
Brighton. *Who was it in Brighton that he knew?* It
turned out to be a woman who may have been an
ex-girlfriend. *So, did she have something to do with it?
Who was she?* Our enquiries showed that she was a
medical student and future doctor. *Surely she wouldn't*

be responsible for such an horrendous crime? But, if not her, then who?

We set about looking to form some sort of hypothesis around what may have happened. The girl in Brighton was one possible suspect, although a reason was unclear at that stage. It also transpired that the victim's father had been murdered. He had been killed in India over some financial arguments, so that was definitely a possible avenue of investigation and one with more credence than a young medical student murdering her ex-boyfriend.

Whichever scenario may have been correct, both needed to be investigated. To our surprise, the one that quickly gained most traction was the medical student. Witnesses told us that the victim had arranged to go and see her that Friday night at 11pm, times which matched the phone and ANPR information. The victim had phoned a friend from outside the student's house, saying that there were two men inside. That friend sent him a text several minutes later, a text that was never answered. That call was the last time our victim was known to be alive. The timings of ANPR for the car travelling back to London meant that whatever happened to the victim was likely to have happened there in Brighton. *So, the student must have been involved somehow.*

If we think back to what is required to form reasonable suspicion for an arrest, two factors have to be met:

- **Reasonable grounds for suspecting an offence has taken place**: Yes, this was clearly a murder.

- **Reasonable suspicion the person is guilty of it**: This woman was almost certainly one of the last people to see our victim and appeared to be the reason he had travelled to the place he was killed.

Given these two factors, the decision was made to raise this student's status to suspect and for her to be arrested as soon as possible.

Before that arrest could take place, she actually came to us. She took herself to Lewisham Police Station, saying that she was probably the last person to see the victim alive. She told us that he had been sending her unwanted texts and she had invited him down to her house that night, presumably to stop those texts. She said there was an argument between them and then he drove off in his car.

She was then arrested and taken into custody. We went to her house in order to secure it as a crime scene. As is often the case, the suspect shared a house with other students. They were spoken to and gave a very different version of events to the one told to us by the woman.

The victim had actually been invited down to Brighton with the intention of 'sorting him out'. There had been a previous incident between our victim and the woman, during which he is alleged to have sexually assaulted her. The woman had arranged for two men to 'greet' the victim. They then beat him in the house before tying him up, wrapping him in a duvet and then placing him in the boot of the car.

He was then driven to Blackheath, where the car was set alight. Distressingly, he was still alive when that happened. It's impossible to know how aware he was of what was happening, but a post-mortem confirmed he was killed by the fire and not by the beating he received at the house.

So, who were the two men? The first one was pretty easy to identify. The housemates knew him by his first name and the medical student's phone records showed she was in heavy contact with a person of that name around that time. *Reasonable suspicion for arrest*? Yes. He was soon taken into custody. It transpired he was actually a friend of the victim.

Both he and the medical student were interviewed and, as is normally the case, denied involvement in the murder. But the evidence against them was strong, so the Crown Prosecution Service authorised charges for murder.

We then had to identify the second man from the flat. This was done via CCTV and intelligence. An image was found of a man at Brighton train station, on the night of the murder, in company with the medical student and the other man charged, so there was little doubt who he was. I was actually the officer who arrested this man. We went to his house and I explained why we were there. I told him we had evidence that he was involved in the murder and then arrested and cautioned him. Now, I've arrested a lot of people for murder. I've seen many different reactions, from disbelief to acceptance. But this man was different. When I told him, I saw no reaction at all. Complete indifference. I even had to ask him, *have you heard what I just said*? He nodded. I said again, *you do understand I've just arrested you for murder*? Again, he nodded. I found his reaction so odd that I made a note of it in the statement I made about the arrest and it formed an important part of my evidence at court.

The second man was charged and all three went to trial at the Old Bailey. The evidence presented showed that the medical student had indeed lured our victim to her house and had done so in order for him to be assaulted by the two men. She denied this. The two men also denied murder.

The jury, having listened to all of the evidence, came back with verdicts that I still struggle to comprehend. They found her not guilty of murder, but guilty of grievous bodily harm, so they accepted she was part of the plan to attack the victim.

They found the man who was friends with the victim guilty of murder.

They found the man I arrested not guilty of murder but guilty of manslaughter.

We will never know how they came to those verdicts. For us, as a team, we had mixed feelings. Of course, we were pleased that someone was found guilty of the murder. However, we felt the other two verdicts just didn't fit the evidence.

How Is the Decision to Arrest Made in Murder Investigations?

So, that is how an arrest can be legally carried out, but in murder investigations, *how is that decision reached*? That is a difficult one to answer conclusively as the decision to arrest is a subjective one but generally, the decision will be made taking into consideration the following:

1. **Is there evidence?** You can't arrest people on a hunch; there has to be *some* evidence. But, as with the arson case, there doesn't need to be a huge amount. Just enough to raise suspicion. Sometimes you may have a *gut feeling* about someone, but that needs to be backed up with something tangible.

2. **What police powers will an arrest allow?** By that, I mean will an arrest provide you with the powers you need to progress the investigation, i.e. the ability to search premises, take samples from the suspect and seize phones? If there is relatively little evidence, this can be strengthened by the use of these powers. For example, if you're able to seize a computer, you may find a search on it for *how to burn a house down*, which could be critical to the case.

3. **Could a suspect interfere with evidence?** If you delay an arrest, it gives the suspect time to dispose of evidence such as clothing, phones and weapons. They may also get at witnesses to prevent them from giving statements.

4. **Will the suspect flee?** It's not unusual for murder suspects to evade arrest, often by leaving the country. The longer you delay, the more time you give them to plan and enact an escape.

5. **What impact would an arrest have on the suspect?** The decision to arrest should not be taken lightly as it is a serious action to take. *How would you feel about being arrested for murder?* You would be forcibly taken from your home. You would be detained in custody for many hours, even days. You might be locked in a cell, having been possibly strip-searched. You would be sleeping on a bench and given horrible food. You'd be interviewed for hours on end, being accused of the most serious crime. It is likely your friends and family will find out, as will the media. Regardless of whether you are charged, you will have that arrest hanging over you. It is not a power that police should use indiscriminately and needs to be well justified.

Myth Buster: *When arresting suspects, no Scotland Yard murder detective will ever carry a gun. Whatever you may see on TV or read in books, it does not happen. Most detectives have never fired a gun in their lives. Ninety-nine per cent of murder arrests are made with no police firearms officers present. In fact, those scenes where there's a shoot-out between suspects and the police are, thankfully, extremely rare. Most arrests are extremely routine. No guns, no violence and no drama.*

What Happens After an Arrest Is Made?

After being arrested, the suspect will be taken to a police station. Once there, the arresting officer will explain the facts to a custody officer, who will decide whether the person should be detained. As long as the grounds for arrest are correct and the person isn't unwell or injured, this is normally authorised.

What rights do they have? In English law, a detained person will be told of three rights by the custody officer:

1. They are entitled to free and independent legal advice.

2. They may have somebody told of their arrest.

3. They can read a book containing the rules of their detention.

They will also have the right to make a phone call or write a letter (I've never known a prisoner to write a letter).

Some of these rights can be delayed under certain circumstances. For instance, the right to have someone informed of their arrest can be delayed because other suspects are being sought, it could lead to interference with evidence or it would hinder the recovery of property. When this happens, it is known as being *incommunicado*.

The person will be searched and have all their property taken from them. This will include any belt and shoelaces, to prevent them from self-harming. They will then be placed in a cell.

How Long Can Suspects Be Detained?

This can get complicated if suspects are moved between different policing areas, but for simplicity's sake, we will look at what would happen to a person who is arrested in London, for a murder that happened there.

Once the sergeant authorises detention, the suspect can be held for up to **24 hours**.

On the authority of a police superintendent, this can be extended by 12 hours to **36 hours**.

Police can then apply to a magistrates' court for up to 36 hours more, making **72 hours**.

A further application to the court can add another 24 hours, making a final total of **96 hours**.

So, that equates to **four days**.

Terrorism is different, allowing up to **14 days**.

THE INTERVIEWING OF SUSPECTS

Myth Buster: *An interview will not be carried out by a DCI or DI. Regardless of what you may see in crime fiction, it does not happen. Interviews are carried out by DCs and occasionally DSs.*

In the past, confession evidence in the UK was a topic of controversy. Suspects were asked to make statements, and then sign them, in a process that was unrecorded and open to abuse. The most high-profile examples were cases against suspected IRA terrorists, in particular the Guildford Four and the Birmingham Six. The prosecutions in each case relied heavily on confessions made to police that were later found to have been obtained through abuse. However, today, the protections in place around police interviews make for an extremely safe and trustworthy process. Custody suites have CCTV that records sound, the computerised custody records make tampering impossible, the interviews themselves are videoed and the rights of the suspect are clearly defined. So, if a suspect confesses to murder, it is evidence that can be safely relied upon. The only problem is that *suspects rarely confess to murder*.

A significant majority of those on trial for murder say nothing in the interview. With few exceptions, suspects are represented at a police station by a solicitor. Before any questioning, the suspect will consult with the solicitor, during which they receive legal advice. That advice is nearly always: *make no comment*.

Do we find no-comment interviews frustrating? Put simply, no. They are what we have come to expect. We are usually more surprised if a person speaks. In fact, when they do, more often than not it is because they are innocent and want to explain that fact. Of all the murder investigations I dealt with, *how many do you think confessed to murder? None.* Nobody confessed to what would constitute an unlawful killing. We had several admit to killing a victim, but only in the context of self-defence or where they were suffering from mental illness. That is in more than a hundred murders. I have no doubt some admitted it to their solicitors, but they would have been told to say nothing and wait until the trial to give their side of the story.

Suspects will sometimes make a *prepared statement*. This is usually a single sheet of paper on which is a short statement denying murder. They may sometimes go into further detail, but generally only to deny or admit presence at the scene of the crime. Once given over in the interview, they will go on to answer '*no comment*' to all questions put to them.

Under the law, they are completely within their rights to do that. It is known as a *right to silence*. You may be asking yourself: *Can that count against them later on*? The answer to that is, *maybe*. At trial, the judge can give a direction allowing the jury to make an inference of guilt from the silence. This may happen if the defendant gave evidence at court but did not give that account at the police station, for example. How much weight the jury gives that direction is impossible to say.

For that inference to be drawn, the defendant would need to have been cautioned at the beginning of the interview. So, let us look at it again, but this time in more detail:

'*You do not have to say anything. But it may harm your defence if you do not mention, when questioned, something which you later rely on in court. Anything you do say may be given in evidence.*'

It's a bit of a mouthful, and probably requires some further explanation to decipher all the legal implications. The easiest way to understand it is to break it into three sections:

1. *You do not have to say anything*: This is to inform the suspect of their *right to silence*.

2. *But it may harm your defence if you do not mention, when questioned, something which you later rely on in court*: If the suspect finds themselves as a defendant in a murder trial, the court will look at what was (or wasn't) said at the police station. If they include anything in their defence that wasn't brought up in the interview, that is when it can go against them.

The implication is that the defendant came up with their story in the months after they were charged, having had the opportunity to see all the evidence against them. The judge will *usually* tell the jury that the omissions from the interview *may* be an indication of guilt. In response, the defence will usually explain that the defendant was only acting on the advice of their solicitor. It is then up to the jury as to how much weight they place on it. It is for that reason I answered, *maybe*, to the question of whether it can go against them. It is impossible to know what a jury will make of it, if anything. Each juror will have their own ideas.

3. *Anything you do say may be given in evidence*: Simply put, the court will be told what the suspect said after the arrest and in the interview, and they can use this information to make their judgement.

Regardless of whether a suspect answers questions or not, they will still be asked them.

Let's now look at the structure of interviews.

Myth Buster: *In real life, interviewers don't bang on tables, shout at suspects or tell lies to trick a person into confessing. They're actually quite tame affairs. At trials, I always sensed disappointment from juries at the mundane quality of this evidence. They were probably expecting fireworks but are usually served up a bit of a damp squib. Also, in the UK, results from polygraphs (lie detectors) cannot be introduced as evidence and so aren't used by police.*

What Is the Structure of an Interview?

All police officers receive a certain level of investigative interview training. As officers progress through their careers, they will be given the opportunity to receive more advanced training. In the police, these different levels are known as *tiers*:

Tier 1: Basic interview techniques taught to new recruits at the training schools.

Tier 2: More advanced techniques taught to all detectives.

Tier 3: Advanced interviewing taught to officers investigating serious crimes.

The Tier 3 course lasts for three weeks and is pass or fail, meaning the detectives need to reach a required standard.

There is also Tier 5 training, which allows an officer, trained to Tier 3, to become an *interview advisor*. This is a role performed by either detective constables or detective sergeants. In more complex investigations with multiple suspects, they will help coordinate the different interviews.

All tiers work around one interview model, known as PEACE. This model has been used by police in England for more than twenty years. PEACE is, you guessed it, another mnemonic. It stands for:

P – Planning and preparation

E – Engage and explain

A – Account clarification and challenge

C – Closure

E – Evaluation

I'll go through each of the elements and what they entail in more detail below.

Planning and Preparation

At this stage, the officers will be making sure everything is in place for an effective interview. They will write an interview plan, considering what topics they want to talk about. What they won't be doing is writing down specific questions, which doesn't work in practice. Put yourself in their position. You are sitting opposite a suspect who you are interviewing. You have a dozen or so areas that you need to cover, which could include many things including the incident, their relationship with the victim, where they were that day, how they travelled to the scene, what phone they use and what gangs they associate with. Now try and think of all the questions that stem from that. It might be hundreds. If you did manage to write them all down, picture yourself using them to interview the suspect. How do you maintain a conversation while keeping track of what questions you have or haven't asked? How do you look them in the eye and listen carefully to their answers? Trust me, it would be impossible. Instead, they will write down headings or use mind maps, which ensures they explore all the topics they need to without being hemmed in by a rigid structure. If the interview goes in sudden, unexpected directions, uncovering previously unknown information, the officers need to be able to adapt and evolve their questioning to capitalise on that. They will also ensure they have a good understanding of the investigation and all the relevant evidence before they go in, including the points they need to prove for an offence to have taken place. As we know, for a murder, those points would be:

- Unlawful killing of a person
- Intent to kill or cause really serious harm

They would be looking to cover these points in detail; they will also establish what defences might be available to the suspect that could be used to refute these points and prepare to question those. For instance, if the suspect is likely to raise self-defence at their trial, this should be explored now. This has the benefit of not allowing a suspect the months between charge and trial to come up with a defence. They can still do so, but if they've been asked about it at this stage, it may go against them if they only address it at court. The inference being, if it were true, they could have told the officers about it back at the interview stage.

It would also be helpful to understand the suspect's background, including any needs they may have due to their age, disability or mental health. This is because interviews must be conducted fairly and a person shouldn't be disadvantaged in any way. So, if they have any issues that could interfere with their ability to answer questions, contingencies need to be put in place, such as another person to help facilitate communication.

Preparation also includes the environment in which the interview will take place. This means ensuring the interview room is fit for purpose and has the necessary equipment.

Engage and Explain

To engage the suspect is to encourage them to speak. As I've already pointed out, that isn't always going to be easy.

Explanation is about ensuring the suspect knows *why* they are being interviewed and *the purpose of it.*

Account Clarification and Challenge

This is the main part of the interview. The account is where the suspect will be encouraged to give their side of the story. The first question will be something like: *Tell me what happened.* It is open-ended to encourage them to give as much information as possible, assuming they are speaking.

The interviewer will then go through what was said, asking them to clarify certain topics and draw out more detail. They will also explore topics not raised by the suspect. Up to this point, the suspect wouldn't be put under a lot of pressure. So, if they have contradicted themselves or if there is known evidence that contradicts their account, that wouldn't be pointed out at this stage. The idea is to obtain as much information as possible, be that truth or lies.

As with the opening question, the interviewer will ask open questions, using the '5WH' (who, what, where, when, why and how). This technique is really important to ensure you get the most information possible without leading the suspect. It's the difference between *what colour was the car?* and *was the car red*? One gives the suspect the chance to volunteer the colour, the other leads them down a path they may not have taken themselves.

The challenge phase is where the interviewer will look to ask the awkward questions, and it's what I always considered the most satisfying part as an investigator. It is the stage where you bring the evidence together, point out inconsistencies in their account, highlight where you think they've been lying and start to bring in the accusatory questioning. If you were to get a person to confess to a crime, it would normally be at this point. To do this well, however, takes practice and experience.

Closure

Before the interview ends, the interviewer will verbally summarise what has been said by the suspect, then ask them if there is anything they want to add or whether they have any questions.

They will then give the date and time, before switching off the recording equipment.

Evaluation

The evaluation stage is where the interviewer looks at whether any further action is required and evaluates their performance, i.e. have they missed anything that they should have covered? As much as you prepare, there is always something that you miss. That is the theory, *but how does it work in real life?*

Case File: For me, the best interviews in my career were with terrorists. At that time, they would be questioned at Paddington Green Police Station. It's the most secure station in the country, having been designed to hold Irish dissidents. Due to the way the IRA operated, there was a chance attempts would be made to spring them from custody, hence the need for high security. The area created to hold prisoners was like a station within a station: heavy doors, high wire and thick walls. It all added to the intensity of the situation.

You usually had two weeks of questioning, and they were not easy interviews to conduct. Terrorists wouldn't talk in interviews *at all*. Not even to answer their name. As somebody who enjoys a challenge, I was always determined to make them crack. Having a whole two weeks allowed me to use a wide variety of techniques to achieve this.

I'm sure you've heard of *good cop, bad cop*. One officer takes up the role of the baddie, with the nice one sweeping in to rescue the suspect, thus gaining their trust. I'm not sure if that works elsewhere, but it is a non-starter in the UK. Any hint of you treating their client badly and the solicitor will be the one sweeping in to save them. That said, I used a similar technique but in reverse, and alone. *Remember the terrorist who missed me when I wasn't interviewing him*? That wasn't just down to my affable nature; I made a real effort to get them to like me. Not in a smarmy or desperate way, which would be obvious, but just by being natural and treating them with respect. In between interviews, they would then be more open to talking. At these points, I would show an interest in them as a person, find common interests and build a rapport.

Then, over days of interviewing, the questioning would become more relaxed. I would begin to sit back in my chair, speaking slowly and softly. If possible, I'd seek opportunities to make the situation light-hearted, even funny. One moment that sticks in my mind was completely unplanned. During an interview, the solicitor farted. It may not sound hilarious now, but, in that intense environment, it resulted in us having a fit of giggles. I also had one colleague who asked daft questions. For instance, one terrorist had a satellite phone which we had seized. Dave told him we were going to test it for pollen so we could find out exactly where in the world he had been. We weren't and we couldn't. It was a silly suggestion that ended up with me, the suspect and the solicitor in tears. That wasn't Dave trying to trick the suspect, he genuinely believed it.

Anybody listening may have thought we weren't taking the process seriously, but that couldn't have been further from the truth. The whole idea was to make the suspect relax and be as comfortable as they could be in the circumstances.

All of this was a build-up to the *challenge*, the point in the interview designed to put pressure on the suspect. If someone isn't speaking, it's hard to put that pressure on them but after ten days of relaxed talking, we had opened the lines of communication. I would then suddenly crank up the pressure. My smile would go. My tone would change. When talking, I would lean forward across the table, imposing myself in their personal space. For them, the *jokey fella* had

changed entirely. He was now not nice at all. This
was all done subtly; it *had* to be. If I went too far
and was overly aggressive or oppressive, the solicitor
would step in immediately and all our hard work
would come to nothing.

This was about luring the suspect into their comfort
zone and then snapping them out of it. At this point, I
would start summarising the evidence – the evidence
that would send them to prison for a long time. They
would have heard it all before, but not all at the same
time and not in that changed environment from
someone they had begun to like. If they were going to
speak, now would be the time.

For one terrorist, that is exactly what happened.

I had been interviewing him for nearly two weeks,
continually building that rapport, acting like his friend.
He was relaxed and comfortable. After all that time,
the questions formed a familiar pattern: me asking, him
saying nothing, then me moving on to the next topic.
At some points, it even felt as if he was enjoying it. But
that suddenly all changed. Without warning, I moved
from my relaxed style to leaning in, with a serious tone,
stacking up the evidence against him.

The look on his face told me it was working. He
was visibly shrinking in his chair, he even had tears in
his eyes. Within a few short minutes he looked like the
world had come tumbling in on him. He looked to
his solicitor for help, but everything I was doing was
within the rules, so there was nothing he could do.

'*Look at this evidence. It's overwhelming. If we hadn't*

stopped you, you and your friends were going to kill hundreds of people.'

I placed photographs of the evidence in front of him, drawing his attention to what was almost certainly going to convict him.

'You were prepared to die in any attack you carried out, but are you prepared to spend the rest of your life in prison?'

As well as going over the evidence, we were also trying to find out if he knew the whereabouts of any explosives, chemicals or firearms. It was the first question we asked and one we regularly revisited. The reason being, there was a real possibility those things were out there. Items that could harm the officers searching for them or members of the public if they were not recovered.

I was about to ask that question again, but this time it was different. Now I was asking him under pressure, which I kept trying to increase:

'Your family, how are they going to feel, seeing your name all over the news? Will they feel proud, or ashamed?

'You know I'm looking for any explosives, chemicals or firearms. You need to tell me if you know where they are.'

This was all asked while leaning into him, voice raised higher, tone harsher and while looking him straight in the eye.

'Don't look away. Look at me when I'm talking to you.

'How will your family feel if innocent people get killed? Children, anybody, any religion. You won't be dead if that happens. You will have to live with that for the rest of your life.'

Now he was crying.

'*If you know the location of any explosives, chemicals or firearms, tell me now.*'

Then I had him. He turned and looked at his solicitor, then at me, and back to his solicitor.

'*Do you need to speak with your solicitor?*'

He nodded his head.

'*OK, you can speak to him, but when I come back, I'm going to ask that same question, and I want an answer.*'

He nodded, then Dave and I left the room. We stood outside, virtually high-fiving each other. Nobody ever got terrorists to speak. If he told us the location of any of those items, the repercussions would be huge. Lives could be saved.

We waited about fifteen minutes, the longest fifteen minutes of my life. Then the solicitor opened the door.

'*He will speak to you now.*'

We went back in and sat down. He was sitting there, looking completely broken. Tears in his eyes, pulling his knees up to his chest.

I restarted the tape recorder, then put the question to him again:

'*Do you know the location of any explosives, chemicals or firearms?*'

He looked at his solicitor, looked at me, and then said: '*No.*'

'*No? You don't know the location of any explosives, chemicals or firearms?*'

'*No.*'

He then looked at his solicitor again and said

nothing. Then he reverted to the usual stance: refusing to answer any questions we put to him.

Were you disappointed with how that story turned out? Imagine how I felt. To say I was deflated would be an understatement. It went from a career-defining moment to *the* biggest disappointment. But when I later reflected, I realised it was actually a small triumph. OK, it didn't turn out as I had hoped, but it was a vindication of my interview technique. He obviously felt immense pressure. So much so that he needed to say something, even if it was just *no*. Due to my words and actions, he couldn't just sit there in silence.

Thankfully, not all criminals are terrorists and others may be more open to talking. So, that technique, honed on them, often worked well on other suspects, including rapists and murderers. Moving them from *no comment* to answering questions. Even if that wasn't always a confession, getting an interviewee to speak, when they were determined not to, can prove extremely beneficial to an investigation.

TO CHARGE OR NOT TO CHARGE?

At some point during a suspect's time in custody, a decision will be made as to what is going to happen to them. The biggest factor in that decision-making process is the strength of the evidence.

As we discussed earlier, to make an arrest, only *suspicion* is needed. In order to charge a suspect, however, the bar is much higher. So, *what are the options to deal with a suspect at the end of their time in custody?*

When There Isn't Enough Evidence to Charge

Release on Pre-Charge Police Bail

What is pre-charge police bail? It is the release of a suspect from custody, with the undertaking they will return to the police station at a specified time and date, at which point they might be reinterviewed or charged with offences. Initially, this is for a maximum of twenty-eight days, but it can be extended with various authorities.

Conditions can be placed on the person while they are on bail. For instance, they could be told to live and sleep at a particular address, observe a curfew or not to contact witnesses.

Release Under Investigation

This is a relatively new concept. The person will be released from the police station, with no undertaking to return. However, the suspect will be made aware the investigation into them will continue. If further evidence is obtained, they can be rearrested.

No conditions can be added to this, so no restrictions will be placed on the person.

No Further Action

If there is no evidence to suggest the person was involved in the offence, they can be released, with no further action.

The person will know they are no longer being investigated. However, if new evidence came to light, they could be rearrested.

When There Is Enough Evidence to Charge

In cases of murder, it is not up to the police whether a suspect should be charged. In England and Wales, it is the Crown Prosecution Service (CPS) that makes that decision.

You may have heard news reports refer to a *file being sent to the CPS*. That is what used to happen but no longer. As with most things in life, this system is now computerised. Essentially, the police write a report outlining the case, including details of the evidence against the suspect. That evidence will include all the topics we have covered: forensics, CCTV, witnesses, phones, etc.

A lawyer will examine this evidence to determine whether, in their opinion, there is a reasonable prospect of a conviction. I have heard mention of percentages being factored into the decision, i.e. to progress a case if there is more than a 50 per cent chance of conviction. In my experience, that isn't the case. It is certainly not a scenario I have encountered and I'm not sure how that could ever be calculated.

There are sometimes disagreements over the best decision to make – I have had a number of them over the years – but, ultimately, the final say is with the CPS. It will always be an experienced lawyer that gives advice. If there are any disagreements between the CPS and police, the decision is raised to someone senior.

As with any working partnership, there can be strains. There will also be lawyers you have a better connection with than others; that is just human nature. But, overall, I would describe the relationship between the CPS and Scotland Yard as a good one in general.

When the CPS Authorise a Charge

If a person is charged with murder, they will not be bailed from the police station. They will remain in custody and be taken before a magistrate. From this stage on, they will no longer be referred to as a *suspect* but as a *defendant.*

In most cases, the magistrates will decide whether the defendant should be remanded on bail or in custody. However, in murder cases, the magistrate does not have that discretion. They have no option other than to remand them into custody, meaning the defendant will be held in prison. They will then appear at a Crown Court, usually within forty-eight hours. It is only from there that bail can be given. In murder cases, the defendant will *usually* remain in prison until their trial.

How long does that take? In London, pre-Covid, this usually took around six months. Since the pandemic, those times have risen dramatically.

SO, THAT'S IT: CASE SOLVED AND JOB DONE!

Hmmm … Not quite. In fact, this is probably where I'd say the hard work begins.

Myth Buster: *Another common misconception is that once a suspect is charged, the case is complete for the detectives involved. It* *probably stems from TV. Rarely do they show what happens after the killer is caught. Getting a person charged is one thing, but putting a case together that stands the rigours of a court trial is something altogether different.*

The activity that follows a charge would not make for interesting reading. It involves paperwork, and lots of it. There will be many hours of reading vast amounts of documents to ensure that no gaps appear in the evidence. If you are to lose a case at court, it is likely as a result of getting this part wrong. The investigating team will have regular conferences with the CPS and prosecution barristers. It is a team effort to get a case ready for trial. Everybody needs to be pulling in the same direction. In every investigation, there will be requirements made by the barristers for police to follow up on further lines of enquiry. Disclosure of evidence is always an important issue here. The murder investigation team disclosure officer will work closely with the CPS lawyer to ensure this is carried out correctly. All of this will be going on in the background, while other murder investigations are also progressing.

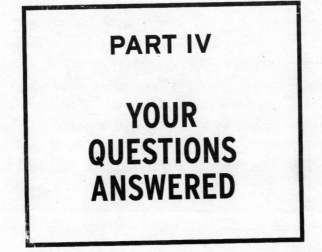

PART IV

YOUR
QUESTIONS
ANSWERED

In the next chapter, we will look at the process of going to trial in more detail, but before then, I want to address a couple of areas that came up in my research. Below are some common questions people had about murder investigations and my best attempt at answering them.

ARE ALL MURDERS INVESTIGATED EQUALLY?

This is a question I often get asked. Either that or: *Are some murders given more attention than others?*

To answer that question, we need to look at it from two points of view:

1. The investigating team
2. The police as an organisation

The Investigating Team

I can honestly say I have never seen an investigation be given anything other than the murder investigation team's full commitment. No matter who the victim is, or the circumstances of the murder, they give everything to solve that crime. It may sound like a cliché, but when police officers swear their oaths, they promise to act *without fear or favour*, and that is what those on MITs do.

I only ever once heard a negative comment about a victim. That person, who wasn't a detective, said something along the lines of *it's just another gang murder*. That attitude is unacceptable, and I made sure they understood that. If they wanted to *pick and choose* whose murders to investigate, they were in the wrong job.

However, as a detective, you may become more emotionally invested in a particular investigation. For me, as a parent, it was always child victims. But that doesn't mean you put more into one case than another. Gang murders often take more effort to solve. Many of those present are unwilling to assist the investigation. Without the cooperation of witnesses, your work is made harder. But MITs' success rates are excellent, despite these hurdles.

The Police as an Organisation

The way in which investigations are categorised does, by its very nature, affect how they are treated by the police. They are categorised as either A, B or C:

Category C: These are murders where the identity of the suspect(s) **is known**.

Category B: These are murders where the identity of the suspect(s) **isn't known.**

Category A: These investigations are a little more complicated. If a murder is high profile, has a significant impact on the community or the police themselves have a potential vulnerability, it would be classified as category A.

For instance, if we look back at our case files, the murder of the two sisters by arson and the man who killed his family and fled to Ghana were both classed as category A investigations (*see also* pages 112 and 223). The former due to the impact on the local community, the latter due to the media interest and concerns with how the missing person enquiry was conducted.

Investigations with potential vulnerability to the police could include cases where an officer was a suspect, or those that may raise issues with previous police investigations – for example, if a person was being investigated for stalking and then went on to kill the victim.

Are category A murders treated differently? The main difference is that more resources are made available to the investigating team for category A murders. That would mean more officers and priority access to supporting services such as forensic scientists.

Is it right that some investigations have access to more resources than others? In my opinion, yes, but not out of choice. In an ideal world, all murders would be given that extra level of resources, but that's just not possible. Resources are finite, particularly during a time when budgets have been cut across all support services. Plus, category A investigations are less common than B or C. They have to be, because otherwise the resources made available to them would be unsustainable. However, I fully appreciate how families involved in other cases may feel. As I write this book, there has been a high-profile case receiving a lot of additional resources. I am aware of at least one relative, in a currently unsolved case, who found it hard to accept that her son's murder had fewer resources dedicated to it. If I were that parent, I would feel the same.

Regardless of the categorisation, every murder investigation will have a team of dedicated, professional investigators, doing all they can to solve the case.

WHAT HAPPENS WHEN MURDERS ARE UNSOLVED?

As successful as MITs are, it would be impossible to solve every crime. In some cases, there won't be the necessary evidence to convict a suspect. Often, the killer *is* known, but that doesn't always equate to evidence. *What happens in those instances?*

If, within the first twenty-eight days of a murder, nobody is charged, a review will take place. For Scotland Yard, that will be carried out by the Serious Crime Review Group (SCRG). This unit is made up of experienced ex-murder detectives who have retired as police officers and return in a civilian role. They will carry out a thorough examination of the investigation, specifically looking for lines of enquiry that may have been missed by the MIT, or any that can be further developed. They will provide the senior investigating officer (SIO) with a series of recommendations indicating where they believe further investigation is needed.

If a case remains unsolved, the MIT will not just give up.

They will exhaust every possible line of enquiry. After that, if there is no likelihood of a suspect being charged, the case will be brought before a panel. It will be for them to decide whether the investigation should continue. That panel is made up of various people, including senior police officers and members of the Independent Advisory Group (IAG). The IAG are members of the public whose role is to represent the community and hold the police to account.

If the panel decide a crime has reached a point where no further investigation is reasonable, the crime will be 'put on hold'. That means no further work will be carried out by the MIT. However, this isn't a quick process. It would take at least two years of investigation to get to this stage, often longer. Even then, the case will be reviewed every two years by the SCRG, who will be looking for any new investigative opportunities or development in techniques such as forensics. So, no case is ever 'forgotten'. Some cases may be subject to a *full review*. If that happens, they are referred to as *cold case reviews*. At any one time, Scotland Yard will have fifteen to twenty cold cases being fully reviewed.

HOW ARE COLD CASES SOLVED?

Essentially, there are three main reasons why cold cases may be solved:

1. **Advances in science**: Techniques exist today that were previously unavailable, which may identify new leads. DNA is the perfect example. If exhibits still exist from years before, their re-examination could lead to the identification of suspects.

2. **New witness accounts**: Over time, people may decide to give information they had previously been reluctant to provide. There can be various reasons for this: changes in loyalty, feelings of guilt or lifestyle changes. Whatever the reason, this new information may be key in progressing an unsolved case.

3. **Deficiencies in the previous investigation**: As I detailed above, there is currently a very robust system for reviewing murder investigations, not only at the stage of crimes being 'put on hold' but also years later. This is to ensure they have been carried out to the highest standard possible, which might not always be the case. For instance, a MIT may fail to follow up certain lines of enquiry or miss an important piece of evidence. In some cases, they could have been pursuing the wrong suspect, an issue that can arise if officers become fixated on a certain person, ignoring contradictory evidence, with *confirmation bias* creeping into their decision-making.

How Many Cases Go Unsolved in London?

So, how many cases actually go unsolved? That is actually an easy question to answer because Scotland Yard release those figures publicly. But, before we look at those, I want you to consider one thing. In this book I have mentioned *budget cuts* on numerous occasions. When I joined a MIT in 2009, there were twenty-nine teams investigating murder. Four of those specialised in shootings within the black community, known as Operation Trident, and one dealt solely with child deaths within the family. In 2013, the Operation Trident and child death teams were disbanded, as were six of the homicide teams, in order to save money. That left eighteen MITs investigating murder in London. Year on year, the Metropolitan Police has had millions of pounds slashed from its funding from government, meaning cutbacks were needed, including to murder investigations and supporting services such as forensics. The impact on MITs was becoming unsustainable, so two additional teams were formed in 2019, putting the number at twenty. *But what was the impact of that cull?* Well, here are the figures for how many murders were solved in London between 2009 and 2019.[xii] [xiii]

Year	No. of Homicides	No. Unsolved	Percentage Solved
2009	129	8	94%
2010	124	6	95%
2011	118	6	95%
2012	106	4	96%
2013	109	8	93%
2014	95	7	93%
2015	119	15	87%
2016	114	15	86%
2017	142	18	87%
2018	138	27	80%
2019	152	44	71%*

*This figure is now likely to be higher due to how long some murders take to solve.

You can see the trend. If the change in numbers was temporary, or a blip, you could put it down to something other than the culling of MITs and the slashing of funding. But it cannot be a coincidence that shortly after teams were disbanded, fewer murders were solved.

Some may feel the numbers aren't hugely different, but I would disagree. Even one unsolved murder is one too many. To double, triple and even quadruple the number of cases going unsolved is, in my opinion, a tragedy. It means many more families are not getting justice for their loved ones. Plus, there are killers walking free. I believe the blame for this lies squarely and firmly with the government. They don't have to face those poor people and tell them: *We haven't been able to catch the person who killed your son or daughter, husband or wife, father or mother.* They won't fall victim to those uncaught murderers who will undoubtedly commit more violent crimes.

HOW DO MIT OFFICERS DEAL WITH WHAT THEY SEE?

A question I have been asked a lot is, *how do MIT officers deal with what they see?* I can only speak for myself, but the honest answer is that I don't think I've been significantly affected. Occasionally, I felt upset at what I saw, although I never carried that upset with me for too long.

When I joined the police, I had never seen a dead body or dealt with injured people. That all changed very quickly. As a new officer, you were sent to the calls involving dead bodies. The first I went to involved a woman who had died on the toilet and hadn't been found for several days. That smell of death was something I had never experienced before and is one that stays with you. It was my first test and, although upsetting, I felt fine dealing with it.

Very early on in our careers, we were made to witness a post-mortem. It was a good way of forcing people to overcome any fears they may have had about dead bodies.

The worst experience I had in a mortuary happened at night. My first station was Greenwich in South East London. The keys to the nearby mortuary were kept there in case the security alarms went off. One night they did, so my colleague and I collected the keys and drove over to check on it. We entered to make sure nobody had broken in. As I was looking around, I noticed a body lying under a sheet. As I got closer, it sat bolt upright. I'm not ashamed to admit that I screamed like a child and ran out. It turned out to be a local initiation, a chance to test the character of new officers. I did laugh, eventually.

During my early career, death and injury became an everyday part of life so, when I joined specialist units, I was prepared for what was to come. The biggest test came after the London bombings on 7 July 2005. At that time, I worked in Scotland Yard's Anti-Terrorist Branch, the department that would investigate any terrorist incidents in London. We were well trained, but for a completely different type of incident: the sort of bombings associated with the IRA. The UK had never witnessed incidents like those first Islamic suicide attacks.

My colleague and I were the first anti-terrorist officers to arrive at one of the scenes. We didn't leave there for two weeks. Most of it was spent on our hands and knees, crawling through a tunnel. Our team was responsible for removing the dead victims, then conducting fingertip searches of the whole scene, collecting all evidence. That included collection of all human remains. This was at the height of summer, in enclosed conditions.

Afterwards, friends and family were concerned about how I was coping. They were worried about whether I had been negatively impacted by the experience. I didn't feel I had been. With so many people asking if I was OK, I became concerned as to why I felt so fine with it all. *Had I lost some part of my humanity?*

I reflected on that and began to understand *why* I didn't seem affected. What I realised is that the way I deal with traumatic events is not to dwell on them. I compartmentalise. Anything that could be upsetting, I shut away. I realised then that this wasn't just a work-related technique, I used it for everything in my life.

I saw this may not be the best coping strategy when my father died. I did the same thing and shut away any emotions without dealing with them. At least until it came to reading his eulogy. That forced me to think about my feelings and, worse still, talk about them. Undoubtedly, that was the hardest thing I've had to do in my life. I struggled a lot and, finally, I cried.

I've always considered the bravest people to be those who deal with trauma by not letting it get to them. What I now realise is that they are the ones who deal head-on with their feelings and emotions. The way I deal with feelings, by hiding from them (although not consciously), is perhaps more cowardly.

I hope I never have to confront all the tragedy I've buried. As my dad's funeral showed me, I may not handle it well.

There is something that I've never shared with anyone apart from those closest to me, which is perhaps telling. I've always had the most vivid dreams and can generally remember them when I wake up. During my time on murder investigation teams, those dreams started to become more and more violent in nature. Most nights I would end up killing someone in my sleep: stabbing, shooting, beating or strangling. I was never worried about those dreams and used to laugh them off – they were just dreams, after all, and I knew I wasn't a violent person. However, when I recently stopped investigating murders, the dreams ceased. *Coincidence*? Probably not. Maybe that was part of my coping mechanism, I don't know. A way of processing everything I had witnessed. I hope it is that and not a sign of some underlying psychopathy! At least now I can go to sleep with pleasant dreams to look forward to.

In terms of any emotional support the police provide, I have noticed a change over the years. After those bombings, we were offered counselling but not in a way conducive to it being accepted. They put a group of us in a room and we were all asked if any of us felt we needed to speak to someone. At that time, the Anti-Terrorist Branch was a male-dominated unit and had a 'macho' culture. In those circumstances, I couldn't imagine many felt comfortable enough to put their hand up, even if they felt they needed help. I don't think it was a coincidence that several officers later had mental health issues.

The next time I was offered counselling was fifteen years later, after we investigated the murder of a police officer. To be fair to the Metropolitan Police, that offer came in a much more personal and private manner, and more than once. The way they now handle mental health is so much better than before. It is recognised as a serious matter, and many more mechanisms have been put in place to provide support. Hopefully, it will prevent some of the issues of the past.

CONCLUSION

So, now you have an insight into what *really* happens in a murder investigation. The stage at which the detectives are the stars of the show. It may have seemed a little heavy with process and legal procedure, but it's important that I give you an accurate understanding of some of the considerations made by MITs, ones that rarely get mentioned by those who report on murder.

Now, when you see that somebody has been arrested for murder, you will have a good appreciation of some of the thought processes that went into making that decision and what will be going on inside the walls of the police station to secure a safe and proper conviction.

All of that has led us to our next chapter, The Trial. It is this moment that everything we have been doing has been building towards: months, or even years, of work in preparation for the courtroom.

CHAPTER 4

THE TRIAL

INTRODUCTION

As you know, a murder investigation team's ultimate goal is to *secure a safe and proper conviction at court*. But *getting* to court doesn't automatically mean a conviction will be secured. There is still plenty that can go wrong. The defence lawyers will rigorously test the prosecution's case, seizing on any opportunity to undermine it.

In this chapter, we will first look at the processes involved in a trial, starting at the place most Scotland Yard investigations end up, the Old Bailey. We will then look at the steps a trial will follow, how mental illness can affect a case, the types of evidence that will be presented, what it's really like to be a witness in this situation and then, finally, the verdict. We won't go into minute detail, as it's unnecessary for this book, but I think it's important for you to have a certain level of understanding to see how we get to the conviction. For MITs, this can be the hardest part of the whole process because they are no longer in control of what happens. Everything they have done up to this point has been for the purposes of bringing evidence to court. Evidence that will now be presented, tested, judged and weighed up by others.

So, let's start where most of Scotland Yard's trials take place, the Old Bailey.

THE OLD BAILEY

The Old Bailey is, arguably, the most famous criminal court in the world. Its official title is actually the Central Criminal Court, but those on MITs know it as 'The Bailey'. It gets this name from the street it's on.

There has been a court here since the sixteenth century. The current building is in two distinct parts, the old side and the new side. The newer building opened around 1970. The old side was opened at the beginning of the twentieth century – a neo-baroque masterpiece including a gold leaf statue of the 'lady of justice' holding scales in one hand and a sword in the other, a symbol of justice in England. As you can imagine, the architecture on each side is vastly different.

The courts in the old building are imposing places, especially Court 1. Whenever I was in there, I was struck by the history of the place. There have been many high-profile trials that have taken place there over the years: Dr Crippen, the Kray twins, Peter Sutcliffe, Ruth Ellis and Jeremy Thorpe, to name just a few. I always found it a humbling experience, if an uncomfortable one. Those old courtrooms were not designed with comfort in mind. If you had to spend several months at court, it was far better for your back if you were in the new building, even if it wasn't anywhere near as special!

Did You Know? *Criminal trials at the Old Bailey are open to the general public. Each court has rows of seats above, where people can sit and watch the trials play out. If you do visit, you won't be allowed to take your phone in – they are banned from that part of the building.*

WHAT IS THE TRIAL PROCESS?

Although no two trials are ever the same, they all follow a set format:

1. **Selection and swearing-in of the jury**: Murder trials can be long affairs and jurors are only asked to give two weeks of service. So, it can take some time to identify twelve men and women who are capable of giving up what could be, potentially, the next three months of their lives. However, most trials are usually around four weeks. Once selected, each juror will swear an oath to *try the defendant and give a true verdict according to the evidence.*

2. **Prosecution opening**: The prosecution barrister will open the trial by explaining to the jury the details of the case.

3. **Presentation of the prosecution case**: This will be in the form of witnesses, playing of CCTV footage and showing of various exhibits as we've discussed earlier in the book. This stage of the trial is usually the lengthiest.

4. **Presentation of the defence case(s)**: If there is more than one defendant, they will present their cases one at a time. This will sometimes start with the defendant giving evidence, although not always, as they are not obliged to do so. The defence may call witnesses.

5. **Prosecution closing speech**: Here, the prosecution barrister will summarise the evidence they say points to guilt. These speeches are for the benefit of the jury, so will be directed at them.

6. **Defence closing speech(es)**: These will follow the same format as the prosecution, although with a different outcome in mind. They will be looking to sow *doubt* in the minds of the jury as to the guilt of their clients.

7. **Judge's summing-up**: The trial judge will summarise the evidence to assist the jury in coming to their verdicts. They will also give directions that the jury must follow to adhere to the law. That is particularly important as juries will not have expertise in this area. As an example, the judge will produce a *route to verdict*, which is a series of questions the jury will need to answer. If they follow that, in sequence, they will arrive at what should be their verdict. In very basic terms, this would be something similar to: *Did the defendant unlawfully kill the victim?* Yes. *Did the defendant intend to kill or cause really serious harm?* Yes – then your verdict should be *guilty of murder*. If the answer to

that last question was 'no', then your verdict should be *guilty of manslaughter.*

8. **Jury deliberations**: The jury will retire to a room where they will decide on their verdict for each indictment. An indictment is essentially the same as a charge, just under a different name for court purposes. The main difference is that alternatives may have to be considered. In cases of unlawful killing, the Crown Prosecution Service (CPS) mostly charge a defendant with murder, but often an alternative indictment of manslaughter will be added at trial for the jury to consider. This is due to the *mens rea* element of murder. If that is lacking, i.e. there wasn't intent to kill, then manslaughter is likely to be the right verdict.

9. **Jury gives their verdict**: The jury can give the verdict of guilty or not guilty in response to the indictments outlined. They may not be able to reach verdicts, which we will discuss later on.

10. **Sentencing**: If a defendant has been found guilty of any indictments, the judge will pass the sentence. In murder cases, this will be a custodial sentence – meaning imprisonment. We will address sentencing in more detail later.

Myth Buster*: In England and Wales, judges do not use gavels (the little wooden hammers). The only banging you will hear is from the judge's door into court. The usher or clerk will knock to inform those in court that the judge is about to enter, signifying for people to stand* *up as a show of respect. People may retake their seats only once the judge has sat down.*

IS PLEA BARGAINING ALLOWED AT TRIAL?

In some countries, there is a system in place that allows plea bargaining. This is where discussions take place between prosecution and defence about the defendant pleading guilty to lesser charges in return for a more lenient sentence. The idea behind this is to reduce the workload of courts.

This *does not* happen in murder trials in England. There may well be pleas entered to lesser charges, but whether those pleas are accepted is not part of any formal bargaining. In numerous cases, before trial, our defendants offered pleas to *manslaughter*. In those cases, they were accepting the act but denying murder as defined in the law. The decision as to whether a plea is accepted, ultimately, falls to the CPS. They will, however, discuss this with other parties, including the police and prosecution barrister. The decision will be based on the evidence and not the convenience of the court. More often than not, that plea is not accepted and a murder trial takes place. Pleas are most often made to lesser charges when mental illness is a factor.

Case File: We were at trial for a stabbing case, for which the defendant, charged with murder, indicated a willingness to plead guilty to manslaughter. We, as the police, did not believe that should be accepted. We discussed this with the CPS and also obtained the views of the victim's family. They were also strongly opposed.

Everybody agreed that a murder trial should take place. He, along with another defendant, was found guilty of murder and sentenced to a minimum of twenty-five years. If we had accepted a plea of manslaughter, he would have received a fraction of this sentence. Yes, we had to have a trial as a result of this and, yes, that trial was at great expense to the public purse, but in this case, it was the right thing to do. Convenience should not come at the expense of justice.

DOES MENTAL ILLNESS AFFECT THE PROCESS FOR A DEFENDANT?

What about cases that have reached court where the defendant is suffering from a mental illness?

If a defendant is suffering from a mental illness, or an *abnormality of the mind*, which had a *significant* impact on them at the time of the killing, it is likely to affect their decision-making process. That is why I separated this from the motives for murder section earlier in Chapter 3 (*see also* page 119). As I said there, murder is a *mens rea* offence, meaning the killer must make a conscious decision to kill or cause really serious harm. If this process is affected by an abnormality of the mind, which *substantially* impaired their ability to understand the nature of what they were doing, form a rational judgement or exercise self-control, then they may be suitable for the *partial defence* of manslaughter by diminished responsibility.

Notice that it isn't enough that the defendant was suffering from a condition, such as schizophrenia. That condition must also be the contributory factor as to why the killing took place.

Who decides if they should be allowed that partial defence? Firstly, it is something that is put forward by the defence. The police may suspect mental health has played a part in a killing, but until the defendant puts forward that defence, they won't know for sure. The defence solicitors will arrange for their client to be seen by a psychiatrist, usually in prison or a secure hospital. This doctor will provide a report in which they will describe the meeting and their findings. They will comment on whether in their opinion:

- the defendant is fit to plead guilty or not guilty;
- the defendant is fit to stand trial; and
- the partial defence of *manslaughter by diminished responsibility* is the right outcome.

The prosecution will then arrange for *their* psychiatrist to assess the defendant and provide their report. They may agree or disagree with the defence doctor. If they agree, the CPS will usually accept this. The result is that the defendant will plead guilty to manslaughter by diminished responsibility, with the murder charge being dropped. If they disagree, a trial is likely to take place where they will face an indictment of murder, with an alternative of manslaughter. The trial will essentially be held on the basis of the state of mind of the defendant at the time of the killing, as the act itself will not be disputed.

This can be a highly emotive and divisive subject, with strong views on either side. Some will have sympathy for the killer, others for the victim. In my experience, each case needs to be looked at on its own merits. I have seen many cases where the right outcome was *manslaughter by diminished responsibility*. The suspects were mentally ill, and that illness was the real cause of why they killed. However, a history of mental illness alone should not mean this defence is automatically accepted.

Case File: At the beginning of the book, I described going to the scene of a killing: a lady who had been stabbed in the street (*see also* page 2). Her killer was a woman under the care of mental health services. She had killed someone previously and had been convicted of *manslaughter by diminished responsibility*, having been diagnosed as schizophrenic. For that, she received a *hospital order*. This order meant she would remain being cared for until deemed well enough to be released.

At the time of this killing, she was under the care of her local mental health team. She was living independently, having been released from her hospital order. Over the course of a weekend, her mental health seemed to decline and she was taken to a hospital for an assessment. This wasn't the hospital she wanted to be at, and she asked to be taken to another, around eight miles away. After being told that wouldn't happen, she became angry, making threats as to what she would do if staff didn't listen to her. She was taken to the psychiatric ward but later walked out. That was possibly because of a staff changeover, when doors were left open to facilitate this.

The killer took a couple of buses, travelling around five miles to a shopping area. There, she went into a supermarket and bought a kitchen knife. She walked outside and immediately attacked a lady waiting at a bus stop. Luckily, that lady managed to get the knife out of her hand. The killer then ran into a butcher's shop, where she stole a large meat knife. She left and, shortly afterwards, attacked and killed the first person she came across – the poor lady in question just happened to be in the wrong place at the wrong time.

She was charged with murder, but due to her mental health history, we feared the most likely outcome would be *manslaughter by diminished responsibility*. If that was the case, sentencing would not reflect the serious nature of her actions and there was the possibility of her being released at some point and killing again.

We made sure that the psychiatrists had her complete history available to them, going back as far as her schooldays. We were not surprised when the two defence psychiatrists confirmed that, in their opinion, she was suffering from an *abnormality of the mind* at the time of the killing and a plea of *diminished responsibility* should be available to her. However, the psychiatrist instructed by the prosecution disagreed. In his opinion, this woman knew exactly what she was doing when she killed and she did so not due to her mental illness but out of anger.

Based on this, we went to trial for murder, where the prosecution psychiatrist gave compelling evidence. Unlike the two defence psychiatrists, he looked at her *whole* life history as opposed to a snapshot. This demonstrated a pattern of behaviour that was consistent with a *personality disorder* and *not* schizophrenia. As I sat in court, hearing all of this play out, it became apparent she had been wrongly diagnosed, not only by the defence doctors but by those currently treating her and, most worryingly, those who assessed her for the previous killing.

When assessed, she claimed to be seeing the world in a 'post-apocalyptic' state; walls falling around her. She was falsely attempting to paint the picture of a psychotic episode. However, we had CCTV footage of her movements during the whole period after she left the hospital when she showed no signs of someone in this form of psychosis. She sat calmly on the bus, playing with her phone. She had the presence of mind to buy the knife at a self-service checkout, speaking coherently to a member of staff. She even went to the toilet to unpackage the knife and hide it about her person. When losing that knife, she knew to go into a butcher's shop for another.

The jury, convinced by the evidence of the prosecution psychiatrist, found her guilty of murder. From a personal point of view, I hope she is never released from prison. Having seen her behaviour before, during and *after* this incident, I'm not convinced she wouldn't kill again. Some may feel she was let down by the system and wasn't given the right sort of care but having heard the evidence, watched the CCTV many times, and being aware of her life history, I know this was the right verdict. All her actions were calculated. She knew exactly what she was doing when she killed that poor lady. Part of her personality disorder included high levels of narcissism. Her sense of self-importance led to anger, triggered by her not being listened to and not being able to get her own way. This was behaviour she had consistently displayed throughout her life. She also displayed a lack of empathy for other people and was highly manipulative.

Case File: In the section on the media (*see also* page 223), I talked about the case where a husband killed his family and fled to Ghana. At one stage, there was a suggestion he would attempt to use the partial defence of diminished responsibility. As you can imagine, this was not an outcome we wanted in a case like this. We met with the Crown Prosecution Service to discuss our options and agreed to instruct the same psychiatrist used in the case where the lady was killed in the street – he was the best I had known, so we were keen to use him again. If mental health was put forward by the defence, he said he would represent us.

As expected, they did go down this route. Less expected, however, was that they were using our psychiatrist. He hadn't been formally instructed by us so was free to represent them. Having seen how persuasive he was in our previous case, we feared he would do the same for this defendant if he felt there was evidence of a mental health issue. To see somebody who had killed his family in such barbaric circumstances found not guilty of murder would have been a real kick in the teeth for us and for the family, but it was now a real possibility. That doctor would see the defendant in prison to make an assessment. His report would then indicate whether he believed diminished responsibility was open to him. All we could do was sit and wait for that report, then instruct another psychiatrist in response. It was a nervous period, but, in the end, our concerns didn't come to fruition. The doctor reported no mental health concerns. In his opinion, the defendant was not suffering from an abnormality of the mind when he killed his family. To say we were relieved would be an understatement. The evidence was overwhelming and without this defence available to him, he had no real option other than to plead guilty to all three murders.

WHAT TYPES OF EVIDENCE ARE PRESENTED AT TRIAL?

There are two types of evidence the prosecution presents to prove a defendant's guilt: direct and circumstantial.

Direct Evidence

This type of evidence goes directly to support the indictment, so in our case, murder. For instance, the account of an eyewitness who sees a defendant stab the victim is *direct evidence*. Other direct evidence could include a confession from the defendant or CCTV footage of the act.

Circumstantial Evidence

If the evidence doesn't go directly to the defendant's guilt, and there could be some other explanation, this would make it circumstantial. As an example, if a witness heard a scream and ran to the noise, then saw the defendant standing over the victim holding a knife, that would be circumstantial evidence. There is an *inference* they stabbed the victim, but something else may have happened, i.e. they found the victim there, then picked the knife up.

Other forms of circumstantial evidence could include DNA, fingerprints and phones. These are all pieces of evidence that could *suggest* a suspect's guilt, but each would have the possibility of other explanations.

You may hear people say that a criminal cannot be convicted because *there was only circumstantial evidence*. In reality, that doesn't matter. Many murderers are convicted based on this type of evidence. A single strand of circumstantial evidence would not convict a person, of course, but several taken together may.

Case File: A group of youths, some on mopeds and others on foot, chased and killed a man they believed to be associated with a rival gang. Two of the defendants stood trial for the murder. An eyewitness described their group as *acting like a pack of wolves*, although they could not identify any of them. There was CCTV footage of the suspects before and after the attack but none of the murder itself. One defendant was seen holding a knife before the attack. It was proven that they got a minicab to the scene, with phone evidence also placing them there. A knife was found nearby, with a DNA profile matching one of the defendants. Clothing was seized from a home address, matching that seen on CCTV. *All of this is circumstantial evidence*, but taken together, it was sufficient for them to be found guilty of murder.

Hearsay Evidence

Hearsay evidence can be either direct or circumstantial evidence. It becomes hearsay only because it has not been directly experienced by the witness reporting it.

In English law, *hearsay* is something said by a person who is not testifying to it themselves. For instance, if a witness says they saw the defendant stab a person, that is evidence. But if a witness says they were *told* the defendant stabbed a person, that is hearsay.

Hearsay is not generally allowed to be admitted as evidence at trial, although there are circumstances where it's permitted. For instance, a police officer could be travelling in an ambulance with the victim, who tells the officer it was *Pete* who stabbed him. The victim then dies, making this a *dying declaration*. Or a witness may not be available to give evidence in person if they are seriously ill or if they have failed to adhere to a summons and all attempts have been made to get them to court. In those circumstances, an application can be made for *hearsay evidence* to be given. It will be for the judge to decide. If they agree, then in the instance of the victim dying, the officer can tell the court, *the victim said he was stabbed by Pete*. In the other examples, the witness's statements can be read to the court and admitted as evidence in the same way as if they had given their testimony in person. The biggest problem with this type of evidence is that the person who it originates from cannot be cross-examined.

Myth Buster: *If you've watched court trials or dramas on US TV, you will have seen lawyers shouting 'objection' whenever their opposing number says something they're unhappy with. The judge will then say whether that objection is 'sustained' or 'overruled'. That may be the case in the States, but it does not happen in English courts. If a lawyer wants to interject in England, they merely stand up from their chair and their opposite number will pause their line of questioning – much more serene.*

WHAT IS IT LIKE FOR A WITNESS AT TRIAL?

In reality, most witnesses won't have to give evidence in court. There is a duty on barristers to try and minimise the number of witnesses who give live evidence at trial. They do this by agreeing on certain facts and reading statements of witnesses whose evidence isn't challenged. However, there will be some witnesses who the barristers will want to give evidence in person.

I won't try and sugar-coat it: giving evidence at court is not a pleasant experience. This is true even for me, someone who has given evidence at court countless times. The problem is, whoever you are, there will always be one side who are trying to undermine your evidence. They may be subtle in how they do that, or not. The way some defence barristers treat witnesses is nothing short of appalling: they are often made to feel it is them on trial.

When I've given evidence in court, I've been accused of all sorts of underhand practices, with no justification whatsoever. However, this is my job and I'm prepared to weather the process. Some barristers will try every trick possible to discredit a witness. It's awful seeing a person who is trying their best to help being called a liar. Their response is usually always the same: *Why would I be lying*? And, it's true, *why would they*? They didn't choose to be a witness to a murder. They certainly don't want to be in a witness box, being humiliated.

Let's consider the typical experience for a witness. They arrive at court daunted, nervous and with no idea of what to expect. There is a witness service, who try their best to look after them while they wait. That wait could be hours or sometimes days. Eventually, they get shepherded into a courtroom where they are made to swear to tell the truth, and then they stand in front of a room full of people having to recount one of the most traumatic experiences of their lives. They try their hardest to remember the important details and then have their evidence picked apart by a barrister. That barrister's sole job is to make them look incompetent, or worse, dishonest. Then, when they've finished, the best they're likely to get is a hollow *thank you* from the judge. They will walk out, emotionally drained, wondering why they bothered helping in the first place.

The truth is that the criminal justice system isn't there for victims or witnesses. It is better than it used to be, but the whole process is geared towards defendants. They have many more rights than witnesses. A witness may be asked to attend court any number of times before they give evidence. No consideration is given to the impact on their lives. You have work? *Well, they will just have to understand.* You have children? *Find a babysitter.*

The Process of Giving Evidence

So, when a witness goes into court, *how will they give their evidence?* The first act will be swearing an *oath* or an *affirmation*.

Oath: They will hold a holy book in their hand, relevant to their religion (Bible/Qur'an/Gita/Torah/Guru Granth Sahib) and say the following words:

I swear by (Almighty God/Allah/Gita/Guru Nanak) that the evidence I give shall be the truth, the whole truth and nothing but the truth.

Affirmation: There will be no holy book. They say the following words:

I do solemnly, sincerely and truly declare and affirm that the evidence I give shall be the truth, the whole truth and nothing but the truth.

For any witness who gives live evidence, there are three stages:

- Evidence in chief
- Cross-examination
- Re-examination

For prosecution witnesses, the prosecuting barrister will ask questions in the *evidence in chief* stage. The defence barrister will *cross-examine*. Finally, the prosecution barrister will ask any questions that arise from the cross-examination, known as *re-examination*.

In the section on witnesses, in Chapter 3 (*see also* page 170), we spoke about *intimidated* and *vulnerable* witnesses. When they are spoken to by police, they give their accounts on video, as opposed to a written statement. To achieve the best evidence from them, that video is likely to be played at court and will constitute their *evidence in chief*. This prevents them from having to give that evidence twice. It is also possible for vulnerable witnesses to be cross-examined *before* the trial, with a recording of that being played in court. That option is not currently available to intimidated witnesses.

Special Measures to Support Witnesses

As we've discussed, giving evidence at a murder trial is not pleasant. If a witness is going into court while in a state of panic or fear, they are unlikely to give their best evidence. In recognition of this, the criminal justice system has put in place mechanisms to help, known as *special measures*. Here is a list of some of those measures that can be made available with permission of the trial judge:

- **Screens**: These mean that only the jury, judge and barristers see the witness. *These are open to most witnesses in murder trials.*

- **Evidence via a live link**: The witness would be in another room, giving evidence via a TV screen. Similar to using Skype or Zoom. *This is only available for vulnerable and intimidated witnesses.*

- **Visual recorded interview**: This is where the witness's visually-recorded account given to police is played as their evidence in chief, meaning they don't have to give that account twice. *This is only available for vulnerable and intimidated witnesses.*

- **Video recording of cross-examination and re-examination**: This would take place away from the trial, with the recordings played in court. However, this is *only available for vulnerable witnesses.*

- **Removal of gowns and wigs by judge and barristers**: This is available for child witnesses, to make them feel less intimidated by the formality of Crown Court.

Another option for some witnesses, although not strictly a special measure, is *anonymity*. In certain circumstances, the witness's identity can be withheld from the court. If this happens, only the prosecution would know who the witness truly is.

Case File: Remember the man on the run with a £20,000 reward out for him (*see also* page 169)? Well, the lady who made the call that resulted in his arrest was required to give evidence at his trial.

For obvious reasons, she was reluctant to attend. Those on trial were dangerous people, capable of extreme violence, so her fears of repercussion were understandable. But if your evidence is required to be given live, you're almost certainly going to be called, with special measures being adopted to try and make the process conducive to giving the best evidence possible. In this lady's case, the judge granted the use of screens. She could give her evidence from behind a curtain, meaning only the judge, jury and barristers would be able to see her.

As the case officer for this investigation, I was responsible for the smooth running of the trial from the police's perspective. Some colleagues brought her to the Old Bailey, where she was taken to a special room for witnesses. I went to see her, to reassure her about the procedures; I wanted her to be as comfortable as possible. I found her in the room and explained what was going to happen. They won't see me, will they? *No, that won't happen.* What about the public gallery? *No, they won't see you either.* She was, understandably, a bag of nerves. Most people would be in her position. *So, are you OK?* Yes, she replied. I left her with a colleague and returned to the court.

The previous witness had finished giving their evidence, so the usher prepared the courtroom for our witness. The curtain was pulled, which prevented the majority of the courtroom being able to see the witness box. From my seat, I couldn't see it either.

I heard the door open, then footsteps to the box. I was expecting her to take a seat before swearing her oath. What I wasn't expecting was for the curtain to be snatched back, revealing her to the whole room. As she did this, she stood staring directly at the defendants – the same people she was terrified of seeing just ten minutes before.

I was surprised, but not as much as the defendants

themselves. *Intimidated*? I think the only people who felt that were the two on trial. She stood staring at the pair for the whole of her evidence, all of which was given vehemently and directly towards them. They looked much more scared of her than she was of them.

The unpredictability of witnesses.

DO DEFENDANTS GIVE EVIDENCE?

Just as a suspect doesn't have to say anything during a police interview, they don't *have* to give evidence at their trial. The decision on whether to do so is generally a tactical one. The defence will weigh up the evidence, consider the character of the defendant and then decide whether them giving evidence would potentially help or harm their case.

In English law, it is for the prosecution to *prove guilt*. The defence does not *need* to prove innocence. Given that fact, it is sometimes more sensible for a defendant to avoid going on the stand. By the very nature of some of those standing trial, they may be volatile, which could turn the jury against them. Also, a prosecution barrister may be able to pick holes in the evidence, making the defendant come across as untruthful. Or, if the defence's case is strong, they may feel they don't need to give evidence, with more to lose than gain from doing so. *Are there repercussions for the defendant if they do not give evidence*? The answer to that is, possibly. The judge will give a direction, similar to the one we spoke about for not answering questions in the interview, i.e. the jury *may* draw an inference of guilt. How much emphasis the jury place on that is always hard to tell.

Case File: Remember the hapless murderer who left his phone at the scene of the crime (*see also* page 220)? He decided not to give evidence. Maybe he had no explanation as to why his phone was under a murder victim. Maybe his advisors thought he would give terrible evidence. It is impossible to know. Whatever the reason, the jury found him guilty.

Case File: Let's go back to the case where the witness lied about using the mobile phone in prison (*see also* page 172). One of the defendants in that case chose not to give evidence. The jury couldn't decide on his guilt which, ultimately, meant he wasn't convicted of murder.

THE JURY DECISION

All the hard work boils down to this one moment: will the jury find the defendant guilty or not guilty?

How do they come to that decision? They will be asked to apply a test to each of the indictments. For instance, a defendant may have several indictments, such as murder, robbery and possession of a firearm. The jury will consider each indictment individually, with a *route to verdict* provided by the judge. The test they will apply is whether they are *sure* the defendant is guilty of each.

You may have heard of this being described as *beyond reasonable doubt*. This is essentially the same as being *sure*. To consider this, the jury will go to a room and deliberate. They will be asked to elect a jury foreman or forewoman, who is expected to chair discussions.

What goes on in a jury room is a matter of speculation. Occasionally, they may send out questions for court. This may give you a clue as to what they are discussing, but you never know for sure.

The time these deliberations take varies greatly. The shortest I have experienced is an hour, the longest was a couple of weeks. Factors that affect this include the number of defendants, the number of indictments, the complexity of the case and the strength of evidence.

How many need to agree? The court will initially be looking for *unanimous* decisions, so this requires the agreement of all twelve jurors.

What if that doesn't happen? After a time, determined by the judge, *majority* verdicts may be accepted. This is where at least ten jurors out of the twelve agree.

And what if ten can't agree? Occasionally, there may be indictments where there is no majority decision and no prospect of there being one. If, as an example, seven are determined to vote one way, and five the other, this will be declared a *hung jury*. In my experience, this doesn't happen often. There is normally an outcome, one way or the other.

What happens if there is a hung jury? At this point, a decision needs to be made by the Crown Prosecution Service (CPS) as to whether to hold a retrial. That would mean the same evidence being presented but with a new jury.

SENTENCING

If a person is found guilty of murder, they will receive a life sentence. In England and Wales, *life* does not mean a person will spend the rest of their life in prison. The judge will pass a minimum recommended prison sentence. They will not be automatically released at that time, however. That is for a parole board to decide, depending on their behaviour while in custody, any plans after release and whether they present a risk of committing further crimes.

In terms of how long those recommended sentences are, it varies according to the circumstances of the offence as well as other factors, such as the age of the defendant and their criminal history. If a knife is used, which was brought to the location by the defendant, the minimum sentence will start at twenty-five years. That may go up or down depending on aggravating or mitigating factors.

Occasionally, a defendant may be handed a *whole life order*, meaning they will never be released. This is given for aggravated murders, often involving multiple killings, although not always, as with those who took the lives of soldier Lee Rigby and MP Jo Cox. These sentences are also handed to those who, having been convicted of one murder, go on to kill again. Child killings are another type of crime that can attract these sentences. At the time of writing, there are around sixty prisoners in the UK who are serving whole life orders.

To give you an idea of typical minimum sentences, here are figures from some of the case studies we have looked at in various sections:

The Crime Scene: Male caught on CCTV robbing and stabbing victim: **twenty-two years**.

The Crime Scene: The man who killed his girlfriend with a breeze block: **Hospital order** (guilty of manslaughter by diminished responsibility).

The Crime Scene: The man who killed his mother and handed himself into police: **Hospital order** (guilty of manslaughter by diminished responsibility).

The Crime Scene: The man with blood on his jacket who used a knife and scissors: **eighteen years**.

The Crime Scene: The dog attack murder: **twenty-four years**.

Investigative Thinking: The two friends who killed the flatmates: **thirty-four years**.

Investigative Thinking: The boy who burned down the house, killing the sisters: **twenty-three years** (his cousin who he persuaded to help him: **twenty-one years**).

Investigative Thinking: The uncle who beat his nephew to death: **seventeen years**.

Investigative Thinking: The terrorist who missed me talking with him: **twenty-six years**.

Lines of Investigation: The passenger on the motorcycle who shot the man in a car: **thirty-two years** (the rider died in prison while awaiting trial).

Lines of Investigation: The two men caught on CCTV attacking the drill artist: **twenty-eight years**.

Lines of Investigation: The robbers of the drug dealer who left the phone behind: **thirty years**.

Lines of Investigation: The ringleader who organised a murder from prison using his phone: **thirty-two years**.

Lines of Investigation: The men who attacked a man coming out of his workplace: **seventeen years**.

Lines of Investigation: The father who killed his wife and two children: **Whole life order**.

The Arrest, Interview and Charging of Suspects: The man burned alive in the boot of the car: The medical student: **six years**. The man guilty of murder: **twenty-two years**. The man guilty of manslaughter: **twelve years**. (The sentences of six and twelve years were not minimum tariffs, so both would have been released earlier.)

The Arrest, Interview and Charging of Suspects: The terrorist who wanted to tell me *no*: **twenty years**.

The Trial: The men who acted like a 'pack of wolves' when attacking their victim: **eighteen years**.

The Trial: The woman who left the hospital and killed a random lady: **thirty-seven years**.

HOW DO THE TEAM FEEL POST-CONVICTION?

I would say there are three distinct feelings when the trial is concluded and the suspect is found guilty.

Firstly, there is a sense of achievement that you, as a team, have reached your goal. When you set out on an investigation, everything you do is to reach this point. In some cases, you may have started with little evidence, but the team's combined efforts mean that you get that conviction. Not all murders are hard to solve, but they all have certain challenges. Even the simplest of investigations can be derailed if they're not conducted properly. Defence lawyers will try their best to undermine your case, using every trick in the book. So, you know that, if you get this far, you've done your job.

Then there is the feeling of personal pride. Investigating murders isn't nine to five, Monday to Friday. The hours can be long and the work hard. You become emotionally invested in the investigation. Sometimes it is hard not to take that home with you. It can harm your health and affect your family. There is an old saying among our kind: *You're not a proper detective unless you've divorced at least once.* There is some truth in that. It is impossible to investigate murders without making some sort of sacrifice in your life, so reaching this point helps make that worthwhile.

Finally, and without doubt most important, is the relief and happiness of having helped the bereaved family. There is nothing we can do to bring their loved ones back, and we can't ever take away the pain they are feeling, but what we can do is bring them a sense of justice. On so many occasions, families have told me that, after the killer has been convicted, they can start to move on with their lives. I can't begin to describe how that made me feel. There can't be many professions that provide that level of job satisfaction. Knowing you have helped people begin the healing process from such a terrible loss is incredibly rewarding.

WHAT ABOUT 'NOT GUILTY' VERDICTS?

I'm not going to lie, they sting. I can honestly say that I have never charged a person I didn't believe was guilty of murder. Even if it wasn't them who pushed in the knife, or pulled the trigger, they were as guilty as the person that did. So, to see those defendants walk free from court and get away with murder was hard but it was part of the job, something you had to get used to. Thankfully, it was in a minority of cases.

The way I dealt with it was by taking solace in the fact we had done our best. I would like to think none of those verdicts were down to us. Although, with a jury system, the reason for a 'not guilty' verdict isn't always obvious.

The worst part was knowing the impact this had on the family, especially when the defence's tactic was to attack the victim's character. That was hard and left you feeling like you had let them down in some way.

APPEALS

Most people found guilty of murder will appeal their conviction. They are also likely to appeal the length of their sentence. They do so as they don't have anything to lose. Rarely, however, will convictions be overturned. In my twelve years of murder investigations, our team never had one.

In the past there have been unsafe convictions, but, in today's criminal justice system, these are rare. Investigations have never before been held to such high standards.

Case File: The verdict is the moment we've all been waiting for after we've painstakingly built a case. It's a moment filled with drama and emotion; a potential turning point for the defendants, the victim's family and us as a team. I wanted to convey the feeling of that experience and so below I've recounted one such occasion in detail.

We received word the jury had reached a verdict. After months of investigation and weeks in court, it all came down to this. As with every trial, it had twists and turns. At some points, your confidence is sky-high and sometimes you are fearing the worst.

As I sat there, waiting for the jury to come into court, I had no idea which way it was likely to go. None of us did. Even the most seasoned detectives, experienced barristers and longest-serving courtroom staff were waiting in anticipation. You could cut the atmosphere with a knife. It was always like that. There was always a buzz of excitement or dread, depending on which side you were on.

As a rule, I don't usually suffer from nerves, except for those critical moments just before the jury take their seats. For nine months or so, you've put your heart and soul into the investigation. You've sacrificed time with friends and family. You've spent sleepless nights working through the evidence in your mind and wondering, *have I missed something? Were my decisions sound? Will the witnesses turn up?* And, if they do, *how will they perform?* All that worry was in the past. All that mattered now was the verdict of those twelve men and women.

The door to the courtroom opened and in walked the family liaison officer (FLO). Directly behind was the victim's family. It was the FLO who told the husband of his wife's murder. She had been there for them throughout the investigation and the trial. She would even go on to be a part of their lives after all this had finished.

During those proceedings, the husband and all the family had carried themselves in that familiar, dignified way that so many bereaved families do. As he took his seat, I saw him glance over at the defendant. It was no more than a fleeting look but enough to tell me what he was thinking: *You have torn my life apart. Now you need to answer for that.*

There was a bang to signify the judge was about to enter. All chatter stopped, and everyone got to their feet. The age-old tradition to show respect. He took his seat, which was our cue to do the same. A minute or so later, the jury was led in by a court usher. They made their way to the same seats they had sat in throughout the trial. A trial through which they had been observers. Now they were the centre of attention: the decision-makers. I always looked for clues as to what they had decided. *Were they looking at the defendant? Were they looking at the family?* It didn't matter, as I would find out soon enough.

The defendant was told to stand and the jury foreman was asked the question: *Have you reached a verdict on which you all agree?* Yes.

I looked back at the defendant, who was trying

to look like she didn't care one way or the other. However, her eyes told a different story. My palms were sweating and my heart racing, and I wasn't the one looking at a long prison sentence. I could only imagine how she must have been feeling.

On the count of murder, do you find the defendant guilty or not guilty?

GUILTY!

It was as if the whole courtroom had let out a simultaneous gasp. The first people I looked at, the first I always looked at, were the family. Their faces showed a sense of relief, not celebration. This verdict wasn't going to bring back their wife and mum but it was so important to them that it was 'murder' and not a lesser conviction. Having sat through the trial and having seen all the evidence, they knew it was the right verdict. Anything less would have been wrong.

Outside the court, every family member shook our hands and some even gave us hugs. I can't put into words how much that meant to us – it was why we did the job.

CONCLUSION

So, we've come to the end of what is the shortest chapter in the book but, in many ways, the most important. We've looked at the process of how the evidence gathered by murder investigation teams is presented, tested and, ultimately, weighed up by the jury. We've identified what the jury will need to consider in coming to their verdict. Throughout the book, we have been looking at this process from the perspective of Scotland Yard's MIT. I hope from this chapter you have recognised how little control they have at the trial. For them, if they haven't got the investigation right before this stage, it is too late. That is why we come back to that *big goal*, the one they need to keep at the forefront of their minds through everything they do: *To secure a safe and proper conviction at court.*

EPILOGUE

At the start of this book, I promised to take you on a journey. It was one I have travelled many times, each as important as the first. It isn't a simple journey, as I hope you can now appreciate. There are many more obstacles to investigating murder than most people will ever know. Most people, but not you. You have peeked behind the curtain to see the complex issues we face and the impossible decisions we make. You would have heard me talk a lot about one specific goal. But the true goal, the one that can't be put into words, is that scene in the courtroom. To hear that guilty verdict and to see the faces of those left behind is the true reward; to feel that immense sense of professional and personal satisfaction that you have done your job well. That is why murder investigation teams do what they do. That, and to fight for the one person who is no longer around to fight for themselves.

If there is one thing I want you to take away from this

book, and it is something I hope came across, it's the passion with which the men and women of MITs do their job. They may not always be successful, they may not always get things right, but they will give their all for the victims and their families. They sacrifice sleep, social lives, time with their own families and, on occasion, their health. But they do so willingly and without looking for credit. Credit they deserve but rarely receive. Sadly, they are more likely to be accused of corruption, incompetence or a lack of caring. All things I hope I have gone some way to dispelling.

Finally, I hope you have sensed the immense admiration I have for those families who've had their worlds ripped apart by murder. It really isn't an exaggeration when I say I was often left in awe at how they dealt with such a tragic and traumatic situation. They have truly been some of the most remarkable people I have ever met.

ABOUT THE AUTHOR

Steven Keogh was a police officer with London's Metropolitan Police for thirty years, with over half of that time spent as a Scotland Yard detective. He was part of the investigations into the killings of over one hundred victims.

He achieved the rank of detective inspector (DI) and was a nationally recognised senior investigating officer (SIO). He not only led murder enquiries but was also a detective constable (DC) and detective sergeant (DS) at Scotland Yard, so has an insight into all levels of investigations.

He was on Scotland Yard's Anti-Terrorist Branch during the time of the London bombings on 7 July 2005. He received a commendation for his work on that investigation from the Metropolitan Police Commissioner, Sir Ian Blair.

As well as a police officer, he is a father of four, with two of his children having followed his career path as serving members of the Metropolitan Police.

ACKNOWLEDGEMENTS

I must start with the person without whom this book wouldn't have been possible, my partner Sophie. *Who knew it would be such a long process?* Without your support, I would never have made it to the end.

To my kids, who saw less of me throughout my career than we all would have liked. For my oldest two, I'm proud of the people you have become, and for my youngest two, I look forward to seeing you grow and fulfil your potential.

My parents, for giving me the grounding to be the person I became (rest in peace, Dad).

I would like to thank those who have helped shape this book, from what it was to where it is now. My amazing editor, Sarah Busby. Your honest and wise feedback was truly brilliant. My designer, Andy Meaden, you have an eye for detail and the patience of a saint.

Those from various backgrounds who made sure I wasn't

talking nonsense: David Videcette, Neil Dawes, Martin Tucker, Dr Matthew Orde, Dr Judith O'Higgins and Bill Crombie.

My fabulous beta readers: MK Turner, Tracy Mullen, Lynn Cantillon, Helen Smith, Lisa Johnson, Gill Smith, Kath Hett, Paul Easson and Katie Barringer.

And those who were with me throughout the ups and downs of my career. You got me through the lows and, without you, none of the highs would have been possible.

The biggest influence on my early career – Paul Sanders, the best I ever worked with. And Jane, you are sorely missed. I hope you are laughing that laugh, wherever you are.

From SO13, Dave, thanks for the laughs. Ian, thanks for the trips.

All those I served with on MIT. There are far too many to mention you all, but some of those who I am most thankful to: Stuart, Damian, Graeme, Richard, Mick, Murph, Vinnie, Pete, Becky, Emma, Charley, Vicky T (RIP), Vicky R, Jason, Simon, Andy, Adam, Mark, Dave, Tom, Kevin, Mark, Chi-Chi, Claire, Jenny, Richard, Neil, Jemma, Manny, Mark, Lee, Nick and all those from MITs 14 and 16.

And finally, I want to thank you, the reader, for coming on this journey. I hope you found it informative and enjoyable. If so (or even if you didn't), please visit the site where you purchased the book and leave a brief review. Your feedback is important to me and it will help others to decide whether to read the book too.

ENDNOTES

i   Spangler, Todd. Variety.com, 5 September 2018. *https://variety.com/2018/digital/news/serial-season-3-premiere-date-podcast-1202927015/*

ii United Nations Office on Drugs and Crime, accessed on 16 July 2021. *https://dataunodc.un.org/content/data/homicide/homicide-rate*

iii House of Commons Public Library, 25 May 2021. *https://commonslibrary.parliament.uk/research-briefings/cbp-8224*

iv Office for National Statistics, 21 February 2021. *https://www.ons.gov.uk/peoplepopulationandcommunity/crimeandjustice/datasets/appendixtableshomicideinenglandandwales*

v   Statista Research Department, 9 July 2021. *https://www.statista.com/statistics/865565/gun-crime-in-london/*

vi Office for National Statistics, 21 February 2021. *https://www.ons.gov.uk/peoplepopulationandcommunity/crimeandjustice/datasets/appendixtableshomicideinenglandandwales*

vii   Home Office statistical bulletin 18/20. *https://assets.publishing. service.gov.uk/government/uploads/system/uploads/attachment_data/ file/903213/statistics-firearm-shotgun-certificates-england-wales-2019-2020-hosb1820.pdf*

viii Office for National Statistics, 21 February 2021. *https://www. ons.gov.uk/peoplepopulationandcommunity/crimeandjustice/datasets/ appendixtableshomicideinenglandandwales*

ix   Office for National Statistics, 21 February 2021. *https://www. ons.gov.uk/peoplepopulationandcommunity/crimeandjustice/datasets/ appendixtableshomicideinenglandandwales*

x   Office for National Statistics, 21 February 2021. *https://www. ons.gov.uk/peoplepopulationandcommunity/crimeandjustice/datasets/ appendixtableshomicideinenglandandwales*

xi   PreciseSecurity.com, 26 August 2021. *https://www. precisesecurity.com/articles/top-10-countries-by-number-of-cctv-cameras/*

xii   Metropolitan Police, 17 June 2020. *https://www.met.police.uk/ SysSiteAssets/foi-media/metropolitan-police/disclosure_2020/july_2020/ information-rights-unit---unsolved-homicides-in-london-from-january-2010-to-june-2020*

xiii Metropolitan Police, accessed on 12 September 2021. *https:// www.met.police.uk/sd/stats-and-data/met/crime-data-dashboard/* and the *Guardian*, accessed on 12 September 2021. *https://www.theguardian. com/news/datablog/2011/oct/05/murder-london-list*